The Patriot's Toolbox

One Hundred Principles for Restoring Our Freedom and Prosperity

College of the Ouachitas

The Heartland Institute

The Patriot's Toolbox

Third Revised Edition
Copyright ©2011
The Heartland Institute

Published by The Heartland Institute
19 South LaSalle Street #903
Chicago, Illinois 60603
phone 312/377-4000
fax 312/377-5000
www.heartland.org

Additional copies of this book
are available from The Heartland Institute
for the following prices:

1-10 copies	$8.95 per copy
11-50 copies	$7.95 per copy
51-100 copies	$6.95 per copy
101 or more	$5.95 per copy

Printed in the United States of America
ISBN-13 978-1-934791-35-6
ISBN-10 1-934791-35-0

Manufactured in the United States of America

Contents

Preface

Rarely have more people in the United States been so deeply concerned about the direction of their country as right now. Since 2008, millions of men and women have literally marched in the streets for political change, and surveys show their views are supported by the great majority of other Americans. They are not demanding new entitlement programs or threatening to strike if their demands are not met. They simply want their country back. As this book's title suggests, they are patriots who want to restore the country's freedom and prosperity.

The most visible part of this uprising, called the Tea Party movement, arose in response to the enormous government bailouts of banks and insurance companies launched by President George W. Bush and overseen by President Barack Obama, and then the massive spending initiatives and government takeovers of formerly private businesses during the first 18 months of the Obama administration. The new patriots perceive that these developments contradict basic American ideals and historical practice. They are right.

This book is offered as a guide to public policy for patriot-activists in the Tea Party movement as well as for candidates for public office, incumbent office holders, civic and business leaders, and journalists assigned to cover the movement. It consists of ten chapters, all previously published by The Heartland Institute as booklets in a series called *Legislative Principles*. Together, they provide a comprehensive collection of practical, evidence-based principles in the major fields of legislation. Additional research and commentary can be found on The Heartland Institute's Web site at www.heartland.org.

The editors and authors of this book do not presume to tell the movement what to think or how to act; this is not a "program" or "agenda" for a movement. The word "patriot" appears in the title because the principles we recommend would return the country to government based on the ideals of the Founders who led the American Revolution: liberty,

limited taxation, and limited government. The word "toolbox" appears in
the title because the principles can be used as tools to fix what is wrong
with the country's politics and public policies. Just as not every tool in a
toolbox is used for every project, we don't expect every reader to find every
chapter and every principle useful to his or her effort.

Four chapters were written by Joseph Bast, president of The Heartland
Institute. The remaining six are based on booklets written by Matthew
Denhart, George Gilder, Leonard Gilroy, Matthew Glans, Hance Haney, Eli
Lehrer, Adrian Moore, Daniel Pilla, Steve Stanek, and Richard Vedder. We
extend our thanks to all of the people who helped write and participated in
the peer review of the original booklets.

Herbert Walberg edited all of the installments in the *Legislative
Principles* series. He and Joseph Bast lightly edited and updated eight
booklets for the first edition of this publication, and then substantially
rewrote Chapter 3 (School Reform) and added two chapters based on two
new *Legislative Principles* booklets that were published in 2010 and early
2011. Diane Bast proofread all the original booklets and then the entire
book. Walberg also wrote the introduction for this volume.

When the Tea Party movement began attracting millions of people to
meetings and protests across the country in 2008, we sensed the *Legislative
Principles* booklets might have found a new audience. We were right: In
2010, tens of thousands of copies of each booklet in the series were
distributed at Tea Party events, and the response from readers has been
overwhelmingly positive. We hope this new edition will find an even larger
audience in 2011 and beyond.

Patrick J. O'Meara proposed combining the booklets into a single
volume, and his generosity made the first edition possible. We thank him
again for his support.

Joseph L. Bast   Herbert J. Walberg
President   Chairman
The Heartland Institute   The Heartland Institute

Introduction

Herbert J. Walberg

The Tea Party movement reveals the disappointment felt by many American voters beginning in 2008 in response to the enormous government bailouts, launched by President George W. Bush, of banks and insurance companies. During the first two years of President Barack Obama's administration, public disappointment grew to outrage as the administration and its Democratic allies in Congress oversaw takeovers of two major automobile companies, a huge increase in government spending financed by borrowing, and a government take-over of the health care industry.

The Rising Tide of Government

Younger people are beginning to realize federal, state, and local governments are incurring trillions of dollars of debt that will have to be repaid through higher taxes during their lifetimes. Middle-aged and older citizens are learning the debt crisis means Medicare and Social Security won't provide the secure health insurance and retirement benefits they were counting on.

More and more voters tell pollsters they believe the biggest threat to liberty and prosperity is not an attack by a foreign power but a rising tide of government power at home. They are right to be concerned. Studies find that government workers are paid considerably more than similarly trained and experienced persons doing the same jobs in the private sector (Edwards 2010).

Some state and local government employees, including educators and police, can retire as early as age 55 with as much as 80 percent of their wages and full health care benefits (Lehrer and Stanek 2010). Nearly 80 percent of government workers qualify for pensions, while only one-fifth of private-sector workers do. At a time of record unemployment, many taxpayers are wondering why the government sector isn't reducing workforces or trimming generous benefits.

The federal government's debt has been a cause for concern for many years, but the eventual day of reckoning always seemed in the distant future, too far away to justify doing anything today. The Great Recession and massive government spending hikes undertaken by the Obama administration and Democratic Party-controlled Congress changed the picture dramatically. The budget deficit in 2010 is an estimated 10.6 percent of Gross Domestic Product (GDP), the highest level since 1945. The combined unfunded liability of Social Security and Medicare in 2009 was nearly $107 trillion. Obama's budget forecasts the national debt will rise from $7.5 trillion (53 percent of GDP) at the end of 2009 to an uncomprehensible $20.3 trillion (90 percent of GDP) at the end of 2020 (Boaz 2010).

The size of the federal debt becomes more comprehensible when presented as the burden to be borne by the average household. An analysis by *USA Today* put the burden at $546,668 in 2008, "quadruple what the average U.S. household owes for all mortgages, car loans, credit cards and other debt combined" (Cauchon 2009). The amount jumped by $55,000 from 2007 to 2008, a 12 percent increase, due to "an explosion of federal borrowing during the recession, plus an aging population driving up the costs of Medicare and Social Security" (*Ibid.*).

States, too, are heavily indebted. The 50 states face a combined budget gap of approximately $200 billion in 2010 (McNichol and Johnson 2010). Simply raising taxes to meet current obligations is self-defeating since successful firms and high earners in high-tax states such as California, Connecticut, Illinois, and Massachusetts tend to move to low-tax states such as Florida, Nevada, Texas, and Utah, which by comparison are thriving with lower unemployment. This migration means fewer and less successful firms and citizens are left with increasing tax burdens.

Similarly, American firms and jobs are migrating to countries not only with low labor costs but also lower taxes. Increasingly, for example, manufacturing is moving to Mexico and Asia while services such as computer programming and legal processing move to India. The steady and substantial increases in taxes in the past few decades have made American economic growth, at around 3 percent, approach the slower rates of Western Europe, in contrast to those of China and India of up to 10 percent. Eastern

Europe and Latin America have prospered with lower taxes, with economic growth rates up to 5 percent in recent years.

Many of the American and European policies are redistributionist: They tax successful citizens more than they tax the unsuccessful and redistribute the money to the growing shares of the population who either work for the government or do not work and do not seek to work. At least since Adam Smith wrote *The Wealth of Nations* in 1776, this "taxing Peter to pay Paul" has been known to impoverish nations. Perhaps the most distinctive and significant part of the great American Experiment was creating constitutional barriers to this destructive tendency of democracies, but those barriers have fallen in recent decades, with calamitous results.

Public Outrage

The public knows who is to blame for this disaster. Bush left office with a job approval rating of only 22 percent, and Obama's approval rating after one year in office was just 29 percent (Earle 2010). Polls conducted in March 2010 found approval ratings of only 19 percent for Congress, 11 percent for U.S. House Speaker Nancy Pelosi, and 8 percent for Senate Majority Leader Harry Reid (Montopoli 2010).

A Gallup/USA Today poll taken in May 2010 found, "Two-thirds of those surveyed this week describe themselves as 'angry' about the way things are going in the USA, the highest percentage in the decade the question has been asked. By nearly 2-1, they would rather vote for a candidate who has never served in Congress over one with experience" (Page 2010).

Fear also is growing about the rising level of government interference in people's lives. Among voters who identified themselves as Independents – the crucial swing voters in recent elections – the percentage of those who said there is "too much government regulation" rose from 38 percent to 50 percent from 2008 to 2009, according to a Gallup poll (Saad 2009). For the first time, surveys show half of American adults think today's American children will grow up to be worse off than people are now (Pew Research Center 2006).

Enter the Tea Party Patriots

The new "Tea Party patriots" recognize that basic American ideals and historical practice are under attack. Their views are radical but only in the original sense of the term, that is, reaching to the roots, foundation, or ultimate sources and principles. They are echoing the ideas of the American Founders including John Adams, Benjamin Franklin, Alexander Hamilton, John Jay, Thomas Jefferson, James Madison, and George Washington.

The Tea Party patriots remind us that the Founders' Declaration of Independence refused to accept "taxation without representation," British Parliamentary supremacy, and the rulings of King George III that violated civil and economic liberties. They call forth memories of events that led up to the Declaration, in particular of the citizens who threw British tea into Boston harbor as a protest against new taxes. Also, leading the American Revolution were Virginia Minutemen, trained to respond to emergencies, whose flags declared "Liberty or Death" and "Don't Tread on Me," popular slogans reproduced on t-shirts and signs at Tea Party rallies occurring around the country.

Unfortunately, traditional big news media staff have been overwhelmingly on the side of big government. They have done their best to ignore the Tea Party movement or, when that is not possible, to underestimate the turnout at its rallies and demonstrations or cast aspersions on the men and women who spend their weekends or use up vacation days during the week to make their opinions known. The Taxpayer March on Washington, on September 12, 2009, was a prime and disgraceful example of media bias. What was by many accounts one of the largest marches on Washington DC in history was simply ignored by most of the print and network media (Pappas 2009). For example, it apparently didn't merit a single picture in *Time* magazine's "Year in Review."

According to the Media Research Center, "surveys over the past 30 years have consistently found that journalists – especially at the highest ranks of their profession – are much more liberal than the rest of America. They are much more likely to vote liberal, and more likely to agree with the liberal position on policy matters than the general public" (Media Research Center, n.d.). Only 21 percent of citizens self-identified themselves as liberals in a recent Gallup poll (Jeffrey 2009).

The growing disconnect between what the liberal-biased traditional media say and what the general public believes is contributing to a major contraction in the size and influence of "old" media. Television networks have lost viewers, hundreds of daily newspapers have folded and others are bankrupt. Citizens have turned to talk radio, cable TV, and Internet-based sources such as Facebook, blogs, and Web sites (Bast 2010).

Although apparently abandoned by politicians and most of the media, the Founders' ideals still prevail in America. A review of international surveys shows continuing "American exceptionalism" (Lipset 1996, 19-27). In contrast to citizens in other nations, 66 percent of Americans agreed "government is almost always wasteful and inefficient." A similar percentage agreed "most government officials don't care what people like me think." The Tea Party movement suggests these views are even more prevalent and strongly felt today.

Overview of the Book

This book was written by policy specialists who know how to make all levels of government accomplish more at less cost, thereby giving citizens the freedom to spend greater shares of their incomes and savings as they think best. Freedom, that elemental value at the very heart of the American experience, is both the means to and ultimate goal of these reforms. Here are a few of the recommendations from each chapter:

■ Chapter 1: "Health Care Reform" shows how we can attain better health care at lower cost by repealing unnecessary regulations, reducing reliance on third-party payers, reforming malpractice insurance, and encouraging people to purchase long-term care insurance.

■ Chapter 2: "Energy and Environment" explains why "energy independence" is an illusionary goal and how nuclear energy, liquefied natural gas, and market-driven prices can provide the energy the nation needs without endangering the environment. It shows how environmental advocacy groups have exaggerated the alleged threats of global warming, air pollution, and mercury.

■ Chapter 3: "School Reform" presents evidence of the success of allowing parents to choose their children's schools, whether public, independent, or parochial, and having tax dollars "follow the students" to schools of choice. Schools that fail to win the approval of parents should not be publicly supported. It describes a new public policy idea, the "Parent Trigger," that would empower parents to demand that their schools be converted to charters or that parents be given vouchers.

■ Chapter 4: "Privatization" documents the worldwide movement to shift the provision of public services from government agencies to private contractors. The chapter presents guidelines to identify privatization opportunities, pick the best outside vendors, structure contracts, and monitor progress.

■ Chapter 5: "Business Climate" reveals the importance of low taxes, avoiding corporate welfare, removing special privileges of labor unions, and reducing entry barriers to allow small innovative firms to compete.

■ Chapter 6: "Telecommunications" describes how new private investments in telecom services could be encouraged by repealing discriminatory taxes, minimizing government's involvement in broadband, and giving a single agency responsibility for consumer protection.

■ Chapter 7: "State Fiscal Policy" explains the importance of keeping taxes low; creating transparent, accountable budgets; privatizing public services to maximize competition; avoiding corporate welfare; and protecting state employees from politics.

■ Chapter 8: "Property and Casualty Insurance" explains how unnecessary regulations are increasing the cost of auto and home insurance. These regulations distort the marketplace and subsidize people who build in flood plains and other high-risk areas.

■ Chapter 9: "Federal Tax Policy" describes the necessary evil that is taxation and policymakers' responsibility to adhere to sound constitutional and economic principles when levying taxes.

■ Chapter 10: "Higher Education Reform" explains the importance of higher education to the advancement of our civilization and our nation's economic productivity and recommends reforms that make it more affordable, more productive, more efficient, and more useful to society.

All 100 principles set forth in this book are presented in the table on the next four pages.

One Hundred Principles
for Restoring Our Freedom and Prosperity

Health Care
1. Health care is a service, not a right.
2. Repeal existing regulations first.
3. Reduce reliance on third-party payers.
4. Help only those who need help.
5. Single payer is not the answer.
6. Encourage entrepreneurship.
7. Expand health savings accounts.
8. Expand access to prescription drugs.
9. Reduce malpractice litigation expenses.
10. Encourage long-term care insurance.

Energy and Environment
1. Energy independence is an illusion.
2. Gasoline prices are market-driven.
3. Global warming is not a crisis.
4. Air pollution is no longer a major public health problem.
5. Mercury is no longer a major public health problem.
6. Biofuels should not be subsidized.
7. CAFE standards sacrifice lives for oil.
8. Electric deregulation is still necessary.
9. Liquefied natural gas is part of the solution.
10. Nuclear energy is part of the solution.

School Reform
1. Allow parents to choose.
2. Funding should follow the child.
3. Schools should compete.
4. Empower school leaders.
5. Empower teachers.
6. Give parents adequate funding with incentives.
7. Allow schools to succeed or fail.
8. Preserve the autonomy of private schools.
9. Teach democratic values.
10. All parents should be free to choose.

One Hundred Principles
for Restoring Our Freedom and Prosperity
(Continued)

Privatization
1. Identify privatization opportunities.
2. Prepare a business case evaluation.
3. Create a council on efficient government.
4. Choose contractors on best value, not lowest price.
5. Use performance-based contracting.
6. Provide effective monitoring and oversight.
7. Bundle services for better value.
8. Prepare a real property inventory.
9. Divest non-core assets.
10. Make the case to the public.

Business Climate
1. Keep total tax burden low.
2. Keep taxes on businesses low.
3. Avoid corporate welfare.
4. Remove privileges enjoyed by labor unions.
5. Lower or eliminate minimum wages.
6. Reduce workers compensation costs.
7. Keep housing affordable.
8. Reduce regulatory burdens.
9. Discourage lawsuit abuse.
10. Attract members of the creative class.

Telecommunications
1. Encourage new investment in telecom services.
2. Repeal discriminatory taxes and fees.
3. Oppose "network neutrality" regulations.
4. Reduce intrastate access charges on telephone calls.
5. End requirements that telcos file tariffs.
6. Give providers greater freedom to set prices.
7. Exempt competitive services from utility commission jurisdiction.
8. End or reform carrier-of-last-resort and build-out obligations.
9. Minimize government's role in broadband deployment.
10. Give a single agency responsibility for consumer protection.

**One Hundred Principles
for Restoring Our Freedom and Prosperity**
(Continued)

State Fiscal Policy
1. Above all else: Keep taxes low.
2. Don't penalize earnings and investment.
3. Avoid "sin" taxes.
4. Create a transparent and accountable budget.
5. Privatize public services.
6. Avoid corporate welfare.
7. Cap taxes and expenditures.
8. Fund students, not schools.
9. Reform Medicaid programs.
10. Protect state employees from politics.

Property and Casualty Insurance
1. Price controls are unnecessary.
2. Emphasize solvency.
3. Minimize residual insurance markets.
4. Avoid tariff barriers to non-U.S. reinsurance
5. Dismantle catastrophe funds.
6. Reform and phase out the National Flood Insurance Program.
7. Don't ban credit scoring.
8. Don't ban territorial rating.
9. Don't interfere in rate-setting.
10. Help only the truly needy.

Federal Tax Policy
1. Simplicity
2. Noninvasiveness
3. Efficiency
4. Stability
5. Visibility
6. Neutrality
7. Economic Growth
8. Broad-based
9. Equality
10. Constitutionality

**One Hundred Principles
for Restoring Our Freedom and Prosperity**
(Continued)

Higher Education
1. Reduce third-party payments.
2. Fund students, not institutions.
3. Increase transparency.
4. Don't push college on everyone.
5. Promote lower-cost alternatives.
6. Emphasize instruction.
7. Restructure university ownership and governance.
8. Raise academic standards.
9. Measure institutional success by student performance.
10. Reduce barriers to entry and encourage accreditation reform.

We hope this brief overview whets the reader's appetite for the chapters that follow. Even more, we hope the principles recommended and the discussion and readings prove useful in developing legislation to help the country's patriots succeed in their goal of expanding and preserving American freedom and prosperity.

References

Bast, Joseph. 2010. There's nothing mainstream about the old media. *The Heartlander*, The Heartland Institute, May-June.

Boaz, David. 2010. The Greek model. Cato@Liberty, May 26. www.cato-at-liberty.org/2010/04/26/the-greek-model/

Cauchon, Dennis. 2009. Leap in U.S. debt hits taxpayers with 12% more red ink. *USA Today,* May 29.

Earle, Geoff. 2010. Poll shows voters abandoning prez in droves. *New York Post,* February 9.

Edwards, Chris. 2010. Overpaid federal workers. Cato Institute, June. www.downsizinggovernment.org/overpaid-federal-workers.

Jeffrey, Terence P. 2009. Conservatives now outnumber liberals in all 50 states, says Gallup poll. CNS News, August 17. www.cnsnews.com/news/article/52602.

Lehrer, Eli and Steve Stanek. 2010. The state public pension crisis: a 50-state report card. *Heartland Policy Study* No. 126, The Heartland Institute, April.

Lipset, Seymour Martin. 1996. *American exceptionalism.* New York, NY: W.W. Norton, 1996.

McNichol, Elizabeth and Nicholas Johnson. 2010. Recession continues to batter state budgets; state responses could slow recovery. Center on Budget and Policy Priorities, May 27.

Media Research Center. n.d. Media bias 101: what journalists really think – and what the public thinks about the media. www.mrc.org/static/biasbasics/MediaBias101.aspx.

Montopoli, Brian. 2010. Poll: low favorability ratings for Pelosi, Reid. CBS News, March 22. www.cbsnews.com/8301-503544_162-20000937-503544.html.

Page, Susan. 2010. Poll finds anger over country' leaders. *USA Today,* May 28.

Pappas, Max. 2009. How many people came to 9/12 taxpayer march on Washington? September 14. www.freedomworks.org/blog/max/how-many-people-came-to-912-taxpayer-march-on-wash.

Pew Research Center. 2006. Once again, the future ain't what it used to be. May 2. pewresearch.org/pubs/311/once-again-the-future-aint-what-it-used-to-be.

Saad, Lydia. 2009. Conservatives maintain edge as top ideological group. October 26. www.gallup.com/poll/123854/conservatives-maintain-edge-top-ideological- group.aspx.

Chapter 1
Health Care

Joseph L. Bast

---

10 Principles of Health Care Policy

1. Health care is a service, not a right.
2. Repeal existing regulations first.
3. Reduce reliance on third-party payers.
4. Help only those who need help.
5. Single payer is not the answer.
6. Encourage entrepreneurship.
7. Expand health savings accounts.
8. Expand access to prescription drugs.
9. Reduce malpractice litigation expenses.
10. Encourage long-term care insurance.

Introduction

This chapter was written in 2007, before the 3,256-page Patient Protection and Affordable Care Act (more popularly known as "Obamacare") was enacted, and therefore that legislation is not mentioned. An excellent critique of the Act, a *Heartland Policy Study* by Peter Ferrara titled "The Obamacare Disaster," is available from The Heartland Institute and can be read on Heartland's Web sites at www.heartland.org and www.healthpolicy-news.org.

This chapter is designed to help concerned citizens find solutions to health care problems by first identifying their causes and true extent – which often are not as they are reported in newspaper stories or touted by special-interest groups – and then by presenting ten principles that ought to guide reform efforts.

Do We Really Spend Too Much?

It often is assumed at the outset that "we spend too much" on health care in the U.S., but who is "we" and what is the "right" amount? Individuals, not nations, earn income and choose how to spend it.

When adjusted for inflation, per-capita health care spending in the U.S. today is about ten times what it was in 1950. By itself, this statistic is not evidence of a problem. Data from around the world show people tend to spend a bigger part of their incomes on health care as they grow wealthier (OECD 2004). Health is what economists call a "superior good," which means spending rises faster than income.

Spending on health care in the U.S. totaled $1.9 trillion in 2004 – an average of $6,430 per person, almost one-sixth of the nation's gross domestic product (NCHS 2006). No doubt some of this increased spending has produced good results. Higher spending on health care is responsible for some part of the significant increases in lifespan and reduced disability during the past half century. Most spending today is on treatments that were unavailable at any cost in the not-so-distant past (Cutler 2004; Gratzer 2006). Health care providers in the U.S. provide a higher level of care than is available in most, and perhaps all, other countries (Brase 2000).

Reasons We Spend So Much

Spending on health care in the U.S. often is compared unfavorably to spending levels in other countries, but there are some good reasons having little or nothing to do with public policies that help explain why health care in the United States costs more than it does in other countries. Among them:

- We invest much more in saving prematurely born infants and extending the lives of our elderly. Other countries withhold care and stop treatment (Wesbury 1990; Wennberg 2006).

- Pregnancy, birth, and abortion rates among girls aged 15 to 19 are higher in the U.S. than in other developed countries (Singh and Darroch 2000).

■   The portion of the U.S. population aged 15 and older that is obese is
    nearly double that of Canada and substantially higher than in other
    wealthy countries (Anderson and Hussey 2000).

The Need for Health Care Reform

Even knowing that a high level of spending on health care is not necessarily
a bad thing, and that there are reasons why we spend more than consumers
in other countries, we might still conclude that we spend too much on health
care in the U.S. In fact, we *should* come to that conclusion.

Waste and inefficiency are easily identified in our hospitals,
government programs, and private insurance markets (Meier 2001b). We
see it in the number of people who lack health insurance, the lack of price
transparency in much of the health care system, the high rate of medical
mistakes in hospitals, and the massive transfers of income – often from the
poor and uninsured to the well-to-do and insured – that the current system
generates.

A "good health care system" wouldn't employ armies of "gatekeepers"
to intrude in the relationship between doctors and patients, wouldn't require
lawsuits to ensure that victims of malpractice get adequate compensation or
that incompetent providers lose their licenses, and wouldn't ration access
to life-saving drugs.

These are the real problems facing health care in America today, and
they each can be traced back to bad public policies. The rest of this chapter
examines these policies and describes the most promising reforms.

Recommended reading: Joseph Bast, Richard Rue, and Stuart Wesbury,
Why We Spend Too Much on Health Care (Chicago, IL: The Heartland
Institute, 1993); D.M. Cutler, *Your Money or Your Life: Strong Medicine
for America's Health Care System* (New York, NY: Oxford University
Press, 2004); David Gratzer, *The Cure: How Capitalism Can Save
American Health Care* (New York, NY: Encounter Books, 2006).

1. Health care is a service, not a right.

Health care is best delivered by the market, just like other important goods and services.

Much of the debate over health care policy begins with two mistaken notions, first that health care is different than other goods and services and therefore does not respond to normal economic rules, and second that it is "too important" to be entrusted to the anonymous forces of markets.

Health Care Services Are Delivered by Markets

Markets exist wherever consumers are allowed to seek the greatest value for their money and producers are allowed to seek profits by providing what consumers want. The interaction of demand and supply creates prices, generates investment, and leads to innovation and progress. Even with current policies and regulations that distort the market for health care, we find normal economic forces working in the same manner as they do in other markets:

- *Price controls lead to shortages.* Medicaid programs set fees for doctor visits below market prices and often below the cost of the visit. As a result, there is a shortage of doctors willing to treat Medicaid patients (Medicare Payment Advisory Commission 2003).

- *Competition reduces prices.* Lasik eye surgery and cosmetic surgery are two areas where providers compete directly and consumers spend their own money. While health care costs overall have risen dramatically in recent years, prices for Lasik and cosmetic surgery have fallen (Cannon and Tanner 2005).

- *Consumers respond to price signals.* Many experiments and other studies have found that consumption of health care changes when prices change. Health plans with increased cost-sharing reduce discretionary spending and unnecessary visits to emergency rooms (Wharam *et al.* 2007).

Health Care Is Not Too Important for Markets

The claim that health care is too important to be left to the market can be turned on its head: Health care is too important to be left in the hands of government bureaucracies that often are unaccountable and unreliable. We need *greater* reliance on markets and normal economic forces, not less, because health care is so important to so many people (Wilson 1989).

Access to and the provision of many important goods and services are generally left to markets, with charitable assistance limited to those who need it. Producers of food, for example, are free to supply whatever they want and sell it at whatever price the market will bear. Regulations help to ensure food safety and some subsidies are offered for a few crops, but beyond that the market for food is generally free from government interference. Food stamps, income subsidies, and private charity allow the poor to purchase what they need in the same markets as everyone else.

Problems with a "Right to Health Care"
The alternative to viewing health care as a service is to view it as an entitlement or right. This view resonates with some health care providers and political and legal philosophers, but it is a deeply problematic idea.

A right is a claim to be treated in a certain way by others, which places an obligation on others to act in certain ways. Negative rights – such as the rights to "life, liberty, and the pursuit of happiness" proclaimed in the Declaration of Independence – are rights to be free from interference and coercion by others, and generally do not contradict the exercise of the same freedom rights of others. Positive rights – such as a claim to free or subsidized health care – are claims to the service, involuntary if necessary, of others. Positive rights therefore bring the risk of contradicting the freedom rights of others (Epstein 1997).

A "right to health care" does not appear in the U.S. Constitution or its Bill of Rights, or in any state constitution, or in the writings of the Founding Fathers or the British intellectual tradition from which they drew their inspiration. This was not an oversight. Positive rights may require that goods and services be produced involuntarily, under the penalty of law. Historically, this has not been an efficient or just way to produce goods and services.

Reformers looking to improve access to quality health care must start by understanding that health care services should be delivered by markets. Policymakers should look for ways to enable normal economic forces to perform their tasks just as they do in markets for other goods and services.

Recommended reading: Richard Epstein, *Mortal Peril: Our Inalienable Right to Health Care?* (Reading, MA: Addison-Wesley Publishing Company, 1997); John C. Goodman and Gerald L. Musgrave, *Patient Power: Solving America's Heath Care Crisis* (Washington, DC: Cato Institute, 1992).

2. Repeal existing regulations first.

Benefit mandates, "guaranteed issue," and "community rating" are among the regulations that unnecessarily increase health care spending.

Policymakers often are anxious to pass new laws and create new programs to "solve" the nation's health care finance problems. But they first should repeal laws and programs that cause those problems or make them worse.

Mandated Benefits

In the U.S. there are 1,843 laws mandating that insurers cover specific providers, procedures, or benefits (Bunce, Wieske, and Prikazsky 2006). These laws often are billed as being pro-consumer but they mostly are pro-producer, needlessly adding to the cost of health insurance and health care services by requiring insurers to cover easily abused services. Higher insurance premiums due to state-mandated benefits are responsible for about 25 percent of the number of uninsured (Jensen and Morrisey 1999).

Mandated benefit laws disproportionately affect those who are self-employed, unemployed, or who work for companies that are too small to afford insurance benefits for their employees. Big businesses typically self-insure and are exempt from state regulations.

"Guaranteed Issue" Laws

Guaranteed issue laws require insurance companies to provide insurance to anyone who seeks it. The Health Insurance Portability and Accountability Act of 1996 requires insurers to offer guaranteed issue policies in the small group (2-50 insured persons) market. Some states also try to impose guaranteed issue on their small group and individual markets, with disastrous effects.

Guaranteed issue drives up the price of health insurance by creating an incentive for people to wait until they are sick before buying insurance. Insurance companies raise premiums to guard against the larger claims of the insured population that tends to be less healthy at any given time. Each round of premium increases causes a new group of healthy people to drop its coverage, causing the insured population to become still more expensive to insure. The result is soaring premiums and rising numbers of uninsured (Meier 2005a; Bast 2004).

"Community Rating" Laws

Community rating requires insurers to charge similar rates to all members of a community regardless of age, lifestyle, health, or gender. Because an insurer cannot adjust its premiums to reflect the individual health risks of consumers, the majority who are healthy see their premiums rise.

Community rating means insurance premiums paid by young and healthy individuals are higher than the benefits they are likely to receive, encouraging them to drop their coverage. Like guaranteed issue, this results in an insured population with higher health care expenses than the average population, requiring higher insurance premiums. Once again, premium increases cause more people to choose to go without health insurance.

States that have adopted guaranteed issue and community rating have higher premiums and fewer insurers competing for customers than states that have not. Guaranteed issue and community rating laws have been especially harmful in states where they have been applied to the individual insurance market (Meier 2005a; NAHU 2005).

Other Regulations

Mandated benefits, guaranteed issue, and community rating are the three most destructive regulations states impose on health insurance companies. Other regulations on insurers and health care providers that limit competition and consumer choices include:

- *Individual and employer mandates.* Maine, Massachusetts, and Vermont are planning to impose mandates on individuals and employers to purchase health insurance. These mandates are unlikely to raise enough money in new premiums or penalties to justify the cost of investigating employers, determining eligibility, overseeing premium collection, and identifying and collecting penalties from the uninsured (Tanner 2006).

- *Certificate of Need.* Many states require health care providers to obtain certificates of need before expanding facilities or opening new centers. Existing hospitals and clinics are allowed to testify against new competitors, and naturally they do. Extensive research demonstrates that certificate of need laws reduce competition and result in higher prices (Barnes 2006; Conover and Sloan 1998; Cordato 2005).

- *Rate reviews and bands.* Most states regulate the rates insurers charge for insurance products in the small group market either by requiring prior approval of rates or by prohibiting insurers from offering rates more than 25 percent above or below a base rate. Sometimes rate review is also imposed on the individual market, and sometimes rate bands of less than 25 percent are proposed. Rate reviews and narrow bands stifle innovation and competition (Wieske 2007).

- *Clean claims and prompt pay laws.* Some states mandate that health insurers pay 95 percent or more of all claims within a certain amount of time after receipt of the claim by the insurer. Such laws can be reasonable, but if the percentage of claims is set too high or the time period too short, compliance costs can soar, causing profit margins to shrink and insurers to stop writing policies (Bunce 2002).

- *Prohibitions on exclusionary waivers.* Some states prohibit insurers in the individual health insurance market from offering policies with either temporary or permanent medical waivers for preexisting conditions. Such waivers enable insurers to offer affordable coverage for all but one or two known conditions, such as allergies, that would otherwise require much higher premiums (Wieske and Matthews 2007).

- *Regulations on PPOs.* Preferred Provider Organizations (PPOs) are groups of providers who agree to offer discounts to insurers, employers, and other plan members. Some states are considering legislation, supported by the American Medical Association, that would limit the ability of insurers and employers to negotiate terms with physician groups. This is likely to lead to higher prices for consumers.

- *Impediments to interstate competition.* Consumers are unable to purchase insurance from out-of-state companies because of the McCarran-Ferguson Act (1945), which grants states the right to regulate health plans within their borders. The patchwork of 50 different sets of state regulations makes it costly and time-consuming for insurers to enter new states (Bast, D. 2005a; Flowers 2007).

States that want to increase the availability of health insurance and make health care more affordable should begin by eliminating or at least reducing the many regulations that currently raise the price of insurance and health care services and limit competition and choice.

Recommended reading: Conrad Meier, *Destroying Insurance Markets: How Guaranteed Issue and Community Rating Destroyed the Individual Health Insurance Market in Eight States* (Washington, DC and Chicago, IL: Council for Affordable Health Insurance and The Heartland Institute, 2005); J.P. Wieske, *State Legislators' Guide to Health Insurance Solutions* (Washington, DC: Council for Affordable Health Insurance, 2007).

3. Reduce reliance on third-party payers.

> Over-reliance on third-party payers is at the root of many health care problems.

Government policies that reward reliance on third parties to pay for routine medical expenses encourage Americans to overuse health care services and reduce the rewards to providers who would otherwise compete on price.

Growing Reliance on Third-Party Payers

Federal tax policies have long encouraged third-party, prepaid medical care over individual insurance or direct payment. Under current tax law, employers can deduct the cost of health insurance premiums from their employees' pre-tax income, so one dollar of earned income buys one dollar's worth of health insurance.

People without employer-provided health insurance, and people with insurance but paying out-of-pocket for expenses below the deductible or for required copayments, typically must use after-tax dollars. This means one dollar of earned income may buy only 50 to 75 cents' worth (depending on a person's tax bracket) of health insurance or medical services. This encourages over-reliance on employer-provided insurance with low deductibles and copayments (Goodman and Musgrave 1992).

Government health care programs for the poor and elderly add greatly to the number of people who depend on third parties to pay for their health care. Government programs for the elderly (Medicare) cost $265 billion and for the poor (Medicaid) cost another $305 billion in 2004. (Kaiser 2005b; Kaiser 2007b). A recent study found that about half of the increase in health expenditures nationwide since 1965 was caused by the creation of Medicare and Medicaid (Finkelstein 2006).

As a result of tax policy and the expansion of Medicaid and Medicare, the amount Americans pay out-of-pocket for health care has fallen precipitously. In 1960 Americans paid about one-half (47 percent) of their medical bills out-of-pocket. By 2004, only 13 cents of every dollar was paid out-of-pocket. The remainder was paid by third parties – employers, insurance companies, and government agencies (CMS 2006).

Consequences of Over-Reliance on Third Parties

Because the party receiving service is not the one paying the bill, reliance on third-party payers reduces the financial incentive for patients to shop for the best deal and to limit their discretionary use of health services. This can be seen in the absence of comparative information about the quality and price of medical procedures now available to consumers. Prices for hospital procedures are rarely posted and bills bear little relationship to actual costs. Consumers seldom seek out such information because they aren't paying the bill, and producers have little reason to provide it because it won't affect whether a patient will choose them over other providers.

Managed care plans emerged in an effort by governments and businesses to combat the rising cost of health care due to these perverse incentives. Government regulations and Health Maintenance Organization (HMO) pre-authorization were substituted for market discipline, the privacy of patients and freedom of doctors were compromised, and a new layer of insurance bureaucracy was created. Since the underlying incentives to over-consume and over-spend were left unchanged, however, spending soon started to rise again.

The Direct Payment Alternative

If consumers paid a larger part of the cost of their care, consumption would fall significantly. The RAND Health Insurance Experiment, conducted during the 1970s, showed that when patients were exposed to greater cost-sharing their medical expenditures fell by about 30 percent with negligible health effects (Newhouse 1993). More recent research on consumers choosing high-deductible insurance and health aavings accounts shows significant reductions in spending without negative effects on health (Wharam *et al.* 2007).

While insurance is necessary and appropriate for expensive and unexpected care, nearly half of all health care spending is for relatively routine and inexpensive treatments best paid directly by patients. Recognizing this, hundreds of doctors have arranged their practices to encourage direct payment for services (Cherewatenko 2002; Meier 2001a). These practices accept only cash, checks, credit cards, or debit cards for health savings accounts (see Principle 7 for more on HSAs). Because they no longer require large staffs to process complex insurance claims or comply with price controls imposed by government programs, they are able to offer prices that are between 25 percent and 50 percent less than the reimbursement paid by Medicare and other insurers.

Direct payment for health care services also reduces the need for claims reviewers and "gatekeepers" who make up the bureaucracy created by managed care programs. Doctors and patients are once again allowed to determine appropriate care without interference.

Direct payment also ends the injustice present in the current system whereby households with the highest incomes, and therefore in higher tax brackets, get the largest tax benefits for employer-provided health insurance. John Goodman estimates that families in the wealthiest quintile of taxpayers get an annual tax subsidy of $1,560 a year, while families in the poorest quintile get only $250 (Thorpe and Goodman 2005).

Policies to Promote Direct Payment

Concerned citizens can promote the movement away from over-reliance on third-party payers by supporting the following policies:

■ End the tax preference for employer-provided health care by replacing it with a tax credit or standard deduction for health care that can be used to purchase individual insurance and make deposits into health savings accounts (Bast, J. 2005);

- Make price information for hospital services more accessible and transparent (Kreit 2006);

- Repeal policies that slow the adoption of high-deductible plans with an HSA, such as mandated first-dollar coverage and state taxes on HSA deposits; and

- Include HSA-like accounts in government programs for the poor and elderly to ensure they have funds for direct payment of health care (Raniszewski Herrera 2006; Konig 2005).

By promoting direct payment, policymakers can reduce unnecessary health care spending, strengthen the doctor-patient relationship, end tax injustice, and reward the most efficient health care providers.

Recommended reading: Michael Cannon and Michael Tanner, *Healthy Competition: What's Holding Back Health Care and How to Free It* (Washington, DC: Cato Institute, 2005); Devon Herrick, "Why Are Health Costs Rising?" National Center for Policy Analysis, *Brief Analysis* No. 437, 2003; John McClaughry, "A Health Care Reform Agenda: Desirable State Changes," *Health Care News*, March 2003.

4. Help only those who need help.

Universal coverage is not the appropriate goal of health care reform.

Despite saturation media coverage of the "crisis" of rising numbers of people without health insurance, the proportion of Americans who lack health coverage has increased little over the past decade: 15.6 percent of the population lacked coverage in 1996, compared to 15.9 percent in 2005 (Census Bureau 2007). The uninsured are a heterogeneous population with diverse needs, priorities, and opportunities.

Being Uninsured Is Not Always Harmful
Being uninsured is similar to losing employment in that most periods without insurance last only a short time. For example, three-fourths of

uninsured individuals regain coverage within 12 months (Census Bureau 2007). We do not assume that everyone who is between jobs needs a government program to provide them with work. Why assume that all of the uninsured need or want government's help to find health insurance?

Brief periods without insurance do not pose either a financial or health threat to the vast majority of individuals who experience them. Access to care can still be obtained through direct payment, many medical services can be postponed until insurance is found or other payment arrangements are made, and hundreds of programs provide drugs and access to insurance for those who want them but believe they cannot afford regular commercial rates (Foundation for Health Coverage Education 2007). Emergency room care cannot legally be denied to the uninsured by hospitals, and hospitals and doctors provide billions of dollars a year in uncompensated care to the needy.

In short, being uninsured does not mean having to go without quality health care. Health insurance is only one way to pay for health care.

Lack of Insurance Often Is Voluntary

Millions of Americans who can afford to purchase health insurance choose to remain uninsured. This should not surprise us since the perverse incentives created by tax policies and regulations have turned health insurance into an expensive way to prepay for routine care, including services most people will never use or would not choose to use if they had to pay for them directly.

The actual "insurance" component of health insurance is small and quite affordable, as revealed by premiums for high-deductible policies in the individual insurance marketplace (Bast, D.C. 2005b). Public health insurance programs that fail to target the needy offer taxpayer-subsidized insurance coverage in direct competition with private insurers, while other welfare programs reduce the risk of going without insurance.

Of the 46 million individuals identified as uninsured in 2005, as many as 14 million already qualify for public coverage but have not enrolled (Blue Cross and Blue Shield Association 2005a). They don't bother because they can always enroll after they become sick. Yet these individuals are included in estimates of the uninsured population.

At the other end of the income spectrum, upper-income families are the fastest-growing segment of the uninsured, yet they plainly can afford to buy private health insurance. The probability of being uninsured in households earning more than $75,000 rose 117 percent from 1996 to 2005 (Herrick 2006c). Approximately 19 percent of the uninsured are in families with income greater than 300 percent of the federal poverty level – $61,950 for a family of four in 2007 (Kaiser 2007a).

Forty-two percent of the uninsured (18.8 million) are between the ages of 18 and 34 (Census Bureau 2007). These young people realize they probably will not incur any medical expenses in the coming year, making health insurance (especially at prices inflated by government regulations) a poor investment.

The Uninsured Typically Get Good Health Care

The uninsured receive care at a level similar to patients insured by Medicare, managed care, and fee-for-service (Asch *et al.* 2006). They receive only about 50 percent of the care received by those covered by low-deductible employer-provided health insurance, but this is testimony to the over-use of routine health care services by the latter rather than denial of service experienced by the former (Hadley and Holahan 2003).

Federal and state governments spend more than $300 billion annually on public health insurance such as Medicaid and state children's health insurance programs (SCHIP). Government and private charity care spending on the uninsured totals about $1,000 per full-time uninsured individual (Thorpe and Goodman 2005).

Focus Efforts on the Needy

Many states are offering subsidized health insurance to middle- and even upper-income families, even though these are not the people who need or merit public assistance. Many previously insured people switch to new state programs simply to take advantage of public subsidies, leaving the uninsured rate unchanged yet costing taxpayers tens or hundreds of millions of dollars.

Government efforts to reduce the number of uninsured should focus on that relatively small group of individuals and families that have low incomes but do not qualify for public aid, can't get employer-provided coverage, and are uninsured for relatively long periods of time (HPCG 2007). Reforms that target their needs include:

■ Establish high-risk pools, which provide subsidized comprehensive health insurance to those with serious medical conditions. Such pools are typically funded by a combination of state subsidies and tax credits for insurer assessments. Thirty-four states had high-risk pools in 2006 (Wieske 2007).

- Replace the tax exemption for employer-provided health insurance with a tax credit or personal deduction that can be used to purchase health insurance and make deposits into health savings accounts.

- Repeal community rating and guaranteed issue laws, particularly in the individual market, that force the healthy to subsidize the unhealthy, driving many people out of the private insurance market.

- Restrict eligibility for government health insurance programs, such as Medicaid and SCHIP, so that private insurers can sell affordable insurance products to middle-income families that can afford to pay the premiums without public aid.

- Expand health savings accounts, which give those who are temporarily uninsured for short periods of time the funds needed to pay directly for health care.

The public policy challenge is not to persuade people to do what is not in their best interest, and certainly not to *force* them to make such a choice. Rather, it is to allow people to buy real health insurance without mandated coverage for seldom-used and less-valued services, and to hold accountable those who decide not to purchase insurance for whatever costs they impose on others.

Recommended reading: J.P. Wieske and Merrill Matthews, *Understanding the Uninsured and What to Do about Them* (Washington, DC: Council for Affordable Health Insurance, 2007); Victoria C. Bunce, J.P. Wieske, and V. Prikazsky, *Health Insurance Mandates in the States 2006* (Washington, DC: Council for Affordable Health Insurance, 2006); J. Hadley and J. Holahan, "How Much Medical Care Do the Uninsured Use, and Who Pays for It?" *Health Affairs,* February 2003.

5. Single payer is not the answer.

Single-payer health systems provide inferior care and fail to provide universal access.

Some nations have substituted central planning for markets for the delivery of health care services. Such programs cause long delays in the provision of care (rationing by queue), low rates of investment and innovation, and inferior health outcomes. They are not a model for the U.S.

Waiting Lines

Single-payer systems use long delays in receiving treatment to ration health care. In Canada, the median average wait for treatment after referral to a specialist was nearly 18 weeks in 2006. Patients in New Brunswick waited on average 31.9 weeks. Patients waited an average of 16.2 weeks to see an orthopedic surgeon, and another 24.2 weeks for treatment to be performed after the initial visit (Esmail, Walker, and Wrona 2006).

Britain's National Health Service (NHS) has more than one million people on waiting lists for care. Multiplied by the time spent waiting for care "produces an astounding fact: Britons already in the queue for medical treatment will wait a total of *one million years* for care" (Young and Butler 2002).

Lack of Investment

The number of physicians per capita is nearly 50 percent higher in the U.S. than in Britain and Canada, resulting in smaller case loads and more individualized attention in the U.S. (Anderson *et al.* 2002). Whereas only a little more than 11 percent of U.S. physicians are general practitioners, in Canada and Britain nearly half are. This means patients in the U.S. have greater access to specialists than patients in other countries (Goodman, Musgrave, and Herrick 2004).

Only a handful of PET scanners, the best tool for diagnosing cancer, are available for use in Canada, compared to more than 1,000 in the U.S. The U.S. has nearly 80 percent more CT scanners per capita than Canada and nearly twice as many as Britain. The U.S. has nearly three times as many MRI scanners per capita as Canada, and more than twice as many as Britain (Goodman, Musgrave, and Herrick 2004; Anderson and Hussey 2000).

Inferior Health Outcomes

Long queues and limited access to specialists and the latest medical equipment mean countries with single-payer health systems have health outcomes that are inferior to those of the U.S. For example, only one-quarter of those diagnosed with breast cancer in the U.S. die of it. The comparable figure is 35 percent in France and 46 percent in Britain and New Zealand. About 19 percent of American men die from prostate cancer once diagnosed. The figures are 30 percent and 35 percent in New Zealand and Australia, respectively, and 49 percent and 57 percent in France and Britain, respectively (Goodman, Musgrave, and Herrick 2004).

The shortcomings of single-payer systems are likely to get worse as populations age and the pace of medical innovation accelerates. A British medical think tank called "Reform" reported in 2005 that despite a massive investment in a new National Cancer Plan, the NHS's response to the rising demand for cancer treatments is characterized by "a huge delay in obtaining scans and pathology before a decision can be made on the best treatment to offer an individual," and the system is "operating in a top down confused bureaucracy." According to the authors, "real improvement will not be achieved by simply giving more dollars to a burgeoning bureaucracy. It requires a serious commitment to reform" (Sikora, Slevin, and Bosanquet 2005).

Violation of Patients' and Physicians' Rights

Inherent in single-payer health care plans is allowing a relatively small number of elected officials and unelected bureaucrats to make life-and-death decisions affecting others, substituting their judgment for the voluntary and better-informed choices of millions of patients and their doctors. When government agencies replace markets, those with the most political clout are rewarded with the best and most timely treatment. Everyone else must wait in lines for treatment and are more likely to die from denial of services.

These findings should give pause to proponents of single-payer health care and other proposals – such as expanding Medicaid and imposing insurance mandates on individuals and employers – that are likely to destabilize private health care markets and lead to single-payer programs.

Recommended reading: John Goodman, Gerald Musgrave, and Devon Herrick, *Lives at Risk: Single Payer National Health Insurance around the World* (Lanham, MD: Rowman & Littlefield, 2004); N. Esmail, M. Walker, and D. Wrona, *Waiting Your Turn: Hospital Waiting Lists in Canada,* 16th Edition (Vancouver: Fraser Institute, 2006); Conrad Meier, *Britain's Deadly Mistake: A First-Hand Report on England's Disastrous Experience with Nationalized Health Care* (Chicago, IL: The Heartland Institute, 2002).

6. Encourage entrepreneurship.

Specialty hospitals, retail clinics, and other innovations can lower costs and improve access to quality health care services.

Entrepreneurs and innovators are developing new ways to deliver health care that are more convenient, higher in quality, and less costly than currently available services. Unfortunately, public policies often stand in their way.

Retail Health Clinics

Retail health clinics, located in shopping malls or big-box retail outlets, are increasingly popular because of their convenience, minimal waiting, low prices, and high quality of care. They typically are staffed by a nurse practitioner (NP) with a masters degree in nursing who focuses on diagnosing and treating relatively common and minor illnesses. Prices are posted and typically lower than a visit to a doctor's office (Martin 2007).

Retail health clinics free up better-trained physicians to focus on more seriously ill patients. Because they often are open on evenings and weekends, these clinics serve patients who might otherwise go to expensive emergency rooms (Parnell 2005a).

These clinics can be hindered by legislation restricting the number of NPs a physician can supervise or limiting the scope of practice for NPs. Some states have considered legislation that would prevent NPs from staffing clinics inside pharmacies, an indirect attempt to ban these clinics (LoBuono 2006).

Specialty Hospitals

Specialty hospitals, typically owned at least in part by the doctors who practice in them, focus on a few areas of care, enabling them to increase efficiency and provide higher levels of care than are provided by general hospitals (Parnell 2005b).

Critics of speciality hospitals, such as the American Hospital Association (AHA), cite concerns about physician self-referral and the loss by general hospitals of the most profitable medical procedures to these more efficient rivals. But specialization and competition lead to better quality and lower prices even in health care. Specialty hospitals have shown how innovations such as redesigned hospital layouts can reduce labor costs, reduce waiting times for patients, and improve patient outcomes.

Medical Tourism

Patients are increasingly traveling outside the U.S. for surgery, often at prices that are one-fifth to one-third as high as in the U.S. Countries with highly advanced medical facilities specifically built or equipped for medical tourists include Belgium, Brazil, Costa Rica, India, Malaysia, Mexico, Poland, Singapore, and Thailand (Herrick 2006d).

Patients considering surgery outside the U.S. can use PlanetHospital.com for assistance. Some insurers are beginning to understand how global competition improves quality and lowers cost and may start to reimburse patients for this choice (Cannon and Tanner 2005).

Telemedicine

The Internet and the spread of high-speed broadband services hold enormous potential for improving the quality and lowering the cost of health care. Patients can contact their doctors by email and get quick answers to questions, schedule meetings, and exchange test results. Doctors can monitor their patients' conditions remotely, store and access medical records more quickly, and minimize the amount of time spent on paperwork (Kleba 2007).

Similarly, greater use of electronic medical records could produce huge savings – $81 billion a year according to a report published in *Health Affairs* in fall 2005, or $77 billion according to a 2005 report by RAND. Firms such as SafetySend and eMedicalfiles offer physicians and hospitals ways to create, send, and store confidential medical files that are safe from theft and fraud (Herrick 2006b).

Public Policy Implications

Entrepreneurship in health care, as in other markets, requires that consumers be free to choose and producers be free to compete with one another. Policymakers should avoid regulations that stifle innovation with red tape and price controls that don't allow reimbursement for new services. Regulations that serve to protect incumbent businesses from new competition should be rejected.

Recommended reading: Michael Cannon and Michael Tanner, *Healthy Competition: What's Holding Back Health Care and How to Free It* (Washington, DC: Cato Institute, 2005); Devon Herrick and John Goodman, "Price and Quality in Health Care: The Coming Revolution in the Medical Marketplace," National Center for Policy Analysis, *Policy Report*, 2007.

7. Expand Health Savings Accounts.

Health savings accounts are a key part of empowering consumers and restoring market discipline to health care providers.

Health savings accounts (HSAs) are the key to reducing reliance on third-party payers. They level the tax treatment of dollars used to pay directly for health care and dollars used to purchase health insurance. They also can (but don't yet) level the tax treatment of dollars spent by businesses on health insurance for their employees and dollars spent by individuals for their own health insurance.

What Are HSAs?

HSAs are privately owned savings accounts funded with pretax dollars. Created by the Medicare Prescription Drug, Improvement, and Modernization Act of 2003, HSAs are similar to 401(k) retirement plans, but rather than allow people to save for their retirement, HSAs allow people to save for future medical expenses.

By law, HSAs must be paired with high-deductible health insurance plans. Since such insurance costs much less than the usual comprehensive insurance provided by employers, the premium savings can be deposited into the account and used to pay routine medical bills up to the deductible. Any money left in the account at the end of each year "rolls over" to the next year.

Popular and Inexpensive

The number of HSA accounts in the U.S. tripled between March 2005 and January 2006. Approximately 3.2 million HSAs are now in use (AHIP 2006a). The Treasury Department predicts 14 million people will own HSAs by 2010 if no changes are made to existing law, and as many as 21 million by 2010 if changes were made to encourage their adoption (Clay Trueman 2006).

In 2006, HSAs were approaching 10 percent of the private benefits market and held more than $1 billion, with the average balance being about $1,000. Surveys, including one conducted in 2005 by McKinsey & Company, find very high levels of consumer satisfaction with HSAs as well as sophisticated understanding of how to manage spending (Agrawal 2005).

HSAs Cost Less and Reduce Spending

The average annual premium for HSA high-deductible health plans in 2005 was $2,772 (single coverage) and $6,955 (family) (AHIP 2006b). This is substantially less than the average annual premium for all health insurance plans, $4,024 (single) and $10,880 (family) (Kaiser 2005a).

Because they spend their own money, patients with HSAs shop more wisely for medical care than do people with conventional low-deductible insurance coverage. Two surveys have found people with HSA plans are about twice as likely to ask about drug costs and 50 percent more likely to inquire about the overall cost of care. Patients were 20 percent more likely to manage chronic conditions and 25 percent more likely to use preventive care and engage in health and wellness programs (McKinsey & Co. 2005; Blue Cross Blue Shield Association 2005b).

Health care providers are responding to HSAs with innovative services including retail walk-in clinics, greater price transparency, discounts for cash payment, and easier access to physicians by phone and email (Herrick 2006a).

A Real Solution to the Uninsured Problem

Whereas government-subsidized health insurance programs often attract people who were previously insured, HSAs are popular with people who were previously uninsured. Between 30 percent and 40 percent of HSA enrollees were previously uninsured (AHIP 2006b; eHealthInsurance 2006).

Between 30 percent and 40 percent of HSA enrollees have annual incomes below $50,000 (EBRI 2005). If HSAs were supplemented with federal tax credits, the program would provide coverage to currently uninsured individuals at an annual cost to the government of $2,761, much less than other proposals, and would cause minimum disruption of the private group insurance marketplace. At least 40 percent of the newly covered would come from the bottom 25 percent of income brackets and 75 percent from the bottom half (Feldman *et al.* 2005).

National Reforms

HSAs would be even more successful if Congress allowed unlimited contributions to HSAs and permitted such accounts to wrap around third-party insurance – paying for any expense the insurance plan does not pay. Short of that, four reforms at the national level that would improve HSAs are:

- Provide tax credits or a personal deduction for those who currently do not have employer-provided health coverage.

- Allow people who do not have employer-sponsored health insurance to pay for health insurance with funds from their HSAs.

- Allow insurers to offer a portable, nationally regulated HSA high-deductible health plan.

- Allow insurers to design their plans so different deductibles and copayments apply to different medical services, with high deductibles for services where patient discretion is possible and low or no deductibles where patient discretion is more difficult or inappropriate.

State Reforms

States can help expand HSAs by adopting policies recommended by the Council for Affordable Health Insurance (CAHI 2007):

■ Ensure that the state's definition of income conforms to the Internal Revenue Code for HSA purposes. Four states in 2007 did not accept or follow the federal tax treatment for HSAs: Alabama, California, New Jersey, and Wisconsin.

■ Adopt laws that exempt HSA high-deductible health plans from state mandated benefit requirements. States with mandated benefits that conflict with HSAs include California, Illinois, Maine, Missouri, New York, and Ohio.

■ Add an HSA option for persons who buy insurance through the state's high-risk pool. Twelve states have done so already.

■ Add an HSA option for state and municipal employees. Eleven states have done so already.

■ Add an HSA option for people enrolled in Medicaid. Four states (Florida, Iowa, New York, and South Carolina) have pilot programs that do so already.

Recommended reading: America's Health Insurance Plans, "HSAs and Account-Based Plans: An Overview of Preliminary Research," 2006; John Goodman, "Making HSAs Better," National Center for Policy Analysis, *Brief Analysis* No. 518, June 2005; CAHI, "A State Implementation Report," Council for Affordable Health Insurance, www.cahi.org (accessed on April 15, 2007).

8. Expand access to prescription drugs.

Prescription drugs cure diseases and reduce hospital costs, but they often are the target of price controls and rationing.

Prescription drugs are extending life, reducing suffering, and making surgery less necessary, yet they are heavily regulated and often rationed.

Prescription Drugs Are a Good Value

Drugs represent only about 11 percent of total U.S. health care spending. Drug therapy is often the most efficient method of caring for patients. A dollar of drug expenditure reduces hospital costs by more than $3.50 (Lichtenberg 1996).

Newer drugs work even better than older ones. Patients diagnosed with conditions that have the greatest number of new prescriptions see larger declines in the number of hospital days. For every 100 new prescriptions, hospital days decline by 16 days (Lichtenberg 2003).

Drug Piracy Is No Answer

Those who lament high drug prices often advocate lifting the ban on imported drugs from other countries via channels that are outside the chain of custody that currently protects the quality of drugs sold in the U.S. But breaking the chain of custody makes drugs vulnerable to counterfeiting, contamination, and improper handling (Giuliani Partners 2005; Meier 2005b; Pitts 2006). And to what end? Countries with pharmaceutical price controls produce too few drugs to provide more than a small fraction of what the U.S. market needs (Goodman 2005a).

Because other countries impose price controls on prescription drugs, pirating drugs manufactured for those markets for sale in the U.S. amounts to importing price controls as well. The availability of cheaper drugs from abroad would make it more difficult for drug companies to charge prices high enough to finance research and development, leading to less investment in new drugs in the U.S. (Turner and Meier 2004).

Drug Rationing Is No Answer

State Medicaid programs and the U.S. Veterans Benefits Administration ration access to drugs by using lists of pre-approved drugs, called drug formularies. In order to appear on the lists, drug companies must offer discounts or pay rebates to the states.

Formularies are used in the private sector, too, but when used to limit the cost of public entitlement programs, formularies act as crude and ineffective price controls. Politicians rather than consumers dictate spending, resulting in pressure on plan administrators to refuse to cover new or expensive drugs requested by doctors and to substitute older or generic ones. For example, the Veterans Benefits Administration formulary covers fewer than 1,300 drugs compared to more than 4,000 available for Medicare

Part D drug plans (Enthoven and Fong 2006). Such restrictive formularies greatly reduce patients' and doctors' choices and endanger lives.

Need for Food and Drug Administration (FDA) Reform

A major reason new drugs are so expensive is the costly and time-consuming approval process used by the Food and Drug Administration (FDA). Since 1962, FDA has required new drugs to pass effectiveness as well as safety trials, causing the new drug approval process to take approximately eight years. Many drug developers cannot afford the substantial fees or the nearly decade-long wait for revenue from drug sales to begin.

A promising way to reform FDA regulation of new drugs is to create a dual-tracking system whereby patients and their doctors could choose either to wait for FDA-approved drugs or use new drugs that have passed Phase I safety trials but still are undergoing clinical trials for effectiveness. Patients choosing early access to new drugs could get complete information about the new drug from a Tradeoff Evaluation Database (Madden 2010).

Ways to Reduce Drug Costs

Policymakers can help their constituents reduce spending on prescription drugs without new legislation (Herrick 2006e):

- Since much of the cost of prescription drugs is the result of retail mark-ups, comparison-shopping often saves consumers 30 percent to 50 percent and sometimes more.

- Requesting a generic substitute for an expensive branded drug can reduce prices as much as 90 percent.

- With a physician's permission, buying larger-dose tablets and an inexpensive pill splitter can cut drug cost in half.

Recommended reading: F.R. Lichtenberg, "The Value of New Drugs," *Milken Institute Review*, Fourth Quarter 2003; Devon Herrick, "Shopping for Drugs: 2007," National Center for Policy Analysis, *Policy Report* No. 293, 2006; Richard Epstein, "How Safe and Effective Is the FDA?" *Medical Progress Today,* June 30, 2006.

9. Reduce malpractice litigation expenses.

Malpractice litigation is costly and often fails to reimburse victims and change the behavior of medical providers.

Malpractice insurance, litigation, and the practice of defensive medicine are responsible for part of the unnecessarily high cost of health care in the U.S. Some of this expense is caused by over-reliance on third-party payers, making it difficult for patients to hold providers accountable for their mistakes without resorting to lawsuits.

The High Cost of Malpractice Litigation

In real terms, malpractice claims grew 10-fold and malpractice premiums tripled during the past 30 years (Frank and Grace 2006). In 2001, 52 percent of malpractice awards were for amounts in excess of $1 million, compared to a median award of less than $500,000 just five years earlier (Manhattan Institute 2003).

Even though doctors win an overwhelming majority of medical malpractice cases, these claims still impose huge costs on doctors and insurers. The average legal cost exceeds $93,000 in cases where the doctor successfully defends against a malpractice case and is nearly $19,000 in cases where a claim is dismissed or dropped (AMA 2006).

Lawsuit abuse leads to "defensive medicine," the practice of physicians, hospital administrators, and other providers to order tests and file reports solely for the sake of reducing the possibility of litigation in the event a patient doesn't get well. The annual cost of defensive medicine has been estimated by the Department of Health and Human Services as being between $60 billion and $108 billion (HHS 2002).

Issues Regarding Legal Reform

The plaintiff's bar and its apologists claim rising malpractice insurance premiums are the result of poor investment decisions and price-gouging by insurance companies, not frivolous lawsuits or giant awards (Hunter 2004). These claims are unpersuasive.

Many malpractice insurers are physician-owned nonprofit mutual companies and their rates are similar to those offered by commercial insurers. It is unlikely doctors are over-charging themselves for insurance. If insurers were making excessive profits there would be new firms entering the market, but the market has seen more exits than entries. Poor investment strategies seem unlikely to be the culprit given that 80 percent of medical-malpractice insurer investments are in bonds rather than stocks. And investment losses should be unrelated to an insurer's decision to sell a profitable product (Frank and Grace 2006).

The plaintiff's bar and even some reform advocates say caps on awards discourage attorneys from taking on risky cases, deny appropriate compensation to victims of medical malpractice, and send a signal to hospitals and doctors that life-threatening mistakes are tolerable (Hyman and Silver 2007). While these concerns are legitimate, caps may be a necessary part of an overall legal reform strategy because the plaintiff's bar opposes other reforms that would reduce their financial windfalls while ensuring that victims receive fair and speedy compensation.

Legal Reforms

States that have passed legislation to reduce the cost of malpractice litigation include Alaska, California, Colorado, Maine, Michigan, and Utah. The Oklahoma legislature passed legislation (SB 507) in April 2007 that is a good model for other states. Specific reforms concerned citizens should support include:

- Cap non-economic damages for pain and suffering, which are difficult to quantify and subject to abuse (Pruitt and Schwartz 2003). Approximately 30 states have imposed caps.

- Create special medical courts to deal exclusively with complex medical malpractice cases requiring specialized knowledge (McCaughey 2003).

- Require state licensing boards and hospitals to conduct quality audits of physicians who are repeat offenders, publicize the results, and report them to the National Practitioner Databank (Hyman and Silver 2007).

- Require malpractice claimants who reject reasonable settlement offers to meet a "beyond any reasonable doubt" standard to win pain-and-suffering damages (Horowitz 1999).

Recommended reading: T. Frank and M.F. Grace, "Faulty Studies from Center for Justice & Democracy Are Stunting the Medical-Malpractice Debate," American Enterprise Institute, *Policy Outlook*, 2006; Manhattan Institute, *Trial Lawyers, Inc.: A Report on the Lawsuit Industry in America 2003,* Manhattan Institute Center for Legal Policy, 2003.

10. Encourage long-term care insurance.

Middle- and upper-income families should privately insure for their long-term care needs.

Many members of America's "baby boomer" generation face a financial crisis as they enter retirement without having made adequate arrangements for retirement income or health care expenses (Goodman and Cordell 1998). Encouraging the purchase of long-term care insurance and saving Medicaid for the truly needy are two ways policymakers can help their constituents and control Medicaid spending.

Long-Term Care and Medicaid
Long-term care (LTC) – commonly defined as nursing home care or home health care for individuals above the age of 65 or with a chronic condition requiring constant supervision – is a growing part of the nation's health care system. LTC expenditures account for about 8.5 percent of total health expenditures in the U.S., or 1.2 percent of gross domestic product. Real expenditures (adjusted for inflation) are expected to triple over the next 35 years (Brown and Finklestein 2004).

LTC can be very expensive, with the average nursing home providing skilled care charging between $150 and $300 per day, or as much as $100,000 a year. Custodial home care costs less, but just three visits per week can cost more than $9,000 a year.

Medicaid was designed to help meet the health care needs, including LTC, of the indigent, but over the years it has become the principal source of payment for nursing home and home health care costs for all Americans. Medicaid paid 44.3 percent of nursing home costs in 2004, while private health insurance paid only 7.8 percent of nursing home bills and 12 percent of home health care costs (Moses 2007a).

Reducing Reliance on Medicaid

"Medicaid's LTC benefit has become 'inheritance insurance' for baby boomers," explains Stephen Moses, "lulling them into a false sense of security regarding their own future LTC needs. Medicaid's loose eligibility rules for LTC create perverse incentives that invite abuse and discourage responsible LTC planning" (Moses 2005).

A cottage industry has emerged to counsel middle- and upper-income retirees on how to shelter their wealth in order to qualify for Medicaid. Most elderly people needing nursing home care can easily qualify for Medicaid-financed LTC, even those with middle- and upper-incomes and substantial assets (Moffit and Moses 2000).

Private insurance for long-term care is available, but only about 15 percent of seniors and 5 percent of baby boomers own such policies. The benefits paid by private LTC insurance are often redundant with Medicaid or make the insured ineligible for Medicaid, amounting to an implicit tax of 60 to 75 percent on the benefits paid from private LTC insurance plans (Brown and Finklestein 2004).

Unless Medicaid policies are changed, it is unlikely the number of people buying private LTC insurance will grow fast enough to prevent a financial crisis in the coming years.

Policy Reforms

States will not be able to fund all the health needs of tens of millions of retiring middle-income baby boomers in the years ahead. The cost would simply be too enormous. To the extent possible under federal law, states should target Medicaid LTC benefits to people truly in need and prevent Medicaid from being free "inheritance insurance" for middle- and upper-income families (Moses 2004; Moses 2007b). Specifically:

- Estimate the savings that could accrue by tightening Medicaid eligibility rules and expanding Medicaid estate recoveries.

- Set up programs to divert applicants for Medicaid to home equity conversion and private insurance.

- Close Medicaid eligibility loopholes such as those related to annuities, trusts, asset transfers, and life care contracts.

- Make Medicaid a loan, not a grant, for middle-income recipients and implement a strong estate recovery program to ensure loans are repaid.

- Use some of the savings to encourage the younger and healthier population to plan, save, invest, and privately insure for long-term care.

Recommended reading: S.A. Moses, *The Long-Term Care Dilemma: What States are Doing Right - and Wrong* (Washington, DC: Council for Affordable Health Insurance and American Legislative Exchange Council, September 2004); S.A. Moses, "Aging America's Achilles' Heel: Medicaid Long-Term Care," Cato Institute, *Policy Analysis* No. 549, September 2005.

References

AHIP. 2006a. Census shows 3.2 million people covered by HSA plans. America's Health Insurance Plans, January.

AHIP. 2006b.HSAs and account-based plans: An overview of preliminary research. America's Health Insurance Plans, June.

AMA. 2006. Medical liability reform – NOW! American Medical Association, July 19.

Anderson, G.F. and P.S. HusseyS. 2000. Multinational comparisons of health system data. Commonwealth Fund, October.

Anderson, Gerard *et al.* 2002. It's the prices, stupid: why the United States is so different from other countries. *Health Affairs*, May/June.

Argrawal, V. *et al.* 2005. Consumer-directed health plan report - early evidence is promising. McKinsey & Co., June.

Asch, S.M. *et al.* 2006. Who is at greatest risk for receiving poor-quality health care? *New England Journal of Medicine* 354 (11), March 16.

Barnes, J. 2006. The failure of government central planning: Washington's medical certificate of need program. *Policy Brief*, Washington Policy Center, January.

Bast, D.C. 2005a. Bill would allow consumers to purchase health insurance across state lines. *Health Care News,* June.

Bast, D.C. 2005b. Individual health insurance is accessible, affordable, study finds. *Health Care News,* October.

Bast, J.L. 2005. Bush health care agenda introduced in congress. *Health Care News*, June.

Bast, J.L. 2004. How community rating and guaranteed issue have destroyed the individual insurance market in eight states. *Health Care News,* February.

Bast, J.L., R.C. Rue, and S.A. Wesbury. 1993. *Why we spend too much on health care.* Chicago, IL: The Heartland Institute.

Blue Cross Blue Shield Association 2005a. The uninsured in america. W20-04-035, January.

Blue Cross Blue Shield Association 2005b. Blue Cross and Blue Shield Association consumer survey shows high rate of satisfaction with HSAs, cites increased reliance on decision-support tools. September.

Brase, T. 2000. WHO belittles U.S. health system. *Intellectual Ammunition,* November/December.

Brown, J.R. and A. Finkelstein. 2004. The interaction of public and private insurance: Medicaid and the long-term care insurance market. MIT and NBER.

Bunce, V.C. 2002. Dirty little secrets about clean claims laws. *Issues & Answers,* Council for Affordable Health Insurance, November.

Bunce, V.C., J.P. Wieske, and V. Prikazsky. 2006. Health insurance mandates in the states 2006. Council for Affordable Health Insurance, March.

CAHI. 2007. HSA state implementation report. Council for Affordable Health Insurance, www.cahi.org, last accessed April 15, 2007.

Cannon, M.F. and M.D. Tanner. 2005. *Healthy competition: what's holding back health care and how to free it.* Washington, DC: Cato Institute.

Clay Trueman, L. 2006. Bush offers wide-ranging health care proposals. *Health Care News,* March.

CMS 2006. National health expenditures by type of service and source of funds: calendar years 1960-2004. Department of Health and Human Services, Centers for Medicare and Medicaid Services.

Census Bureau. 2007. Health insurance coverage: 2005. U.S. Census Bureau, Housing and Household Economic Statistics Division.

Cherewatenko, V.S. 2002. The simplecare story. *Health Care News,* February.

Conover, C.J. and F. Sloan. 1998. Does removing certificate of need regulations lead to a surge in healthcare spending? *Journal of Health Politics, Policy and Law* 23 (3), June.

Cordato, R. 2005. Certificate-of-need laws: it's time for repeal. Nathaniel Macon Research Series, No. 1, John Locke Foundation, October.

Cutler, D.M. 2004. *Your money or your life: strong medicine for America's health care system.* New York, NY: Oxford University Press.

EBRI 2005. Early experience with high-deductible and consumer-driven health plans: findings from the EBRI/commonwealth fund consumerism in health care survey. Employee Benefit Research Institute, December.

eHealthInsurance. 2006. Health savings accounts: January 2005-December 2005. May.

Enthoven, A. and K. Fong. 2006. Medicare: negotiated drug prices may not lower costs. *Brief Analysis* No. 575, National Center for Policy Analysis, December 18.

Epstein, R.A. 1997. *Mortal peril: our inalienable right to health care?* Reading, MA: Addison-Wesley Publishing Company.

Epstein, R.A. 2006. How safe and effective is the FDA? *Medical Progress Today,* June 30.

Esmail, N., E. Walker, and D. Wrona. 2006. *Waiting your turn: hospital waiting lists in Canada.* 16th edition. Vancouver: Fraser Institute.

Feldman, R. *et al.* 2005. Health savings accounts: early estimates of national take-up. *Health Affairs*, November/December.

Finkelstein, A. 2006. The aggregate effects of health insurance: evidence from the introduction of medicare. National Bureau of Economic Research, April.

Flowers, A.T. 2007. National market could cure America's health care crisis: policy analysts. *Health Care News*, January.

Foundation for Health Coverage Education. 2007. The health care options matrix. www.coverageforall.org last accessed April 15, 2007.

Frank, T. and M.F. Grace. 2006. Faulty studies from Center for Justice & Democracy are stunting the medical-malpractice debate. *Liability Outlook*, American Enterprise Institute, April.

Giuliani Partners 2005. Examination and assessment of prescription drug importation from foreign sources to the United States. Report commissioned by PhRMA, April.

Goodman, J.C. 2005a. Drug reimportation: The free trade solution. *Brief Analysis* No. 503, National Center for Policy Analysis, February.

Goodman, J.C. 2005b. Making HSAs better. *Brief Analysis* No. 518, National Center for Policy Analysis, June.

Goodman, J.C. and D.E. Cordell. 1998. The nightmare in our future: elderly entitlements. *Policy Report*, National Center for Policy Analysis, January.

Goodman, J.C. and G.L. Musgrave. 1992. *Patient power: solving America's health care crisis*. Washington, DC: Cato Institute.

Goodman, J.C., G.L. Musgrave, and D.M. Herrick. 2004. *Lives at risk: single payer national health insurance around the world.* Lanham, MD: Roman & Littlefield.

Gratzer, D. 2006. *The cure: how capitalism can save American health care.* New York, NY: Encounter Books.

Hadley, J. and J. Holahan. 2003. How much medical care do the uninsured use, and who pays for it? *Health Affairs,* February.

Herrick, D.M. 2003. Why are health costs rising? *Brief Analysis* No. 437, National Center for Policy Analysis, May.

Herrick, D.M. 2006a. Transparency helps patients shop for care. *Health Care News,* April.

Herrick, D.M. 2006b. Telemedicine provides benefits, but security and privacy risks abound. *Health Care News*, June.

Herrick, D.M. 2006c. Crisis of the uninsured: 2006 update. *Brief Analysis* No. 568, National Center for Policy Analysis, September.

Herrick, D.M. 2006d. Medical tourism is prompting price discussions. *Health Care News,* October.

Herrick, D.M. 2006e. Shopping for drugs: 2007. *Policy Report* No 293, National Center for Policy Analysis, November.

Herrick, D.M. and J.C. Goodman. 2007. Price and quality in health care: The coming revolution in the medical marketplace. *Policy Report,* National Center for Policy Analysis, January.

HHS. 2002. Confronting the new health care crisis: improving health care quality and lowering costs by fixing our medical liability system. U.S. Department of Health and Human Services, July.

Horowitz, M.J. 1999. Suited for reform. *American Outlook*, Hudson Institute, February.

HPCG 2007. Principles for health insurance coverage for children and families. Health Policy Consensus Group, Galen Institute, April.

Hunter, R. 2004. *Medical malpractice insurance: stable losses/unstable rates 2004.* Americans for Insurance Reform, October.

Hyman, D.A. and C. Silver. 2007. Medical malpractice litigation and tort reform: it's the incentives, stupid, *Vanderbilt Law Review* 59 (4).

Jensen, G.A. and M. Morrisey. 1999. Mandated benefit laws and employer-sponsored health Insurance. Health Insurance Association of America.

Kaiser 2005a. Employer health benefits 2005 annual survey. Kaiser Family Foundation.

Kaiser 2005b. Medicare spending and financing fact sheet. Kaiser Family Foundation, April.

Kaiser 2007a. Characteristics of the uninsured. Kaiser Family Foundation, February.

Kaiser 2007b. Medicaid program at a glance. Kaiser Family Foundation, March.

Kleba 2007. A health link hits home. *Governing*, March.

Konig, S. 2005. Medicaid reform: Florida, South Carolina lead the way. *Health Care News,* August.

Kreit, B. 2006. Transparency provision removed from federal bill. *Health Care News,* October.

Lichtenberg, F.R. 2003. The value of new drugs, *Milken Institute Review*, Fourth Quarter.

Lichtenberg, F.R. 1996. The effect of pharmaceutical utilization and innovation on hospitalization and mortality. *NBER Working Paper* No. 5418, National Bureau of Economic Research, January.

LoBuono, C. 2006. When pharmacies compete for patients, prices drop. *Health Care News*, November.

Madden, B.J. 2010. *Free To Choose Medicine.* Chicago, IL: The Heartland Institute.

Manhattan Institute. 2003. Trial lawyers, inc.: a report on the lawsuit industry in America 2003. Center for Legal Policy, Manhattan Institute.

Martin, T. 2007. *Research & commentary on retail health clinics*. The Heartland Institute, April.

McCaughey, B. 2003. Medical courts would heal infirmities of legal system. *Investor's Business Daily*, July 17.

McClaughry, J. 2003. A health care reform agenda: desirable state changes. *Health Care News*, March.

McKinsey & Company 2005. Consumer-directed health plan report – early evidence is promising. June.

Medicare Payment Advisory Commission. 2003. 2002 survey of physicians about the Medicare program. March.

Meier, C.F. 2001a. Fee-for-service health care makes a comeback. *Health Care News*, March.

Meier, C.F. 2001b. Does managed care cause medical errors? *Health Care News*, March.

Meier, C.F. 2002. *Britain's deadly mistake: a first-hand report on England's disastrous experience with nationalized health care*. Chicago, IL: The Heartland Institute.

Meier, C.F. 2005a. *Destroying insurance markets: how guaranteed issue and community rating destroyed the individual health insurance market in eight states*. Washington, DC and Chicago, IL: Council for Affordable Health Insurance and The Heartland Institute, October.

Meier, C.F. 2005b. Campaign for drug importation falters. *Health Care News*, February.

Moffit, R.E., R. Teske, and S. Moses. 2000. How to cope with the coming crisis in long term care. *Heritage Lectures*, The Heritage Foundation, April.

Moses, S.A. 2004. *The long-term care dilemma: what states are doing right - and wrong.* Washington, DC: Council for Affordable Health Insurance and American Legislative Exchange Council, September.

Moses, S.A. 2005. Aging America's Achilles' heel: Medicaid long-term care. *Policy Analysis* No. 549, Cato Institute, September.

Moses, S.A. 2007a. Bias in long-term care favors nursing homes, government. *Health Care News,* February.

Moses, S.A. 2007b. States can fix long-term care problems. *Health Care News*, April.

NAHU. 2005. Analysis of state-level health insurance market reforms. National Association of Health Underwriters, October.

NCHS. 2006. Health, United States, 2006. U.S. Centers for Disease Control and Prevention, National Center for Health Statistics.

Newhouse, J. 1993. *Free for all?* Cambridge, MA: Harvard University Press.

OECD. 2004. Health spending in most OECD countries rises, with the U.S. far outstripping all others. Organization for Economic Cooperation and Development, www.oecd.org last accessed April 17, 2007.

Parnell, S. 2005a. Nurse practitioners offer effective, low-cost care. *Health Care News*, October.

Parnell, S. 2005b. Specialty hospitals offer savings, improved care in future. *Health Care News,* January.

Pitts, P. 2006. Pharmaceutical fakery is health care terrorism. *Baltimore Sun,* August 15.

Pruitt, S. and V. Schwartz. 2003. Placing constitutional limits on punitive damages: state legislatures may help. *ALEC Policy Forum*, American Legislative Exchange Council, April.

Raniszewski Herrera, C. 2006. Pressure for market-based Medicaid reform rises. *Budget & Tax News*, June.

Sikora, K., M. Slevin, and N. Bosanquet. 2005. *Cancer care in the NHS.* London: Reform.

Singh, S. and J.E. Darroch. 2000. Adolescent pregnancy and childbearing: levels and trends in developed countries. *Family Planning Perspectives* 32 (1).

Tanner, M. 2006. Individual mandates for health insurance: slippery slope to national health care. *Policy Analysis* No. 565, Cato Institute, April.

Thorpe, K.E. and J.C. Goodman. 2005. *Reforming the health care system*. Muncie, IN: Miller College of Business, Ball State University and The Heartland Institute.

Turner, G. and C.F. Meier. 2004. Prescription drug importation: just the facts. *Health Care News,* June.

Wennberg, J.E. *et al.* 2006. The care of patients with severe chronic illness: an online report on the medicare program. The Center for the Evaluative Clinical Sciences, Dartmouth Medical School.

Wesbury, S. 1990. Why other nations' Rx won't work. *Healthcare Executive* 5 (4), July/August.

Wharam, J. Frank *et al.* 2007. Emergency department use and subsequent hospitalizations among members of a high deductible health plan. *Journal of the American Medical Association,* March.

Wieske, J.P. 2007. *State legislators' guide to health insurance solutions*. Council for Affordable Health Insurance.

Wieske, J.P. and M. Matthews. 2007. *Understanding the uninsured and what to do about them*. Washington, DC: Council for Affordable Health Insurance.

Wilson, J.Q. 1989. *Bureaucracy: what government agencies do and why they do it*. New York, NY: Basic Books.

Young, M. and E. Butler. 2002. Britain's million-year wait. *Health Care News*, June.

Additional Resources

- *PolicyBot*, The Heartland Institute's free online clearinghouse for the work of other free-market think tanks, contains thousands of documents on health care issues. It is on Heartland's Web site at www.heartland.org.

- *www.healthpolicy-news.org*, a Web site devoted to the latest news and commentary about health policy issues. Read headlines, watch videos, or browse the thousands of documents on health policy reform available from *PolicyBot*.

- *Health Care News*, a monthly publication from The Heartland Institute. Subscribe online at www.heartland.org.

Directory

The following national organizations support sound policies on health care reform and are good sources of additional research and commentary on this issue.

American Action Forum, www.americanactionforum.org
Cato Institute, www.cato.org
Commonwealth Foundation, www.commonwealthfoundation.org
e21, www.obamacarewatch.org
Ethics & Public Policy Center, www.eppc.org
Galen Institute, www.galen.org
Heritage Foundation, www.heritage.org
Hoover Institution, www.hoover.org
HSA Coalition, www.hsacoalition.org
Institute for Policy Innovation, www.ipi.org
Maine Heritage Policy Center, www.mainepolicy.org
National Center for Policy Analysis (NCPA), www.ncpa.org
Pacific Research Institute, www.pacificresearch.org
State House Call, www.statehousecall.org

Chapter 2
Energy and Environment

Joseph L. Bast

---

10 Principles of Energy and Environment Policy

1. Energy independence is an illusion.
2. Gasoline prices are market-driven.
3. Global warming is not a crisis.
4. Air pollution is no longer a major public health problem.
5. Mercury is no longer a major public health problem.
6. Biofuels should not be subsidized.
7. CAFE standards sacrifice lives for oil.
8. Electric deregulation is still necessary.
9. Liquefied natural gas is part of the solution.
10. Nuclear energy is part of the solution.

Introduction

Energy issues are rising to the top of the agenda in many states, compelling elected officials to take positions on topics as wide-ranging as subsidies to biofuels producers and restrictions on mercury emissions from coal-burning power plants. Energy issues often are complex and frequently changing, with changes in technology, prices, and policies adopted in other states and other countries all affecting what policymakers do.

This chapter covers ten of the most important energy issues facing the country, with each section ending with recommended actions and recommended reading. A bibliography appears at the end of the chapter.

Three Themes

Three themes appear frequently in this chapter:

- Energy issues are often environmental issues, and vice versa. Restrictions on access to energy are often defended in the name of environmental protection.

- Newspaper stories and advocacy spin are often at odds with sound science and facts.

- Markets usually do a better job than governments at giving consumers what they want and directing capital and other scarce resources to their best and most efficient uses.

The first theme explains why this chapter addresses such issues as air quality, global warming, and mercury emissions. All are implicated in the use of fossil fuels, and solutions to these problems (or possible problems) have major effects on the supply and cost of energy.

The second theme, sound science, is in response to the fact that debates over energy policy often are driven by exaggeration and scare tactics used by advocates to boost public support for their agendas. Environmental groups embrace these tactics as a way to generate public sympathy for their cause, while business groups embrace them to secure subsidies for themselves or regulations that harm their competitors.

The final theme of this chapter, that markets tend to be more efficient than government at solving social and economic problems, is one of the lessons of the twentieth century. The collapse of the Soviet Union, the fall of the Berlin Wall, and the rise of Pacific Rim economies, China, and India give testimony to the power of free minds and free markets. The ideas of socialism and central planning, so influential at the beginning of the century, are now viewed by many policymakers as flawed and discredited by real-world experience.

The Policy Question

How do we balance energy and environmental concerns with the individual rights and freedoms we hold dear?

Those who say we must not utilize our least-expensive fuel sources are putting small and hypothetical risks ahead of better-understood costs and benefits. We know that coal, natural gas, and nuclear power can be used to generate electricity safely and cleanly. If we fail to do so, we risk supply interruptions and rising costs, which in turn will reduce economic growth and job creation.

Unhindered and unsubsidized competition among energy technologies is the best means to discovering tomorrow's new energy sources. Elected officials should not try to pick winners, even though doing so may score points with one group or another in the short term.

In the long term, the individual choices of people and businesses, not governments, will lead to a more diversified fuel supply, reliable energy technology, and environmental protection that is effective as well as efficient. Market-driven energy policies will generate the wealth necessary to maintain a healthy environment and provide our homes and businesses with affordable and reliable electricity.

Recommended reading: Joseph Bast and Sandy Liddy Bourne, *Energy Policy for America: A Guidebook for State Legislators* (Chicago, IL: The Heartland Institute, 2007); Robert L. Bradley, Jr. and Richard W. Fulmer, *Energy: The Master Resource* (Dubuque, IA: Kendall/Hunt Publishing Company, 2004); Stephen Moore and Julian L. Simon, *It's Getting Better All the Time: 100 Greatest Trends of the Last 100 Years* (Washington, DC: Cato Institute, 2000).

1. Energy independence is an illusion.

Markets, not politics, should determine how much energy we import.

"Energy independence" has become the rallying cry for many environmental and anti-war activists who seek to wean businesses and consumers in the U.S. from reliance on imported fossil fuels. But can energy independence be achieved, and if so at what cost?

How Dependent Are We?

Our dependency on imports is primarily in the transportation sector. Some 96 percent of energy used for transportation comes from oil, and slightly more than half of the oil consumed by the U.S. is imported. By 2020, imports are expected to amount to two-thirds of the U.S. oil supply. This is up from approximately 35 percent in 1973 and 37 percent in 1980 (Energy Information Administration 2008).

We are not dependent on imported fossil fuels for our electricity needs. Virtually all electricity in the U.S. is produced from domestic coal (52 percent), nuclear (21 percent), natural gas (14 percent, some of which is imported), hydroelectric (7 percent), and other renewable (2 percent) energy sources. Only 2.2 percent of the country's electricity comes from oil-fired plants.

The U.S. has sufficient reserves of coal and other energy resources to become energy independent. The U.S. has the world's largest coal reserves, with 264 billion short tons of recoverable coal reserves from a demonstrated reserve base of 491 billion short tons (Energy Information Administration 2007). Coal can be and increasingly is burned cleanly, though mining, transportation, and disposal of ash and sludge have negative environmental impacts. Coal also can be liquified and gasified for use in transportation, home heating, and other applications.

The U.S. is the third largest producer of oil, behind Saudi Arabia and Russia, and has the tenth largest proven reserves of oil in the world. Alaska's Arctic National Wildlife Refuge (ANWR) holds at least 4.5 billion barrels of oil and possibly as much as 11.5 billion barrels.

Federal lands in the U.S. contain some 635 trillion cubic feet of recoverable natural gas, but development of much of this is prohibited by federal laws. For example, more than 40 percent of natural gas reserves in the Rocky Mountain West is off-limits to development, and only 24 percent of U.S. offshore oil and gas prospects is open to exploration and drilling (Innis 2008).

Nuclear power also holds great promise and is seeing a worldwide resurgence (Domenici 2004). New innovations such as pebble bed reactors are likely to reduce costs and further increase safety, but once again, environmentalist activism obstructs new investment.

Why Do We Import Energy?

We import energy for two reasons. First, laws ban commercial access to billions of barrels of oil, trillions of cubic feet of natural gas, and billions of tons of low-sulfur coal in the U.S. These laws were passed supposedly to protect wilderness areas, but the actual intent and their effect have been to restrict access to domestic sources of energy.

The second reason we import oil (and increasingly natural gas) is economic: When the cost of imported oil is low, it is plainly in the interests of U.S. businesses and consumers to buy it, just as buying other goods and services from other countries when they are inexpensive is a boon to American consumers. Free trade benefits both parties to every transaction, and by encouraging greater specialization of labor it boosts productivity and therefore total wealth.

When the cost of imported oil is high, as it currently is, we import energy until domestic producers, alerted to profit opportunities by the higher prices, resume or increase their production. Domestic supplies eventually increase, thereby moderating prices and once again benefitting consumers. This response, however, takes time, and it can be slowed or even stopped by government policies such as restrictions on drilling and mining on public lands and "windfall" taxes.

Why Energy Independence Is an Illusion

Genuine energy independence would require energy *isolationism* – the erection of barriers to free trade with other countries – which is known to slow economic growth, invite retaliation by trading partners, and raise prices. Free trade, not isolationism, is the way to enhance energy security and world peace.

According to Robert Ebel, head of the energy program at the Center for Strategic and International Studies, "It makes absolutely no sense to talk about energy independence. ... We cannot produce our way to energy independence, and we cannot use efficiency or conservation to achieve energy independence. It's just not going to happen, at least in my lifetime" (Cassidy 2004).

The benefits of energy independence are also an illusion. Reducing oil imports from the Middle East would not substantially affect the U.S. because oil from the Middle East accounts for only 11 percent of all U.S. oil imports (Shughart 2008). Canada and Mexico are the two largest sources of oil imported to the U.S., and boycotting our neighboring allies would make no sense at all.

Oil is bought and sold in global markets, so even if the U.S. stopped buying oil from the Middle East, other countries would buy it instead, freeing up oil that the U.S. could then import. The U.S. cannot de-fund Middle Eastern terrorists by reducing its oil imports from the region (Taylor and Van Doren January 2006).

America's military is not in Iraq because of oil, although the Mideast's large oil reserves contribute to its political instability. The U.S. has historically maintained a military presence in the Mideast for several reasons, including to stop Soviet expansionism, protect Israel from its Arab neighbors, and most recently to stop the spread of terrorism.

Policy Recommendations

Since some progress toward self-sufficiency could make our energy supplies more secure, policymakers should focus on removing public policies that restrict the development of domestic energy supplies, including nuclear power and domestic fossil fuel reserves. The following steps are recommended:

- Support the repeal of federal and state restrictions on coal, natural gas, and oil extraction from public lands and offshore.

- Remove regulatory barriers and policies that allow anti-nuclear and NIMBY ("not in my backyard") activists to stop or delay the construction of new facilities.

- End subsidies and preferences for all types of energy – fossil fuels as well as renewables – and allow energy technologies to compete on a level playing field.

- Repeal state "renewable portfolio standard" laws that force electric utilities to purchase highly subsidized wind power.

Recommended reading: Roy Innis, *Energy Keepers - Energy Killers, The New Civil Rights Battle* (Chicago, IL: Merril Press and The Heartland Institute, 2008); Energy Information Administration, *Annual Energy Outlook 2008 with Projections to 2030*, 2008.

2. Gasoline prices are market-driven.

Government policies, not greedy oil companies, are responsible for high and rising gasoline prices.

The climb of retail gasoline prices to historically high levels in the summer of 2008 led to claims that oil companies are manipulating prices, calls for price controls, and talk of the need to achieve "energy independence." Closer analysis shows market processes are working well and a very different set of public policy changes is in order.

Oil Industry Profits

While large in absolute dollar amounts, oil industry profits are modest when measured as net income on each dollar of revenue. Over the past five years, the industry's net income was only 5.7 cents per dollar of revenue, hardly different than the 5.5 cents average for all industries (Stanek 2006).

Oil industry profits are also highly cyclical. The oil industry goes through repeated boom and bust cycles as prices vary but high levels of investment in capital and exploration must be maintained. Today's high profits pay for investments made in the past that did not generate returns for investors because of low gasoline prices.

Finally, the oil industry pays high taxes already. ExxonMobil reported net after-tax earnings of $40.6 billion in 2007, paid $30 billion in corporate taxes that year, and had an effective tax rate of about 40 percent, much higher than other industries (ExxonMobil 2008). Other oil companies reported similarly high tax rates.

How High Are Gasoline Prices?

Gasoline prices in 2008, adjusted for inflation, exceeded the record-high prices of the early 1980s. Nationally, the average retail price exceeded $4 a gallon in July 2008.

The good news is that Americans today spend only about 4 percent of their household income on motor fuels, a third less than the 6 percent of household income spent in the early 1980s (Newman 2008). Consumers are beginning to cut back on the distances they drive: Miles traveled fell 4.3 percent in March 2008 compared with March 2007, and families are choosing the most fuel-efficient car in the garage for various trips. Overall, the miles per gallon of households with two or three cars has risen about 12 percent since 2000 (*Ibid.*).

Causes of Price Increases

Gasoline prices have risen because global demand for oil has risen dramatically, attributable in large part to rapid industrialization in China and India, while global production has not kept pace. The wars in Iraq and Afghanistan and Hurricanes Katrina and Rita each interrupted crude oil production, transport, or refining capacity, contributing to price spikes.

Public policies are partly to blame for high gasoline prices. An expansive monetary policy has made the U.S. dollar fall relative to most other currencies, while also making commodities such as oil an attractive target for international investment. Overly restrictive environmental regulations at the federal and state levels have placed most new U.S. oil resources off-limits, preventing domestic producers from increasing their output to help meet rising demand.

Regulatory requirements for 50 different blends of reformulated fuels for individual cities and regions in the U.S. add 10 to 13 cents to the price per gallon of gasoline and create temporary bottlenecks in supply. Federal and state ethanol mandates have increased gasoline prices by approximately 25 to 30 cents per gallon (Bourne August 2006).

High taxes on oil company profits combined with high excise taxes on retail sales increase the price of gasoline substantially. Nationwide, excise taxes on gasoline average 46 cents per gallon. In Chicago, the nation's highest motor fuel taxes raise the price of a gallon of gasoline by more than 80 cents.

Recommended Policies

Concerned citizens can support specific steps to lower gasoline prices:

- Lower excise taxes on motor fuels.

- End subsidies and mandates for ethanol and other biofuels.

- Support ending restrictions on oil and gas exploration and production on public lands and in offshore and coastal areas.

- Call for reducing the number of boutique fuels required by federal laws.

Recommended reading: Jerry Taylor and Peter Van Doren, "Economic Amnesia: The Case against Oil Price Controls and Windfall Profit Taxes," *Policy Analysis*, Cato Institute, January 2006; Jonathan Williams and Scott Hodge, "Large Oil Industry Tax Payments Undercut Case for 'Windfall Profits' Tax," *Tax Facts* No. 48, Tax Foundation, January 31, 2006; Alastair J. Walling, "The Very Boring Reasons Behind High Gas Prices," *Regulation*, December 2005.

3. Global warming is not a crisis.

Concerns over global warming do not justify higher energy taxes or carbon "cap-and-trade" programs.

The use of fossil fuels to generate energy produces carbon dioxide (CO_2), a greenhouse gas which, everything else being equal, could lead to some warming of the global climate. Most scientists believe the Earth experienced a small rise in temperatures during the 1990s, but they are unsure how large a role human activities may have played.

The important questions from a public policy perspective are: How much of the warming is natural; how sure are we that it will continue; and would continued warming be beneficial or harmful? The answers, in brief, are: Probably two-thirds of the warming in the 1990s was due to natural causes; the warming trend has already stopped and forecasts of future warming are unreliable; and the benefits of a moderate warming are likely to outweigh the costs.

Natural or Man-Made?

The Intergovernmental Panel on Climate Change (IPCC), an agency of the United Nations, claims to know with certainty that the warming in recent decades was due to human activities. During the 1980s and 1990s, that warming appeared to be occurring at the rate of between 0.15 and 0.17 degrees Celsius per decade, for a possible increase over the next century of 1.5 to 1.7 degrees C.

Many climate scientists disagree with the IPCC on this key issue. They say it is impossible to tell if the recent small warming trend is *natural*, a continuation of the planet's recovery from the recent "Little Ice Age," or *unnatural*, the result of human greenhouse gas emissions (Idso and Singer

2009). A 2003 survey of climate scientists found only 9.4 percent "strongly agreed" that climate change is mostly the result of human activity while 10.2 percent "strongly disagreed." Nearly half (44.2 percent) disagreed or were uncertain (Bray and von Storch 2007).

How Much Warming?

While the global climate warmed slightly during the 1980s and 1990s, it has not warmed at all since 2000, and there is some evidence that a cooling trend has begun (Taylor 2007). This contradicts the predictions of the IPCC and poses a challenge to the theory that CO_2 concentrations play a major role in global temperature trends. However, it confirms the views of many less-politicized climate scientists who acknowledge that the global climate is always warming or cooling (Michaels 2005; Christy 2006).

When asked if computer climate models "can accurately predict climate conditions in the future," only a third (35.1 percent) of climate scientists say they agree, while 18.3 percent were uncertain and nearly half (46.6 percent) disagreed. Majorities of the scientists say the current state of scientific knowledge is inadequate to provide reasonable predictions of climate variability on time scales of ten years, 100 years, or greater than 100 years (Bray and von Storch 2007).

The scientific community's lack of certainty about future climate trends is rooted in the shortcomings of computer models. These models are the centerpiece of the IPCC's reports, yet it is widely recognized that they fail to account for changes in precipitation, water vapor, and clouds that are likely to occur in a warmer world. It is a case of "garbage in, garbage out."

Global Warming Benefits as Well as Harms

Alarmists claim global warming will cause massive flooding, more violent weather, famines, and other catastrophic consequences. Once again, these claims are not supported by most scientists.

Sea levels are unlikely to rise by more than several inches, weather may actually become more mild, and most warming occurs at night and during the winter season, meaning it has little adverse effect (and some positive effect) on plants and wildlife. Hurricanes are likely to diminish, not increase, in frequency or severity (Spencer 2008; Singer and Avery 2008). Higher levels of CO_2 have a fertilizing effect on plants and make them more drought-resistant. Warmer temperatures are also likely to be accompanied by higher soil moisture levels and more frequent rain.

The current best estimate is that, if left unaddressed, by 2060 global warming is likely to have a small (0.2 percent of GDP) positive effect on the U.S. economy and a small (1 to 2 percent of GDP) negative effect on the global economy (Mendelsohn and Neumann 1999). These estimates are very small and speculative.

Reducing Emissions Is Expensive

While the likelihood that global warming would be a crisis was never large and is getting even smaller as new research is reported, we know the cost of reducing man-made greenhouse gas emissions would be high.

An analysis of a carbon "cap-and-trade" proposal considered by the U.S. Senate in 2008 – the Lieberman-Warner Act – found it would destroy between 1.2 and 1.8 million jobs in 2020 and between 3 and 4 million jobs in 2030; would impose a financial cost of $739 to $2,927 per year by 2020 on national households, rising to $4,022 to $6,752 by 2030; and would increase the price of gasoline between 60 percent and 144 percent by 2030 and the price of electricity by 77 percent to 129 percent (National Association of Manufacturers/ACCF 2008).

States that try to reduce emissions on their own are likely to incur costs *ten times* greater than a national program because businesses and residents would find it easier to move to nearby states with lower energy costs or less burdensome regulations and because states would have to rely on more costly command-and-control regulatory approaches (Bast, Taylor, and Lehr 2003).

The record of existing emission trading programs gives little basis for supposing a massively bigger regime would work. The sulfur dioxide trading program, often pointed to as a model, succeeded only because railroad deregulation made low-cost, low-sulfur coal available from the Powder River Basin (Johnston 1998). European emission trading programs have been characterized by low trading volumes, high price volatility, and mostly paper transactions that do not result in actual reductions in emissions. Most European countries are far behind schedule in meeting their emission reduction goals under the Kyoto Protocol.

Recommended Policies

Legislators should address the issue of global warming by endorsing the following policies:

- Oppose higher energy taxes or carbon "cap-and-trade" programs.

- Support research independent from government research programs that are biased toward alarmism.

- Remove barriers to energy conservation embedded in state and local laws and regulations, such as restrictive building codes and zoning ordinances.

- Support research and, if appropriate, capital investments in *adapting* to climate change rather than trying to prevent it.

- Pursue win-win strategies that produce enough benefits to pay their way apart from their possible effect on climate.

Recommended reading: Craig Idso and S. Fred Singer, *Climate Change Reconsidered: 2009 Report of the Nongovernmental International Panel on Climate Change (NIPCC)*, Chicago, IL: The Heartland Institute, 2009; Roy W. Spencer, *Climate Confusion* (New York, NY: Encounter Books, 2008).

4. Air pollution is no longer a major public health problem.

Air quality has improved dramatically, making new regulations unnecessary.

Air quality is better today in virtually all parts of the U.S. than at any time since measurements began. According to the Environmental Protection Agency (EPA), emissions of the six "criteria" air pollutants dropped 57 percent between 1970 and 2007, while GDP increased 207 percent, vehicle miles traveled increased 179 percent, energy consumption increased 47 percent, and U.S. population grew by 49 percent (EPA 2008).

Concentrations of particulate matter (PM_{10}) have decreased by 28 percent and of fine particulate matter ($PM_{2.5}$) by 11 percent nationally since

1990. Virtually the entire nation meets federal standards for carbon monoxide, sulfur dioxide, nitrogen dioxide, and lead (*Ibid.*).

No Public Health Effects

Reliable empirical research demonstrates that ambient levels of ozone and $PM_{2.5}$ are too low to have adverse health effects (Enstrom 2005). Indoor air quality, which EPA does not regulate, is typically of lower quality than outdoor air and poses a greater (though still trivial) health risk.

EPA's own technical analyses show reducing ozone levels in cities with the dirtiest air to levels necessary to meet the stringent new federal eight-hour ozone standard would at best reduce respiratory-related hospital admissions and emergency room visits by only a few tenths of a percent (Hubbell *et al.* 2005).

Claims that ambient concentrations of $PM_{2.5}$ cause fatalities are based on studies showing small statistical correlations between daily pollution levels and daily deaths, but such correlations fall well short of proving causation. High $PM_{2.5}$ levels are correlated with *fewer* deaths in about one-third of the cities studied (Schwartz 2006a). A long-term government study that followed thousands of children in California reported that higher ozone levels were associated with a *lower* risk of developing asthma (*Ibid.*).

Counterproductive Rules

EPA rules may be causing ozone levels to be higher than they would be otherwise. EPA and state regulators assume that reducing both oxides of nitrogen (NO_x) and volatile organic compounds (VOCs) is necessary for attaining the federal eight-hour ozone standard. NO_x and VOCs interact to form ozone, the main ingredient of smog.

But research suggests that too little NO_x can actually increase the amount of ozone created. This is happening in cities across the U.S. every weekend, as NO_x emissions decline by as much as 50 percent to 60 percent due to fewer diesel trucks and equipment in use, but ozone levels stay the same or even rise (Schwartz 2006b).

Current Standards Are Too Stringent

EPA has reduced the 24-hour $PM_{2.5}$ standard from 65 ug/m³ (micrograms per cubic meter of air) to 35 ug/m³, even though no new scientific evidence showed tightening the standard was necessary. In fact, EPA's analysis shows the 1997 PM standard is more protective than EPA had assumed when it first issued the standard (Bourne 2006a).

Since 1997, several clean air regulations were adopted whose effects won't be fully realized until 15 to 20 years from now, including the Tier 2 Mobile Source Rule, Highway Diesel Rule, Off Road Diesel Rule, Clean Air Interstate Rule, Clean Air Visibility Rule, and Clean Air Mercury Rule.

The cost of complying with the new $PM_{2.5}$ standard, estimated to be between $20 billion and $60 billion a year, far outweighs any possible benefits. Public resources that could be used for schools, police, and other valuable services will be used instead to pave the shoulders of rural roads, street-sweeping, car and truck emissions testing, and other services producing no public health benefits.

Recommended Policies

Concerned citizens can be for clean air without calling for unnecessary rules and regulations:

- Call on EPA to back off from new NO_x and PM emission standards.

- Oppose adoption of state clean air standards that are more strict than those of EPA. In particular, oppose adoption of California's more stringent auto emission standards.

Recommended reading: Indur M. Goklany, *Cleaning the Air: The Real Story of the War on Air Pollution* (Washington, DC: Cato Institute, 1999); Kay H. Jones, "NAAQS's 'Where's Waldo?' Problem," *Regulation*, Cato Institute, December 2004; Joel Schwartz and Steven Hayward, "Emissions Down, Smog Up. Say What?" American Enterprise Institute, January 2004.

5. Mercury is no longer a major public health problem.

The public health effects of mercury emissions from coal-burning power plants do not justify restrictions on the use of coal.

The mainstream media is filled with alarming stories about the potential health hazards of mercury. While exposure to high concentrations of mercury can pose a threat to human health, the media and environmental groups that supply them with information have overlooked important facts that put the risk in perspective.

Man-made Versus Natural Sources
Mercury is a naturally occurring element that is ubiquitous in the environment. It is also produced during some manufacturing processes and is emitted by coal-fired electric generation plants. Naturally occurring mercury emissions dominate the world mercury "budget," with power plants in the U.S. contributing no more than a fraction of 1 percent of annual global mercury emissions into the air (Pombo and Gibbons 2005).

Mercury emissions from industrial sources in the U.S. have fallen by 90 percent since the 1970s. Power plants are responsible for about 40 percent of remaining emissions. EPA rules require U.S. power plants to reduce their mercury emissions by 70 percent below current levels by 2018 (Taylor 2004).

No Human Health Risk
Environmental activists have scared people, and especially pregnant women, away from including fish in their diets. However, even pregnant mothers were not harmed by very high mercury exposure in the Seychelles Islands. An ongoing, comprehensive Rochester Medical Center mercury exposure study of 643 children (from birth to 9 years of age) in the Seychelles Islands finds that even after maternal consumption of 12 to 14 fish meals per week and mercury blood levels about six times those found in U.S. citizens, there were "no detectable adverse effects" (Myers *et al.* 2003, 1686-92).

The average concentration of mercury in fish found in American grocery stores ranges from non-detectable to about 0.4 parts per million (ppm) – well below the Food and Drug Administration's action level of 1.0 ppm (Ferguson 2004).

Most of the fish consumed in the U.S. are harvested from many places around the world; such fish are not directly affected by domestic power plant emissions. Mandating mercury emission reductions on U.S. electric generation plants will have no effect on mercury concentrations in fish consumed here.

EPA's Standards Are Too Strict

EPA's overly strict mercury standards threaten the public's health (Charnley 2005). EPA sets its safety standard for mercury in fish at 0.3 ppm or lower based on the most restrictive consumption "reference dose" of no more than 0.1 microgram of mercury per kilogram of body weight per day. This standard, the most stringent in the world, has been widely acknowledged to be based on a flawed study of a remote population that consumed large amounts of whale meat and fats contaminated by other toxic chemicals.

EPA's unrealistically low standard has resulted in freshwater fish advisories being issued for rivers and lakes in almost every state. Unfortunately, many people have been frightened away from eating fish entirely.

People with heart disease and various types of cancer, Alzheimer's disease, and type-2 diabetes realize many health benefits from including fish in their diets. Studies have consistently shown regular consumption of fish reduces the risk of heart disease.

Nutritional benefits of protein and omega-3 fatty acids in fish are particularly important for pregnant mothers and their developing babies. Scientists agree the nutritional value of fish in the mental development of children in the womb far outweighs any alleged negative effects of trace amounts of mercury found in fish.

Recommended Policies

Concerned citizens should oppose alarmism over the possible effects of mercury.

- Stress that fish is safe to eat. It has great nutritional benefits and no risk of harm from trace levels of mercury.

- Oppose proposals to impose on power plants and other sources mercury emission standards more strict than federal laws.

Recommended reading: James M. Taylor, "Illinois Governor Ignores Science, Pushes Mercury Cuts," *Environment & Climate News*, April 2006; Richard Pombo and Jim Gibbons, "Mercury in Perspective: Fact and Fiction About the Debate Over Mercury," U.S. House Resources Committee, February 2005; Gail Charnley, "Regulating Mercury Emissions from Power Plants: Will it Protect Our Health?" American Council on Science and Health, October 2005.

6. Biofuels should not be subsidized.

Ethanol and other biofuels do not produce environmental or economic benefits that justify their subsidization.

Biofuels are liquid and gaseous fuels made from organic matter and include ethanol, biodiesel, and methanol. Interest in expanding the use of biofuels is high, spurred by a variety of concerns, some legitimate and some based on public misunderstanding.

Current Production of Biofuels
In 2007, 6.5 billion gallons of ethanol and 450 million gallons of biodiesel were produced in the U.S., about 5 percent of total U.S. oil consumption (Renewable Fuels Association 2008; National Biodiesel Board 2008). Most ethanol made in the U.S. comes from corn. Its production consumed 3.3 billion bushels of corn in 2007, nearly 25 percent of the entire U.S. corn crop (13.3 billion bushels).

Ethanol has been promoted as a fuel additive to reduce emissions, increase octane, and extend the gasoline supply. E10 (a 10 percent ethanol and 90 percent gasoline blend) is widely available. E85 (an 85 percent ethanol and 15 percent gasoline blend) is available mainly in corn-producing states; vehicles must be factory equipped or modified to use this fuel.

Current Mandates and Subsidies

Section 211(o) of the Clean Air Act, as amended by Congress in 2007, sets a requirement for 36 billion gallons of total renewable fuels by 2022, including 21 billion gallons of advanced biofuels (Caruso 2008). Federal and state subsidies for ethanol totaled between $5.8 billion and $7 billion in 2006 and for biodiesel totaled between $0.53 billion and $0.65 billion (Grain Journal 2007).

Congress protects domestic ethanol producers by imposing a 2.5 percent tariff and 54 cents per gallon duty on imports. Ethanol producers with plants with annual production capacity of up to 60 million gallons are eligible for production incentives of 10 cents per gallon on the first 15 million gallons of ethanol produced each year.

According to Jerry Taylor and Peter Van Doren, "in 2006, the subsidies translated into $1.05 to $1.38 per gallon of ethanol, or 42 percent to 55 percent of its wholesale market price." Subsidies to oil producers in 2006, in contrast, were "certainly less than $1 billion – which translates to 0.3 cents per gallon of gasoline" (Taylor and Van Doren 2007).

Why Do We Subsidize Biofuels?

Proponents of biofuels say increased production will increase the supply of transportation fuels and therefore lead to lower prices. But critics point out that ethanol costs more, not less, than gasoline, and current mandates have *increased* prices at the pump by approximately 25 to 30 cents per gallon. Ethanol has a lower energy content than does gasoline, meaning it is a poor value for most consumers (Grunwald 2008).

Using ethanol does not improve air quality because it reduces only carbon monoxide emissions, which are no longer a public health concern. It increases ozone production, which is still a problem in some cities at some times of the year.

Biofuels are said to reduce carbon dioxide emissions, thought to contribute to "global warming." But the latest research on this issue, published in *Science*, finds the production and use of a gallon of ethanol produces more carbon dioxide than does a gallon of gasoline (Fargione *et al.* 2008; Searchinger *et al.* 2008).

Biofuels are a "homegrown" and renewable energy source, so they extend the life of domestic reserves of fossil fuels. But we are at little risk of running out of fossil fuels, globally or in the U.S., for many years

(Carroll 2006; Huber and Mills 2005). Fear of running out of oil is no reason to bring biofuels online now.

Recommended Policies

Concerned citizens should oppose subsidizing any fuel, including biofuels:

- Oppose mandates and subsidies for ethanol and other biofuels.

- The path toward increased use of ethanol cannot be built by mandating blends that fall between E10 and E85 blends because doing so would require costly modifications to, and might cause performance problems for, existing vehicles.

- If the main justification for encouraging biofuels production is rural economic development, any subsidies for biofuels should come out of the budgets of current economic development and agriculture price support programs.

Recommended reading: Michael Grunwald, "The Clean Energy Scam," *Time*, March 2008; National Taxpayers Union, "Ethanol: Bumper Crop for Agribusiness, Bitter Harvest for Taxpayers," *Policy Study* #121, July 20, 2006; Dennis Avery, "Farming for Ethanol Would Have Serious Consequences for Forests, Food Production," *Environment & Climate News*, July 2006.

7. CAFE standards sacrifice lives for oil.

CAFE standards needlessly increase highway fatalities and don't significantly reduce emissions.

Increasing federal Corporate Average Fuel Economy (CAFE) standards is a common part of the legislative agenda of those who seek to solve environmental and energy problems by restricting the types of vehicles Americans can purchase and drive. But there are more cost-effective ways to save fuel, and CAFE standards have a terrible unintended consequence: needless highway deaths.

Understanding CAFE

CAFE standards, created by the 1975 Energy Policy Conservation Act, require manufacturers to achieve minimum targets for average fuel economy, expressed in miles per gallon (mpg).

CAFE currently mandates fuel economy of 27.5 mpg for passenger cars and 22.2 mpg for light trucks, rising for light trucks to between 21.3 and 28.4 mpg by 2011, depending on the size or "footprint" of the vehicle. The 2007 Energy Independence and Security Act (EISA) requires new cars and light trucks sold in 2020 to deliver a combined fleet average of 35 miles per gallon.

Under rules proposed by the Department of Transportation in April 2008, fleet-wide fuel economy would increase by 4.5 percent annually through 2015. For passenger cars, fuel economy would rise from the current 27.5 mpg to 35.7 miles per gallon by 2015, while for light trucks, fuel economy would rise from 23.5 mpg in 2010 to 28.6 mpg in 2015 (Peters 2008). California is seeking a waiver from EPA to impose even higher standards.

Higher CAFE Standards Don't Benefit Consumers

The idea that consumers can be made better off by restricting their freedom to choose – the presumption that lies at the bottom of all proposals to impose or raise CAFE standards – is false. Consumers are better positioned than regulators to choose the size, fuel economy, and other features of the cars and trucks they buy. Fuel economy information is plainly posted on new car price stickers, and the price of gasoline is advertised on every street corner.

The National Highway Traffic Safety Administration (NHTSA) claims the proposed CAFE standards for model year 2015 would produce private net benefits (to car and light truck owners) of $13.3 billion (NHTSA 2008). But an independent analysis concluded NHTSA over-estimated the consumer benefits by some $16 billion, and the actual effect would be an annual net *cost* to consumers of $2.6 billion (NERA Economic Consulting 2008). CAFE advocates grossly over-estimate the value consumers place on fuel economy and under-estimate the value they place on other features such as performance and cargo space.

Doesn't Promote Energy Independence

Reducing gasoline consumption does not mean less reliance on foreign sources of oil. In fact, it could mean just the opposite. Reduced demand for gasoline caused by higher CAFE standards would cause gasoline prices to be lower than they would be otherwise. Lower gasoline prices *increase* our reliance on imported oil, measured as a percentage of total oil consumption, because domestically produced oil is more expensive than imported oil.

A more sensible strategy is not to mandate energy efficiency standards but rather to increase energy diversity – the ability to rapidly switch from petroleum to other fuels in the event of an oil supply disruption. Encouraging car manufacturers to make flex-fuel vehicles – which can run on up to E85 fuel – is an example of this kind of policy.

An Ineffective Way to Combat Global Warming

Car and light truck emissions in the U.S. account for only 1.5 percent of all human-caused greenhouse gas emissions, a fraction that will become even smaller as emissions from developing countries rise. Raising CAFE standards even to 40 mpg would reduce the car and light truck share of greenhouse gases by less than one-half of 1 percent – a negligible amount.

Ian Parry and coauthors, with Resources for the Future, write: "It makes no sense to focus exclusively on automobiles when the huge bulk of the low-cost opportunities for carbon reduction lie in power generation" (Parry 2004).

An Ineffective Way to Improve Air Quality

Limits on vehicle emissions of hydrocarbons, carbon monoxide, and nitrous oxide are set in grams per mile and are identical for every passenger car or light truck, as appropriate, regardless of their fuel economy. Higher CAFE standards, therefore, would not reduce air pollution.

Higher CAFE standards could actually *increase* emissions by encouraging more driving (called the "rebound effect"), discouraging ride-sharing, and diverting investment and innovation from genuine breakthrough technologies into compliance with regulations that have little to do with real-world environmental effects (Kleit Fall 2002).

CAFE Trades Lives for Oil

CAFE standards caused between 1,300 and 2,600 traffic deaths every year since they were established in 1975 (National Academy of Sciences 2002). This is because the best way to achieve fuel economy is to build lighter cars, which do not protect passengers as well as heavier vehicles during traffic accidents.

The new CAFE standards adopted in 2007 reduce somewhat the incentives for car manufacturers to subsidize the sale of very lightweight cars, but they still will increase the cost of highway accidents – including the costs of fatalities, injuries, and property damage – by at least $885 million a year (NHTSA 2008).

Anti-war activists, many of them environmentalists, sometimes accuse the Bush administration of "trading lives for oil" by deploying troops in the Middle East. But CAFE, which seeks to save a little oil, kills far more Americans each year than die in Iraq and Afghanistan. Why are there are no protests when politicians and bureaucrats trade real American lives for the illusion of energy independence?

Social Costs of CAFE Exceed the Benefits

Some CAFE advocates claim the benefits of purchasing cars and trucks with better fuel economy are undervalued by buyers because they are shared with other people. This would be the case if CAFE mandates helped the nation achieve energy independence, fight global warming, or achieve other social benefits. But even the NHTSA believes this is false (NHTSA 2008).

NHTSA's analysis of the costs and benefits of CAFE for the 2015 model year found social costs would exceed benefits by $1.35 billion a year, even though NHTSA exaggerated the benefits of reducing CO_2 emissions and underestimated the negative effects of increased congestion caused by the "rebound effect." NERA Economic Research puts the real social cost at $4.9 billion in 2015. (NERA Economic Research 2008).

Recommended Policies

Policymakers should express their opposition to federal CAFE standards and especially oppose the even stricter standards being proposed by California. There is no public policy justification for taking away people's freedom to choose their vehicles.

Recommended reading: James D. Johnston, *Driving America: Your Car, Your Government, Your Choice* (Washington, DC: American Enterprise Institute, 1997); Andrew N. Kleit, "CAFE Changes, By the Numbers," *Regulation,* Vol. 25, No. 3, Fall 2002; NERA Economic Consulting, *Evaluation of NHTSA's Benefit-Cost Analysis of 2011-2015 CAFE Standards*, 2008.

8. Electric deregulation is still necessary.

The deregulation of electric utilities, begun in the 1990s, needs to be completed.

Rising electricity rates are prompting some regulators and elected officials to reconsider the wisdom of steps taken in the 1990s to deregulate electric utilities. However, electricity deregulation was necessary and finishing the job remains an important part of the energy agenda in many states.

Deregulation Fumbled, but Still Necessary

Plentiful, reliable, and inexpensive electricity is closely correlated with strong economic growth and rising standards of living (Moore and Simon 2000). The increasing electrification of American homes and industries is one reason air pollution emissions are falling even though population and the production of goods continue to expand.

Regulating electric companies as public utilities, while successful in terms of producing bountiful and inexpensive power for the nation's growing population, was increasingly unable to take advantage of new opportunities created by technological and institutional changes (Klitgaard and Reddy 2000). During the 1990s, 24 states took steps to restructure their electricity markets.

In California, restructuring had disastrous consequences in 2001 (Taylor and Van Doren 2001). As economist Jim Johnston wrote in 2003:

> The electricity restructuring in California forced all transactions into the spot market and made it very difficult to operate under a regime of stable prices. The restructuring also forced a separation of power generation from transmission. Unappreciated was the value of vertical integration in absorbing short-run surges in electricity supply and demand. Also unappreciated was the danger of maintaining retail price controls (Johnston 2003).

Restructuring placed too much focus on competition and too little on reliability (Johnston 1997b). Vertical de-integration created competition in some areas, but it also destroyed the natural price hedge that exists when the same corporate entity controls both production and distribution (sale).

Instead, opportunities were created for the gaming of capacity reservations, in order to profit from short-term price fluctuations.

The Need to Encourage Investment

Several states, such as Illinois, combined deregulation with temporary price caps or roll-backs, to be lifted by a date certain or when the industry met certain benchmarks of competitiveness. Partly as a result of these agreements, electricity prices rose only 1.1 percent per year between 1985 and 2000 (Edison Electric Institute 2006).

During the past few years, just as utilities are coming out from under years of temporary price controls, they often are hit with rising fuel costs, mandates that they buy expensive power from wind and solar energy producers, and legal challenges to the licensing of new electric power plants. While utilities are announcing plans to raise prices, state legislatures are threatening to renege on their promises to lift the price caps.

Extending price caps and blocking construction of new power plants are harmful to the long-term health of electric markets. Because demand for electricity tends to be inelastic in the short run, limited supplies can cause price spikes and shortages. Electric utilities compete with each other and other industries for capital, and price controls and lengthy permitting battles scare off investors. According to one recent report, demand for electricity is increasing approximately three times as fast as investment in new electricity supplies (Smith 2006).

Recommended Policies

Concerned citizens should pursue real deregulation to encourage new investment in and market-based pricing of electricity. Recommended policies include:

- Honor commitments to end temporary price caps or roll-backs that were part of state electric deregulation in the 1990s.
- Support the licensing of new generation capacity and oppose mandates to purchase expensive solar and wind power.

- Do not mandate vertical de-integration of the electric industry and review laws passed in the 1990s that required it.

- Explore and promote innovative patterns of ownership, such as joint ventures and regional system organizations, instead of top-down efforts to redesign the electric industry.

Recommended reading: Robert J. Michaels, "Vertical Integration and the Restructuring of the U.S. Electricity Industry," *Cato Policy Study* No. 572, Cato Institute, July 2006; Jim Johnston, "Anti-manifesto," *White Paper*, The Heartland Institute, 2003.

9. Liquefied natural gas is part of the solution.

LNG is a clean and safe source of energy that is at risk because of environmentalist and NIMBY opposition.

In an attempt to maximize clean power generation, electricity providers during the past decade have turned to natural gas. The rise in demand combined with regulatory constraints on domestic supply have led to greater imports of liquefied natural gas (LNG). Unfortunately, environmentalists and NIMBY (not in my backyard) activists have raised baseless concerns about LNG safety.

About Liquefied Natural Gas (LNG)

LNG is natural gas cooled to minus 260 degrees Fahrenheit, at which point it condenses into liquid form. It is colorless, odorless, non-toxic, and non-combustible in this form. Upon reaching a destination port, the LNG tanker anchors offshore and pumps the LNG through specially designed pipes into onshore storage and containment facilities. The LNG is then warmed at the onshore storage facility and delivered through pipelines to domestic destinations.

Demand for LNG rose sharply in recent years. Domestic conventional production of natural gas in the lower 48 states of the U.S. is expected to decline from 4.8 trillion cubic feet in 2004 to 4.2 trillion cubic feet in 2030 (Energy Information Administration 2008). Imports, mainly in the form of LNG, are expected to make up much of the difference between supply and demand.

To accommodate this increase in imported LNG, EIA predicts "the total capacity of U.S. LNG receiving terminals increases rapidly, from 1.4 trillion cubic feet in 2004 to 4.9 trillion cubic feet in 2015, when net LNG imports total 3.1 trillion cubic feet."

Environmentalist Opposition

Environmentalists and NIMBY (not in my backyard) activists have opposed new LNG terminals, claiming they are dangerous; incompatible with fishing, tourism, and other competing uses of seaside property; and lead to "increased dependence on imported fossil fuels, a dependence which would add to global warming and discourage development of alternative and renewable bio-friendly energy sources" (Green Party 2006).

Although some opposition to economic and technological change is always to be expected and in some cases is justified, the case against LNG terminals is weak. Appeals to "global warming" and renewable fuels are used to oppose all investments in conventional energy sources, even though we depend on those sources for 90 percent or more of our electricity and expect to do so through most of the twenty-first century.

Safety Concerns Addressed

LNG transportation and storage facilities are safe (Foss 2003). LNG is shipped in multi-containment storage chambers monitored with elaborate, multi-tiered, computer monitoring systems ensuring that no rupture or leakage occurs unnoticed. In its liquid form, natural gas is non-combustible. The LNG must warm and gasify for there to be a risk of combustion. However, because LNG is lighter than air, as it warms it rises and dissipates, making ignition unlikely. Moreover, a very precise ratio of natural gas to air (a narrow window between 5 and 15 percent natural gas) is necessary for such ignition to take place.

LNG is kept at significant distances from population centers and other land-based facilities. LNG tankers must dock offshore, the liquefied gas is pumped through specially designed pipelines to shore, and the onshore storage facilities form their own separate community isolated from other facilities and population centers. "In the past 40 years there have been more than 33,000 LNG ship voyages without a significant accident or cargo security [incident]" (Federal Energy Regulatory Commission 2008).

Recommended Policies

Concerned citizens should recognize the long-term value and national potential of new LNG import facilities. They should favor the following LNG policies:

- LNG terminals should not be singled out or demonized; they are a critical part of America's energy policy.

- The siting of LNG terminals must involve community members and include measures to mitigate any possible negative impact on neighbors.

Recommended reading: Bill Cooper, executive director, Center for Liquefied Natural Gas, "Testimony before the Maryland Senate Finance Committee and the House Economic Matters Committee," March 22, 2006; Michelle Michot Foss, "LNG Safety and Security," Center for Energy Economics, University of Texas - Austin, October 2003.

10. Nuclear power is part of the solution.

Regulatory barriers to the expansion of nuclear power ought to be removed.

Nuclear power is an important part of the nation's energy portfolio. Nuclear power plants generate approximately 20 percent of the electricity and 8.1 percent of all energy consumed in the U.S. There are 103 active nuclear power plants in the U.S. and an additional 339 plants worldwide.

The U.S. has more nuclear power plants than any other nation, but some other nations rely more heavily on nuclear power than does the U.S. France, for example, relies on nuclear power for 78 percent of its electricity.

Nuclear Power Is Safe

Nuclear power plants use a "Defense in Depth" philosophy that combines multiple, diverse, and reliable safety features (Domenici 2005). The systems use a redundancy technique that provides for two or more safety systems to perform key functions independently to ensure a backup mechanism if there is a failure of a plant system or component. New nuclear plant designs also include passive safety features that automatically shut down the nuclear reactor in the unlikely case of accidents. One feature is for cooling water to flow via gravity rather than requiring pumps, which might not operate during a power outage or which can experience mechanical failures.

Several physical barriers at each plant safely contain radiation and provide emergency protection against uncontrolled releases of radiation. Uranium fuel pellets are ceramic, sealed inside rods, and contained within thick steel reactor vessels. The reactor itself is inside a reinforced steel and concrete structure.

Permanent Storage of Spent Fuel

Nuclear power plants produce only incidental amounts of any of the criteria pollutants regulated by the Environmental Protection Agency (EPA) and no greenhouse gases. After more than 30 years of operation, nuclear plants have produced only 54,000 tons of spent fuel, all of which has been safely stored (Foulke and Burnett 2005).

Permanent storage of spent fuel at Yucca Mountain, Nevada is safe and necessary (Cravens 2007). Used nuclear fuel is currently stored in more than one hundred above-ground facilities in 39 separate states. One centralized, underground, and specially designed storage area would be inherently safer than having so many storage areas near 39 separate population centers. For more than 20 years, world-class scientists have performed thousands of safety studies at Yucca Mountain.

One uranium fuel pellet about the size of your fingertip contains as much energy as almost a rail car full of coal, but today's reactors utilize only 3 percent of that energy. Reprocessing can recover up to 95 percent of the remaining energy. If the United States joined France, Britain, and Japan in recycling used fuel, existing and future spent fuel rods would provide a long-term supply of nuclear fuel.

Cost Competitive

Nuclear power is cost-competitive with other sources of electricity. The operating costs of the average nuclear facility have declined from 2.46 cents per kilowatt hour in 1995 to 1.7 cents per kilowatt hour today (Foulke and Burnett 2005). The cost savings are attributable to streamlined re-licensing at the federal level, consolidation of nuclear facilities in the industry, and improved efficiency in operations.

Recommended Policies

Concerned citizens should support removing regulatory barriers to the expansion of nuclear power by adopting the following policies:

- Encourage national elected officials to approve use of the Yucca Mountain storage facility.

- Neither subsidize nor discourage through regulation the selection of nuclear power as one of the sources of new generating capacity.

- Facilitate the permitting process for new nuclear power plants so there are no unnecessary delays or expenses incurred when new plants are proposed and built.

- Ensure that nuclear energy policies provide for safe transportation of nuclear waste materials for appropriate storage or disposal.

Recommended reading: Gwyneth Cravens, *Power to Save the World* (New York, NY: Knopf, 2007); Larry Foulke and H. Sterling Burnett, "Burning Bright: Nuclear Energy's Future," National Center for Policy Analysis, *Brief Analysis* #511, March 28, 2005.

References

Avery, Dennis. 2006. Farming for ethanol would have serious consequences for forests, food production. *Environment & Climate News*, July .

Bast, Joseph L. and Sandy Liddy Bourne. 2007. *Energy policy for America: A guidebook for state legislators.* Chicago, IL: The Heartland Institute.

Bast, Joseph L., James M. Taylor, and Jay Lehr. 2003. State greenhouse gas programs: an economic and scientific analysis, *Heartland Policy Study*, No. 101. The Heartland Institute, February, www.heartland.org/article/11133.

Bourne, Sandy Liddy. 2006a. Consumers should blame uncle sam for today's high gasoline prices, *Heartland Perspective*, August 1.

Bourne, Sandy Liddy. 2006b. A State legislator's guide to ozone and particulate matter. In *Energy policy for America: a guidebook for state legislators,* eds. Joseph L. Bast and Sandy Liddy Bourne, 5-7. Chicago, IL: The Heartland Institute.

Bradley, Robert L. Jr. and Richard W. Fulmer. 2004. *Energy: the master resource.* Dubuque, IA: Kendall/Hunt Publishing Company.

Bray, Dennis and Hans von Storch. 2007. The perspectives of climate scientists on global climate change. GKSS National Research Center.

Carroll, Joe. 2006. Global oil output won't peak until 2030, Yergin says. Bloomberg, November 14.

Caruso, Guy. 2008. Statement of Guy Caruso, administrator, Energy Information Administration, U.S. Department of Energy, before the Committee on Energy and Natural Resources, U.S. Senate. March 4.

Cassidy, John. 2004. Pump dreams: is energy independence an impossible goal? *The New Yorker*, October.

Charnley, Gail. 2005. Regulating mercury emissions from power plants: will it protect our health? American Council on Science and Health, October.

Christy, John R. 2006. Questions surrounding the 'hockey stick' temperature studies: implications for climate change assessments. Testimony, House Committee on Energy and Commerce, Subcommittee on Oversight and Investigations, July 27.

Cooper, Bill. 2006. Testimony before the Maryland Senate Finance Committee and the House Economic Matters Committee. March 22.

Cravens, Gwyneth. 2007. *Power to save the world.* New York, NY: Knopf

Domenici, Pete V., with Blythe J. Lyons and Julian J. Steyn. 2004. *A brighter tomorrow: fulfilling the promise of nuclear energy.* Lanham, MD: Rowman & Littlefield.

Edison Electric Institute. 2006. Assessing rate trends. Prepared by Pacific Economics Group, LLC, January.

Energy Information Administration. 2007. Coal reserves current and back issues. U.S. Department of Energy, October.

Energy Information Administration, Annual energy outlook 2008 with projections to 2020. U.S. Department of Energy.

Enstrom, James. 2005. Fine particulate air pollution and total mortality among elderly Californians, 1973-2002. Jonsson Comprehensive Cancer Center, University of California, Los Angeles, and Scientific Integrity Institute.

Environmental Protection Agency. 2008. Air trends: basic information, www.epa.gov/airtrends/sixpoll.html, last viewed June 30.

Environmental Protection Agency. March 2006. Clean alternative fuels: ethanol, *Fact Sheet*.

ExxonMobil. 2008. *2007 Annual Summary Report*.

Fargione, Joseph *et al.* 2008. Land clearing and the biofuel carbon debt, *Science* 319: 1235-8.

Federal Energy Regulatory Commission. 2008. LNG – safety & inspections. www.ferc.gov, last viewed July 5.

Ferguson, Robert. 2004. *How safe are we from the fish we eat?* Science and Public Policy Institute, September.

Foss, Michelle Michot. 2003. LNG safety and security. Center for Energy Economics, University of Texas at Austin, October.

Foulke, Larry and H. Sterling Burnett. 2005. Burning bright: nuclear energy's future, *Brief Analysis* No. 511, National Center for Policy Analysis, March 28.

Goklany, Indur M. 1999. *Clearing the air: the real story of the war on air pollution.* Washington, DC: Cato Institute.

Grain Journal. 2007. New International Institute for Sustainable Development study expects U.S. biofuel subsidies to reach $92 billion between 2006-2012. October 23.

Green Party. 2006. Pacific Green Party opposes liquid natural gas facilities in Oregon. News Release, August 21.

Grunwald, Michael. 2008. The clean energy scam. *Time*, March.

Hubbell, Bryan J., Aaron Hallberg, Donald R. McCubbin, and Ellen Post. 2005. Health-related benefits of attaining the 8-Hr ozone standard, *Environmental Health Perspectives*, January.

Huber, Peter W. and Mark P. Mills. 2005. *The bottomless well.* New York, NY: Basic Books.

Idso, Craig and S. Fred Singer. 2009. *Climate Change Reconsidered: 2009 Report of the Nongovernmental International Panel on Climate Change (NIPCC).* Chicago, IL: The Heartland Institute.

Innis, Roy. 2008. *Energy keepers - energy killers, the new civil rights battle.* Chicago, IL: The Heartland Institute.

Johnston, James D. 1997a. *Driving America: your car, your government, your choice.* Washington, DC: American Enterprise Institute.

Johnston, Jim. 2003. Anti-manifesto. *White paper*, The Heartland Institute.

Johnston, Jim. 1998. Emissions trading for global warming. *Regulation* 21 (4).

Johnston, Jim. 1997b. Ensuring reliability in a competitive environment. In "The future of electricity: reliability in a competitive world," *Heartland Policy Study* No. 79, proceedings of a conference, The Heartland Institute.

Jones, Kay H. 2004. NAAQS's 'Where's Waldo?' problem, *Regulation* 27 (4).

Kleit, Andrew N. 2002. Short- and long-range impacts of increases in the corporate average fuel economy (CAFE) standard. Competitive Enterprise Institute, February 7.

Kleit, Andrew N. 2002. CAFE changes, by the numbers. *Regulation* 25 (3).

Klitgaard, Thomas and Rekha Reddy. 2000. Lowering electricity prices through deregulation. *Current Issues in Economics and Finance*, Federal Reserve Bank of New York, December.

Mendelsohn, Robert and James E. Neumann, eds.. 1999. *The impact of climate change on the United States economy*, Cambridge, MA: Cambridge University Press.

Michaels, Patrick. 2005. *Shattered consensus: The true state of global warming.* Lanham, MD: Rowman & Littlefield.

Michaels, Robert J. 2006. Vertical integration and the restructuring of the U.S. electricity industry. *Policy Analysis,* Cato Institute, July.

Milloy, Steven. 2005. U.S. Senate squelches mercury panic. *Environment & Climate News*, November.

Moore, Stephen and Julian L. Simon . 2000. *It's getting better all the time: 100 greatest trends of the last 100 years.* Washington, DC: Cato Institute.

Myers G.J. *et al.* 2003. Prenatal methylmercury exposure from ocean fish consumption in the seychelles child development study. *Lancet,* May 17.

National Academy of Sciences. 2002. *Effectiveness and impact of corporate average fuel economy (CAFE) standards.*

National Association of Manufacturers / American Council for Capital Formation. 2008. Study of the economic Impact from the Lieberman-Warner Climate Security Act.

National Biodiesel Board. 2008. U.S. biodiesel production capacity. January 25.

NHTSA. 2008. *Corporate average fuel economy for model years 2011-2015 passenger cars and light trucks: Preliminary regulatory impact analysis.* April.

National Taxpayers Union. 2006. Ethanol:. Bumper crop for agribusiness, bitter harvest for taxpayers. *Policy Study* No. 121, July 20.

NERA Economic Consulting. 2008. *Evaluation of NHTSA's benefit-cost analysis of 2011-2015 CAFE standards.*

Newman, Rick. 2008. The repercussions of $4 gas. *US News and World Report*, March 7.

Parry, Ian W.H., Carolyn Fischer, and Winston Harrington. 2004. Should corporate average fuel economy (CAFE) standards be tightened? *Resources*, Resources for the Future, December.

Peters, Mary. 2008. CAFE standards announcement. Washington, DC: U.S. Department of Transportation, April 22.

Pombo, Richard W. and Jim Gibbons. 2005. Mercury in perspective: fact and fiction about the debate over mercury. U.S. House Resources Committee, February.

Renewable Fuels Association. 2008. 2007 final ethanol production and demand. News Release, March 4.

Schwartz, Joel. 2006a. Health risks of ozone are exaggerated. *Environment & Climate News*, April.

Schwartz, Joel. 2006b. Finding better ways to achieve cleaner air. *Environment & Climate News*, July.

Schwartz, Joel and Steven Hayward. 2004. Emissions down, smog up. Say what? American Enterprise Institute, January.

Searchinger, Timothy *et al.* 2008. Use of U.S. croplands for biofuels increases greenhouse gases through emissions from land-use change, *Science* 319: 1238-40.

Shughart, William F. II. 2008. No one holds us over a barrel. *The Times-Tribune*, June 1.

Singer, S. Fred and Dennis Avery. 2008 *Unstoppable global warming – every 1,500 Years.* Lanham, MD: Rowman & Littlefield (revised edition).

Smith, Rebecca. 2006. U.S. electricity demand is outpacing new resources, report warns, *The Wall Street Journal*, October 16, p. A2.

Spencer, Roy W. 2008. *Climate confusion*, New York, NY: Encounter Books.

Stanek, Steve. 2006. Oil industry posts record profits in 2005. *Budget & Tax News*, March.

Taylor, James M. 2007. Little ice age may return soon, Russian scientists say. *Environment & Climate News,* February.

Taylor, James M. 2006. Illinois governor ignores science, pushes mercury cuts. *Environment & Climate News*, April.

Taylor, James M. 2004. Study shows fear of mercury 'hot spots' unfounded. *Environment & Climate News*, August.

Taylor, Jerry and Peter Van Doren. 2007. The ethanol boondoggle. *The Milken Institute Review*, January.

Taylor, Jerry and Peter Van Doren. 2006. Economic amnesia: the case against oil price controls and windfall profit taxes. *Policy Analysis*, Cato Institute, January.

Taylor, Jerry and Peter Van Doren. 2001. California's electricity crisis; what's going on, who's to blame, and what to do. *Policy Analysis*, Cato Institute, July.

Walling, Alastair, J. 2005. The very boring reasons behind high gas prices. *Regulation,* December.

Williams, Jonathan and Scott Hodge. 2006. Large oil industry tax payments undercut case for 'windfall profits' tax. *Tax Facts* No. 48, Tax Foundation, January 31.

Additional Resources

- *PolicyBot*, The Heartland Institute's free online clearinghouse for the work of other free-market think tanks, contains thousands of documents on environment and climate issues. It is on Heartland's Web site at www.heartland.org.

- *www.environmentandclimate-news.org*, a Web site devoted to the latest news and commentary about environment and climate issues. Read headlines, watch videos, or browse the thousands of documents on energy and environment issues reform available from *PolicyBot*.

- *Environment & Climate News*, a monthly publication from The Heartland Institute. Subscribe online at www.heartland.org.

Directory

The following organizations produce reliable information on energy and environment topics. For contact information for more organizations, visit The Heartland Institute's Web sites at www.heartland.org and www.environmentandclimate-news.org.

American Legislative Exchange Council, www.alec.org
Cato Institute, www.cato.org
Center for the Study of Carbon Dioxide and Global Change,
     www.co2science.org
Climate Audit (Steve McIntyre), www.climateaudit.org
Climate Depot, www.climatedepot.com
Competitive Enterprise Institute, www.cei.org
Heartland Institute. www.heartland.org
Heritage Foundation, www.heritage.org
International Climate and Environmental Change Assessment Project
     (ICECAP), www.icecap.us
JunkScience.com, www.junkscience.com
National Center for Policy Analysis, www.ncpa.org
Roger Pielke Jr.'s Blog, www.rogerpielkejr.blogspot.com

Roy Spencer, Ph.D., www.drroyspencer.com

Science and Environmental Policy Project, www.sepp.org

Science and Public Policy Institute, www.scienceandpublicpolicy.org

State Policy Network, www.spn.org

Watts Up With That? (meteorologist Anthony Watts),
    www.wattsupwiththat.com

World Climate Report, www.worldclimatereport.com

Chapter 3
School Reform

Joseph L. Bast

---

10 Principles of School Reform

1. Allow parents to choose.
2. Funding should follow the child.
3. Schools should compete.
4. Empower school leaders.
5. Empower teachers.
6. Give parents adequate funding with incentives.
7. Allow schools to succeed or fail.
8. Preserve the autonomy of private schools.
9. Teach democratic values.
10. All parents should be free to choose.

Introduction

In 1983, the National Commission on Excellence in Education warned, "the educational foundations of our society are presently being eroded by a rising tide of mediocrity that threatens our very future as a Nation and a people." Nearly 30 years later, the tide has yet to subside.

Public Schools Are Under-Performing

The failure of public schools to graduate students who are academically prepared to become productive members of society is well documented:

■ Fewer than one in three (30 percent) eighth-graders scored at proficient or above in the 2003 Urban National Assessment of Educational Progress (NAEP) reading test. In Chicago, the figure was only 15 percent, and in Cleveland and the District of Columbia, the figure was only 10 percent (Clowes 2004a).

■ The U.S. high school graduation rate for 2007-08 was only 75 percent, indicating that one in four students drops out before graduating. Latino and black graduation rates are only 63.5 percent and 61.5 percent, respectively (NCES 2010).

■ Relatively few American students achieve at levels as high as those of students in other economically advanced nations, and U.S. students make smaller achievement gains during their K-12 school careers than students from other economically advanced countries (OECD 2010).

The problem is not a lack of spending: Between 1980 and 2000, expenditures per pupil increased by 22.9 percent in constant dollars (Clowes 2001). Research by dozens of scholars has found no consistent relationship between higher spending and improvement in academic achievement (LeFevre 2006).

Declining Productivity

Productivity – the ratio of inputs to outputs – is a key measure of quality and success in all enterprises, whether public or private. Like achievement scores, measures of productivity reveal a national school system in crisis.

Harvard economist Caroline Hoxby divided average student achievement scores by per-pupil spending to estimate the change in productivity between 1970–71 and 1998–99. She found American school productivity fell by between 55 and 73 percent, depending on the skill and age cohort tested (Hoxby 2001a). According to Hoxby, if schools today were as productive as they were in 1970–71, the average 17-year-old would have a score that fewer than 5 percent of 17-year-olds currently attain.

The falling productivity of government schools can be traced to three developments inside the public school establishment (Hanushek 1996, Vedder 1996). The first is growth of a vast bureaucracy of nonteaching personnel. Government schools in the United States report a higher ratio of nonteaching personnel to teachers than government schools in any other developed country (OECD 2007). In 2005, teachers comprised just 51.2

percent of all the staff employed by public elementary and secondary school systems in the U.S. (NCES 2008, Table 80)

The second trend is the fall in average class size. The number of teachers rose significantly faster than school enrollment after 1970, although not as rapidly as nonteaching personnel. The ratio of students to teachers in public schools fell from 17.6 in 1987 to 15.4 in 2007, a decrease of 12.5 percent (Ibid., Table 61).

The third reason for the low productivity of government schools is a dropout rate that has not fallen despite large increases in spending and personnel. Students who drop out before graduating increase the cost per graduated, or finished, student.

Recommended reading: Martha Naomi Alt and Katharin Peter, "Private Schools: A Brief Portrait," in *The Condition of Education 2002* (Washington, DC: U.S. Department of Education, 2002), www.nces.ed.gov/pubs2002/2002013.pdf; *A Nation at Risk* (Washington, DC: National Commission on Excellence in Education, 1983), www.nces.ed.gov/pubsearch/pubsinfo.asp? pubid=2003060.

1. Allow parents to choose.

Parents and other legal guardians should be allowed to choose the schools their children attend. They should not be penalized financially for choosing a private secular or religious school.

Parental choice in education today is officially discouraged. Parents who choose private schools for their children forfeit the public funds collected to educate their children, including tax dollars they themselves pay. Parents who send their children to public schools are given either no choice or a choice among only a few similar schools governed by the same school district authorities, none of which may be satisfying to them.

Parents Have the Legal Right to Choose

Parents in the U.S. can properly assert the right, recognized by long tradition and law, to direct the education of their children (Skillen 1993). Some legal experts place the right of parents to control the schooling of their children at the foundation of all other civil liberties (Arons 1997; McCarthy *et al.* 1981).

The U.S. Supreme Court ruled in *Pierce v. Society of Sisters* (1925) that "the fundamental theory of liberty upon which all governments in this Union repose excludes any general power of the state to standardize its children by forcing them to accept instruction from public teachers only. The child is not the mere creature of the state; those who nurture him and direct his destiny have the right, coupled with the high duty, to recognize and prepare him for additional obligations."

In *Zelman v. Simmons-Harris* (2002), the U.S. Supreme Court upheld Cleveland's school voucher program, with the majority writing, "in keeping with an unbroken line of decisions rejecting challenges to similar programs, we hold that the program does not offend the Establishment Clause."

Parents Can Be Trusted to Choose Wisely

The current system of school finance is based on the notion that "local government agents make better school assignments for individual children they have never met than would the family, even were the family to be supported by professional counseling" (Coons and Sugarman 1978 rev. 1999, 47). But this is patently untrue. Parents are more likely to know their children's individual needs and concerns, and they have much stronger incentives to choose the right schools for their children than bureaucrats do. Parents usually care deeply about their children and may anticipate having to rely on them in their old age (Bast and Walberg 2004).

Surveys reveal parents typically rank schools the same way experts do, indicating they have sufficient information to make informed choices (Solmon 2003; Hoxby 2001). Surveys also show most parents who choose independent schools do so on the basis of academic quality rather than athletics, convenience, or other considerations less indicative of a school's quality (Witte 2000).

Parental Choice in Education Is Spreading

Giving public funds to consumers in the form of vouchers is not a radical idea. Existing voucher programs include food stamps, low-income housing vouchers, the GI Bill and Pell Grants for college students, federal day-care grants, and Social Security (Savas 2000). Social Security, for example, distributes about $700 billion annually to millions of seniors to spend as they wish. The seniors spend their retirement tax dollars on the goods and services of their choice, including donating some to charities, churches, temples, and mosques.

Using vouchers to fund schools is also no longer a radical or untried idea. School voucher and scholarship tax credit programs are operating in 12 states and the District of Columbia, serving nearly 200,000 children (Alliance for School Choice 2011). Participation in the Milwaukee Parental Choice Program has grown from 341 students in the 1990–91 school year to approximately 20,000 in 2010–11.

Public support for expanding school choice is strong. The 2004 Phi Delta Kappa International/Gallup Poll found 57 percent of parents with children now attending public schools would send them to private schools if vouchers were available (Clowes 2004b). A 2010 survey of registered voters in six states found 64 percent would favor tax credit scholarships versus 24 percent who oppose such a system, and 65 percent would favor school vouchers while 28 percent would oppose the idea (DiPerna 2010).

Recommended reading: John E. Coons and Stephen D. Sugarman, "Amid Perplexity, Who Should Decide?" in *Education by Choice: The Case for Family Control* (Troy, NY: Educator's International Press, Inc., 1999), www.schoolreform-news.org/article/15845.

2. Funding should follow the child.

Tax dollars raised for education should go to schools chosen by parents, not to bureaucrats far from the classroom.

Americans have decided, as a society, to use taxes to finance some or all of the schooling of children regardless of their parents' ability to pay tuition. This creates a potential conflict with the right of parents to control the education of their children. With certain precautions, that conflict can be addressed by allowing tax dollars to follow the child to whichever school his or her parents choose.

Current Funding Practices Empower Bureaucracies
About half of the taxes collected for education flow from taxpayers to federal or state departments of education, and from there to local school

districts and finally to public schools and teachers. The other half of funding comes from local property taxes that typically go to local school districts or to state agencies for redistribution to "property poor" school districts.

Because of bureaucracy, two of every five tax dollars raised for schools do not make it to the classroom (Bonsteel and Brodt 2000). This system concentrates authority in the hands of small groups of largely unelected officials, often far removed from the classroom. Over time, this system has become heavily bureaucratic, wasteful, and resistant to change.

Funding follows a different set of rules in the private school sector. There, parents pay tuition directly to the educators they choose for their children, so funds automatically follow the child. The freedom to choose motivates parents to study their choices closely and let educators know what kinds of schools they want. Competition for tuition leads educators to modify and improve their offerings, and unnecessary and expensive bureaucracies are not tolerated.

Vouchers and Tax Credits

The way public schools are funded can be made to more closely resemble private school funding by requiring that tax dollars follow students to the schools chosen by their parents or guardians. Two ways to do this are vouchers (sometimes called "choice scholarships") and tuition tax credits.

Under a voucher plan, parents are allowed to choose the schools they consider best for their children and receive tax-funded vouchers or certificates good for tuition (up to some set amount) at participating schools (Walberg and Bast 2003; Hakim *et al.* 1994; Friedman and Friedman 1980). Schools then compete for students. The amount of the voucher, which schools may participate in the program, and what kinds of regulations should be imposed on participating schools are choices to be made during the school choice program's design process. (See the principles below for specific legislative suggestions.)

The second way is to provide tax relief to parents who pay tuition to private schools or to individuals and corporations who make donations to pay for private school tuition (Olsen and Brouillette 2000; Bast 2001). Illinois, Iowa, and Minnesota have laws that allow taxpayers to get back from their state governments some part of the amount they spend on private school tuition. Arizona, Florida, and Pennsylvania offer tax credits to corporations and individuals who finance scholarships for children from low-income families.

School Choice Is Working

It is widely acknowledged that students attending private schools, where school choice is practiced, outperform public school students on most measures of academic achievement. According to the U.S. Department of Education, "Students at grades 4, 8, and 12 in all categories of private schools had higher average scores in reading, mathematics, science, and writing than their counterparts in public schools. In addition, higher percentages of students in private schools performed at or above 'proficient' compared to those in public schools" (Alt and Peter 2002).

On average, the costs of private schools are about half that of public schools, and their graduates are more often admitted to elite universities (Salisbury, 2003).

Scholars have carried out large surveys and smaller scale studies of charter schools, private schools, and students using vouchers to attend private schools. They have also compared schools in districts with more or less school choice based on the number of schools in each district or their geographic concentration. The studies looked at student achievement gains, per-student cost efficiency, parent satisfaction, citizens' favorable regard, and students' constructive citizenship attitudes and their social behavior in school.

Most of the large-scale studies and surveys find beneficial effects of school choice and are conclusive rather than merely suggestive. Caroline Hoxby (2004), for example, compared achievement data from 99 percent of the nation's charter schools with nearby traditional schools and found a achievement to be higher on average in charter schools especially those that had been in operation longer. Hoxby's results showed that poor and Hispanic students performed particularly well in charter schools and that charter school students did particularly well when in states with strong charter school laws that gave the schools autonomy and insured that they got a substantial fraction of the total per-pupil funding of traditional schools.

Hoxby also found a constructive competitive effect of charter schools on nearby traditional public schools. Similarly, Bryan Hassel (2005) reviewed 26 rigorous studies of charter schools and found 16 showed superior charter school effects – this, despite the fact that many of the charter schools were newly begun.

With respect to voucher programs, Jay Greene (2001) summarized seven random assignment studies and three nonrandom assignment studies of voucher programs. The authors of all ten studies found achievement benefits of the programs.

Paul Peterson (2006) found that parents of voucher students reported less fighting, truancy, tardiness, and cheating in their children's private schools than in their children's previous public schools. Voucher parents also reported the private schools kept them much better informed about their children's behavior and academic progress.

Parents and citizens view charter and private schools more favorably than traditional public schools (Public Agenda, 1999). Most voucher programs are oversubscribed, and many students must be turned away. Because states and municipalities limit the number of charter schools, they must also turn students away. (For details of these and many other studies and summaries of studies of school choice, see Walberg, 2007).

Recommended reading: Herbert J. Walberg and Joseph L. Bast, *Education and Capitalism* (Stanford, CA: Hoover Institution Press, 2003), www. hoover.stanford.edu/publications/books/edcap.html; Milton Friedman and Rose Friedman, *Free to Choose* (New York, NY: Harcourt Brace Jovanovich, 1980).

3. Schools should compete.

To finance their operations, schools should have to rely on tuition, including tax-funded tuition, paid by parents who choose their children's schools.

Schools should receive taxpayer dollars only if parents willingly choose to send their children to them. Schools that consistently fail to persuade enough parents to trust them with their children should not be rewarded with funding, as is now often the case with public schools. Instead, such schools should be closed so their students can attend better schools and their staffs and other resources can be put to better use elsewhere.

Competition Brings Out the Best in People

Competition brings out the best in people and organizations, not because it appeals to greed or selfishness, but because the desire to innovate, earn the esteem of others, and be best in one's field is deeply and widely instilled (Olson 2000; Novak 1996). Competitors provide benchmarks against which to measure individual efforts and also invaluable lessons in what to do and what not to do. Rewards for high achievement are common in all fields, from athletics to music, business, restaurants, medicine, and science.

Requiring that schools compete should not be controversial. Competition is relied upon to provide food, clothing, shelter, transportation, medicine, and countless other essential goods and services. Competition among providers of pre-school and after-school services and higher education is allowed and encouraged. Yet constructive competition among primary and secondary schools is suppressed by assigning students to public schools and withholding public funds from private schools.

Schools Improve When They Compete

A survey of more than 35 studies of the effect of competition on public schools found "a sizable majority of these studies report beneficial effects of competition across all outcomes" (Belfield and Levin 2001, 1). Caroline Hoxby (2002) reports student achievement in public schools improves as public inter-district choice increases and as the share of students who attend private schools in the metropolitan area rises. In other research, Hoxby (2001b) also found schools in metropolitan areas with maximum choice among districts are 35 percent more likely than schools in areas with minimum choice to have curricula that reach high standards in English, math, science, social studies, and foreign language.

A 2010 study of the effects of school choice on students in Florida found "that greater degrees of competition are associated with greater improvements in students' test scores following the introduction of the program; these findings are robust to the different variables we use to define competition" (Figlio and Hart 2010).

Lack of Competition Breeds Mediocrity and Waste

When protected from competition, even talented and well-intentioned public officials are motivated to act in ways intended to increase their income, authority, prestige, or leisure (Borcherding 1977). The usual bureaucratic approach is to minimize choices for people for whom services are to be provided and to routinize procedures as much as possible, usually in the name of fairness and efficiency but often simply to reduce the bureaucrats' workload. The result in public education has been large and impersonal schools, assignment of students to schools based on where their parents live rather than the special needs of students, and school codes and collective bargaining agreements that stifle creativity and mandate mediocrity (Gatto 2001).

The absence of competition and choice in public schooling has allowed school administrators to be dominated by teacher unions representing the employees they are supposed to be managing (Lieberman 2007). Union leaders influence political decisions affecting school budgets and restrict access to information needed to implement regulations. The interests of union leaders are often different from and therefore compete with those of the students.

Recommended reading: Caroline M. Hoxby, "How School Choice Affects the Achievement of *Public* School Students," in Peter T. Hill, ed., *Choice With Equity* (Stanford, CA: Hoover Institution Press, 2002), pp. 141-178; Myron Lieberman, *The Educational Morass: Overcoming the Stalemate in American Education* (Lanham, MD: Rowman and Littlefield).

4. Empower school leaders.

Principals and other school leaders should be free to create missions and programs they believe will be most attractive to students and parents.

Many public schools fail because they are over-regulated. Regulations grew over time because school leaders face conflicts of interest that lead them, in the absence of competition, to act against the interests of students. Allowing parents to choose and requiring schools to compete would restore a proper incentive system, making deregulation possible.

Relying on Politics Requires Regulation

Regulations are the price we pay for choosing to rely on political systems instead of markets to detect and prevent inefficient or corrupt behavior (Wilson 1989; Olson 2000). Each layer of government or bureaucracy attempts to restrict the range of discretionary decision-making by the layer below it by imposing rules, requiring reports, and naming oversight committees. The more complex the service, the more costly, complicated, and detailed the rules become and the less responsive its delivery is to the needs and desires of its beneficiaries.

Federal and state officials, for example, direct the annual spending of many billions of dollars for "categorical" or "compensatory" programs. In theory, these funds go to special classes and services for children categorized as poor, migrant, bilingual, racially segregated, or psychologically impeded – groups superintendents might otherwise be tempted to neglect because they represent few voters or are unlikely to complain about poor service. In practice, the programs have created huge bureaucracies that are counterproductive for learning.

When parents turn to their elected representatives in federal and state government for help, the situation simply grows worse. Those officials have imposed so many mandates, categorical aid programs, and political and regulatory oversight agencies and conflicting and unnecessary restraints on school-site personnel that "virtually everything of consequence is either forbidden or compulsory" (Jencks 1972).

Conflicts of Interest Flourish in Public Schools

Public schools are regulated especially heavily because their employees operate in an institutional setting rife with conflicts of interest. For example, superintendents set standards, make policy, and propose budgets, while at the same time they are responsible for delivering the service: hiring and managing the teachers, choosing and maintaining the facilities, and so on. They face powerful incentives to set low academic standards in order to make them easier to reach, to raise the budget in order to avoid difficult negotiations with teacher unions, and to defer maintenance of facilities, since this will be little noticed during their tenure.

The plight of district superintendents is made worse by the bargaining unit of the teacher union. A dissatisfied union steward can leak information to the school board that contradicts the superintendent's reports, leading to embarrassment and conflict with the board. Faced with the need to discipline an incompetent teacher, the superintendent is torn between doing the right thing and appeasing union representatives (Brimelow 2003).

School Choice Empowers School Leaders

School choice frees school leaders from the burden of excessive regulation by replacing politics with markets. Accountability comes "from the bottom up" – from parents making informed choices for their children – rather than "from the top down" by bureaucrats and other officials imposing detailed rules.

School choice ends the superintendents' conflict of interest by separating responsibility for providing schooling from responsibility for producing it. "The distinction between providing or arranging a service and producing it is profound. ... [I]t puts the role of government in perspective" (Savas 2000, 65). State and local school boards and superintendents would be responsible only for providing funds to schools chosen by parents that met certain standards of financial and academic accountability, civil rights, and safety. Responsibility for actually *producing* schooling would rest in the hands of the leaders of individual schools competing for students and public funds.

Recommended reading: Peter Brimelow, *The Worm in the Apple: How the Teacher Unions are Destroying American Education* (New York, NY: Harper Collins, 2003); John Taylor Gatto, *The Underground History of American Education* (New York, NY: Oxford Village Press, 2001).

5. Empower teachers.

School choice would free teachers from their current dependency on teacher unions, allowing them to act as true professionals.

Compared to professionals in other fields, public school teachers are surprisingly unfree. In order to teach in most states they must take courses at teachers colleges that are often condemned as being useless or even counterproductive in the classroom. They must join teacher unions and have hefty dues withheld from their paychecks, largely for use in political campaigns without their consent. Merit pay is off-limits in nearly all public school systems (Hess 2004).

Teachers Today Are Unfree
The lack of competition among schools within districts takes negotiating power away from teachers and puts it in the hands of public school

administrators. Districts can hire teachers for less, give them less choice of subjects to teach, workloads, and working conditions, and not worry that good teachers would seek work at schools that offer better terms. Teachers are especially vulnerable to this kind of treatment because they often are their household's second wage-earners, so they are not free to move to another city or state, and because their skills do not qualify them for better-paying employment in other fields (Merrifield 1999).

Public school teachers lost the rights that other professionals take for granted because the market forces that protect and reward professionals do not operate inside the public school system. The logic of bureaucracy rewards centralization of authority, resulting in school districts and high schools that are too large for a single curriculum to be best for most students. With multiple and constantly changing curricula, however, there can be no certainty as to what students should have mastered in earlier grades, making it difficult for school boards, superintendents, and principals to accurately assess the performance of individual teachers (Sykes 1995; Evers and Walberg 2003).

Teacher Unions Protect Teachers, but at a High Price

With objective measures of professional competence missing, teachers rightly fear favoritism and other kinds of managerial abuse. Powerful teacher unions offer protection in the form of insurance and detailed collective bargaining agreements that severely limit the principals' managerial prerogatives. In some respects this strategy works: Teachers are almost never terminated for incompetency, and even the most troubled schools are seldom shut down. But this state of affairs has badly damaged the teaching profession and children.

Teaching has become a widely disrespected profession. "[N]ew students [entering teacher colleges]] are drawn disproportionately from the bottom third of American college students," as measured by their score on high school achievement tests (Hoxby 2003b, 93). Average real teacher pay rose 12 percent between 1982 and 2002, but pay rose faster for college graduates as a group and in comparable professions; for example, 17 percent for nursing (Finn 2003).

School Choice Offers a Better Route for Teachers

There is a better path for teachers to follow. School choice would allow public school teachers to recover their lost freedoms while boosting the productivity of K-12 schools.

Private schools offer a glimpse of how school choice benefits teachers. The 2007–2008 Schools and Staffing Survey (SASS), a national survey of teachers and principals conducted by the U.S. Department of Education, found public school teachers are twice as likely as private school teachers to say the stress and disappointments they experience at their schools are so great that teaching there isn't really worth it, and they are more than twice as likely to say they plan to leave teaching as soon as they are eligible for retirement (SASS 2008).

If parents were allowed to choose schools for their children and if public funds followed the child, the tactics used by superintendents, school boards, and teacher unions to avoid accountability would no longer be necessary or possible. Superintendents would have no incentive to mislead parents or voters. Accurate consumer reports containing school-level information about student achievement and professional competence would become widely available, similar to those now available on automobiles, hospitals, and other goods and services.

School choice would allow a variety of curricula to be applied consistently based on the needs of students and preferences of parents. This would make possible more accurate evaluation of each teacher's contribution to a student's learning. Schools that retain incompetent or dangerous employees would quickly lose students to those with merit-based employment policies.

Most teachers, in short, would benefit from a more open and competitive education industry. The teaching profession has as much to gain from increased choice and competition as students do. That is probably why the Association of American Educators, the nation's largest non-union teacher organization, supports school choice (Beckner 2011).

Teachers Would Earn More and Start Their Own Schools

Successful schools would pay more for teachers with proven ability since by doing so they could attract more students and consequently have greater resources, from privately or publicly financed tuition, from which to pay teachers. Excessive bureaucracy would not be tolerated, and more of the tax dollars raised for education would reach teachers and classrooms. Principals would no longer be prevented from offering higher pay to exceptional teachers or those teaching difficult topics such as calculus and physics.

Under a system of school choice, teachers would be free to start their own schools free of bureaucracy and regulations (Zuelke 1996). While innovation has flourished in other fields, the practice of teaching hasn't seen nearly as many changes. Colleges, for-profit tutoring services, and businesses providing online courses seem to be reaping the benefits of the Internet and other technological advances, leaving teachers behind. Expanding school choice would allow more teachers to take advantage of these new trends (Walberg 2010).

A wide range of opportunities would emerge as old assumptions and dogmas, kept alive for more than a century behind the walls of monopoly and bureaucracy, are finally subjected to competition and fall before new and better ideas.

Recommended reading: William M. Evers and Herbert J. Walberg, *School Accountability* (Stanford, CA: Hoover Institution Press, 2003); Myron Lieberman and Charlene K. Haar, *Public Education as a Business* (Lanham, MD: The Scarecrow Press, Inc., 2003); D.E. Leisey and C. Lavaroni, *The Educational Entrepreneur: Making a Difference* (San Rafael, CA: Edupreneur Press, 2000).

6. Provide adequate funding.

Tax credits and vouchers should be of sufficient value to allow parents to choose high-quality schools, while also creating incentives to choose more efficient and lower-priced schools.

Tuition vouchers or tax credits should be sufficient to enable parents to choose high-quality schools, including parochial schools as well as secular schools that are not subsidized by churches, temples, or mosques.

Setting the Value of Vouchers and Tax Credits

Ideally, the amount of tax dollars following students to the schools chosen by their parents should be the same no matter what kind of school it is: public, private, charter, secular, or religious. The current weighted per-pupil funding formulas used by many public school systems could be the basis for setting the voucher or tax credit level.

If parents of children already attending private schools become eligible for tax dollars or tax credits, spending on public schools would have to be reduced or overall public spending would have to increase, perhaps requiring tax increases. To avoid these politically unpopular alternatives, voucher and tax credit advocates have proposed limiting eligibility to students currently attending public schools or setting the voucher or credit amount below current public school per-pupil spending (Merrifield 2001; Bast 2002a).

Various levels of support have been proposed, ranging from tax deductions of $250 or less to vouchers worth $10,000 to $12,000 per year for children from the poorest 20 percent of families (Reich 2000). Milton Friedman, one of the earliest proponents of vouchers, originally called for them to be set at levels equal to the current per-pupil spending of public schools (Friedman 1962). He later recommended a lower voucher value reflecting the ability of the private sector to produce goods and services at approximately half the total cost of the public sector (Friedman and Friedman 1980).

Allow Parents to Add to Vouchers and Tax Credits

The lower the dollar value of school vouchers and tax credits, the greater is the need to allow parents to pay part of the tuition directly. Such "tuition add-ons" have the advantage of coaxing parents to become more closely involved in their children's education (Coulson 1999).

Opponents of vouchers, and some voucher proponents as well, oppose tuition add-ons fearing they would worsen socioeconomic stratification and racial segregation in education (Witte 2000; Coons and Sugarman 1978, rev. 1999). Such fears are misplaced.

Most private schools in most parts of the country are not characterized by ethnic or social segregation; many already educate large numbers of low-income and minority students (Alt and Peter 2003). In fact, by some measures, public schools in major cities are more segregated than private schools (Peterson *et al.* 2001). Current pilot voucher programs show that even low-value vouchers make effective and integrated schools available to low-income and minority students (Rouse 2000; Moe 2001). Given this range of considerations, what is the most productive solution?

Reward Parents who Choose Less-Expensive Schools

If voucher or tax credit levels were set at current public school spending levels, schools that currently spend less could raise their tuition to the amount of the voucher or tax credit. Parents, insulated from the true cost of the schooling their children receive, would not be price-conscious shoppers, and schools would not be encouraged to become more efficient.

To avoid this problem, voucher proposals can establish Education Savings Accounts (ESAs) in the name of each qualified student, into which parents can deposit the difference between the voucher value and the actual tuition charged (Bast 2002; Ladner and Dranias 2011). If a voucher were worth $7,000, for example, and a parent chose a school charging $6,000 for tuition, the $1,000 difference would be deposited in the student's ESA. Withdrawals from the ESA would be permitted only to pay for tuition, tutoring, and other educational expenses for the student. When a student reaches a certain age (19, 21, or 23 are often suggested), anything left in the account would revert to taxpayers.

Recommended reading: John Merrifield, *The School Choice Wars* (Kent, England: Scarecrow Press, Inc., 2001); Matthew Ladner and Nick Dranias, "Education Savings Accounts: Giving Parents Control of Their Children's Education," Goldwater Institute, January 28, 2011.

7. Allow schools to succeed or to fail.

Entrepreneurs and teachers should be free to start or manage schools, and schools that fail to attract students should be allowed to close.

One reason many public schools achieve poor academic results is that they are neither free to succeed nor free to fail. Schools that succeed against the odds are often penalized by losing supplemental grants or their best personnel to schools that "need help." Schools that fail to achieve satisfactory results often receive *more* funding as elected officials and the school bureaucracy attempt to fix the problem (Sykes 1995).

Reward Success and Penalize Failure
The inability to recognize and reward success and penalize failure cannot be addressed by passing accountability legislation, holding annual awards ceremonies, or even mandating frequent achievement tests with real

consequences for students and school personnel. The problem, as described above (see Principle 3 – "Schools should compete"), is inherent in public schools so long as they are government agencies accountable to distant officials rather than directly to the parents of their students.

The solution is to allow parents to choose schools and require schools to compete for students. When the money follows the student, schools that fail to satisfy parents lose income and either shrink or close. Schools that parents find attractive grow in enrollment and justify a premium price from parents, allowing them to use the additional funds to improve further and enabling their staffs to benefit financially from the schools' success. There is no need for thick manuals filled with regulations or layers of bureaucracy to "manage change."

Many Educators Are Eager to Become Entrepreneurs

School choice works only if school leaders and teachers can organize and operate their schools as they see fit, subject to the discipline of market competition and parental choice. This must include rewards for success and penalties for failure, which in turn require the freedom to create new schools and expand successful ones as well as a genuine risk of closure in the event of failure (Merrifield 2001).

The private sector injects new ideas and resources into K-12 schooling. Teachers across the country are forming "private practices" and offering their services to schools or directly to parents the way lawyers, doctors, and other professionals do (Zuelke 1996; Leisey and Lavaroni 2000). The Education Industry Association, a trade association, represents some 400 companies that already supply services to and often compete directly with public schools (Seibert 2004). Groups such as PAVE (Partners Advancing Values in Education), a nonprofit organization in Milwaukee, are helping voucher and charter schools "write business plans, understand the financing of multi-million-dollar projects, and place schools in the context of being a neighborhood resource" (Sweet 2003).

The Fate of Failing Schools

In a system of expanded school choice, the number of children needing to be educated would remain the same, so educators will be as much in demand after the plan takes effect as before. Good teachers and skillful administrators may face the inconvenience of taking new positions at different schools, but otherwise they should not fear a competitive marketplace. Unlike the present system, better performers would be rewarded with higher compensation.

John E. Coons' original voucher proposal provided guaranteed loans and similar assistance to community groups that founded voucher schools (Coons 1971). A revolving loan fund for such a purpose could be established with the funds earned from the sale or lease of public school space. Richard Vedder has proposed profit-sharing and an employee stock ownership plan (ESOP) that would enable public school teachers to own their schools and subjecting them to the rewards and risks that would entail (Vedder 2000).

A new public policy idea called the "Parent Trigger" would empower parents to demand that their public school be closed, converted into a charter school, or that parents be given vouchers to enroll their children in nearby private schools (Bast *et al.* 2010). Failing schools in this case could become charter schools or be leased to teachers or entrepreneurs to become voucher schools.

Recommended reading: M. Sweet, "The Supply Side of Educational Choice," *Report*, Wisconsin Policy Research Institute, 2003; R. Vedder, *Can Teachers Own Their Own Schools?* (Oakland, CA: The Independent Institute, 2000).

8. Preserve the autonomy of private schools.

The autonomy of private schools should be recognized as being in the public interest. New regulations should not be imposed on private schools.

Competition, not inspection by government agencies or compliance with myriad rules and regulations, is the surest guarantor of quality in education. Legislators should ensure that a voucher or tax credit program does not lead to the imposition of new regulations on private schools.

Private Schools Exempt from Many Rules

At present, private schools enjoy greater autonomy than do public schools, but this is a privilege to be preserved. State constitutions typically allow for heavy regulation of private secular schools regardless of whether those schools receive any government funding. Vouchers and tax credits do not *per se* open any doors for government regulators that are not already open to them. Religiously affiliated schools are protected by the First Amendment against federal or state regulations that interfere with the freedom of religion regardless of whether or not they participate in a voucher or tax credit program.

School choice legislation should be written to ensure that private schools retain their authority over curriculum, textbook selection, and student admissions, retention, and discipline. Private schools should continue to be exempt from statutes that guarantee tenure and contract renewal and that restrict transfers and demotions. Private schools also should continue to enjoy protection against the assertion of special constitutional rights by school employees, for example, to belong or not to belong to unions and professional associations (Lieberman 1986; Valente 1985).

Some Concessions Can Be Made

Parental choice advocates may concede to the public's concerns over the accountability of private schools that accept public dollars (Moe 2001). They can preempt some criticism by placing in their proposed legislation language prohibiting participating schools from teaching the hatred or expounding the inferiority of any person or group on the basis of race, ethnicity, color, national origin, religion, or gender, or discriminating in their admissions policies on the basis of race, color, or national origin (Bast 2002b).

Voucher proponents may also agree to require participating schools to administer standardized achievement tests of each school's choosing and make test results available publicly and on request. Because most private schools already administer such tests, this is unlikely to be a burdensome regulation, and it addresses the common complaint that some parents are unable to monitor the performance of the schools their children attend.

In a competitive marketplace, good schools would have sufficient motivation to publish and even advertise performance-based information. Several independent tests of student achievement are recognized in most states. The government need only enforce the test mandate, and perhaps only for a limited time.

Four Strategies to Prevent New Regulations

Four strategies are available to legislators seeking to reduce the risk of a voucher or tax credit program increasing regulations on private schools (Walberg and Bast 2003, 260-264). The first is to include language establishing that the autonomy of private schools is in the public interest and that all regulations affecting private schools are "frozen" at their pre-voucher levels.

A second strategy is to give opponents of increased regulation the legal standing and tax funding they need to protect school autonomy. This ensures that private schools can retain quality legal representation when needed. A third means is to require any government body with regulatory powers over participating private schools to have a membership equally balanced between government and private school interests.

A fourth means to limit regulation is to combine with the voucher plan an initiative to deregulate public schools. This could put public and private school leaders and teachers on the same side of the issue, so they could work together to resist new regulations.

Recommended reading: Frederick Hess, *Spinning Wheels: The Politics of Urban School Reform* (Washington, DC: Brookings Institution Press, 1999); Joseph L. Bast, "Why Conservatives and Libertarians Should Support School Vouchers," *Independent Review*, Vol. 7, No. 2 (Fall 2002), pp. 265-276.

9. Teach democratic values.

> The failure of public schools to teach civics and democratic values is a compelling reason to adopt school choice.

Schools play a key role in democracies, but that does not justify the current arrangement in which tax dollars are allocated exclusively to public schools while parents who choose religious or secular private schools for their children are financially penalized. Indeed, the urgent need to do a better job teaching civics and other democratic values favors school choice.

Many Public Schools Fail to Teach Civics

Many public schools today do a poor job teaching civics and democratic values. According to a 2006 assessment conducted by the National Assessment of Educational Progress, 27 percent of fourth-grade students, 30 percent of eighth graders, and 34 percent of 12th graders ranked below "basic" in their civic knowledge and understanding, meaning they were unable to answer correctly even simple questions about the U.S. Constitution and the role of citizens (NAEP 2007). These results were essentially unchanged since the prior assessment in 1998.

Students perform poorly on the NAEP assessments because civics isn't being taught in the country's public schools. Writing in 2004, Stephen Macedo observed that "until the 1960s, it was common for high-school students to take as many as three courses in civics, democracy, and government. Today, however, most students take only one government-related course" (Macedo 2004). He also noted that NAEP tests for civics knowledge only every ten years, which "sends the signal that civic education matters very little."

Government-run schools are unlikely to give parents an affirmative experience with self-government. By taking from them any authority to choose the schools their children attend, and then rejecting their input on curricula, staffing, and other operational matters, government schools are more likely to diminish than promote the civic and democratic impulses of parents. What civics lessons do students learn when they observe their parents being systematically excluded from meaningful participation in their schools?

Democratic Values and Capitalism

Critics of private schools assert there is a fundamental conflict or tension between the promotion of democratic values and reliance on civil institutions such as churches and markets to operate schools. This is surely untrue, since America's educational system relied on competition, choice, and privately paid tuition for some two centuries before the arrival of the modern public school, and it successfully educated generations of Americans.

Economic historians contend the institutions of capitalism – private property rights, freedom of exchange, and the Rule of Law – are necessary for creating the peace and prosperity that enable democracies to succeed (Pipes 1999; Bethell 1998). The institutions of democracy – open elections, political equality, and majority rule – divide and check political power, an essential condition for the preservation of individual liberty and capitalism

(Olson 2000). Historically, capitalism and democracy emerged side by side, each the guarantor of the other. They promote and protect rather than contradict one another.

The claim that private schools cannot prepare citizens for democracy also overlooks an opposite concern: How wise is it to allow a government to control the schooling of its own citizens? Such control undermines the independence of its citizens and weakens the mediating institutions such as the family and voluntary private organizations that help create and protect democracy (Mill 1859, repr. 1947, 108).

Recommended reading: National Assessment of Educational Progress (NAEP), *The Nation's Report Card: Civics 2006,* U.S. Department of Education, 2008; J.P. Greene, "Civic Values in Public and Private Schools," in P.E. Peterson and B.C. Hassel, eds., *Learning From School Choice*, Chapter 4 (Washington, DC: Brookings Institution Press, 1998), pp. 83-106.

10. All parents should be free to choose.

The goal should be to allow every parent to choose, require every school to compete, and give every child the opportunity to attend a safe and effective school.

All children would benefit if parents were given greater freedom of choice, and therefore all parents should be allowed to participate in school choice programs. A program designed only for poor people, Milton Friedman (1998) warned, will be a poor program. Middle- and upper-income voters are unlikely to rally in support of a program that does not benefit themselves, leaving interest groups free to take over and run the program for their own benefit.

Better and more just, then, that programs give all parents a choice and every child a safe and effective school. However, politics often requires compromises and patience.

Phase-in Provisions May Be Necessary
Because school choice advocates face powerful opposition from organized interests that benefit from the status quo, they must form alliances with

groups that disagree with them on some issues. A common compromise is to phase in an ambitious voucher plan over several years.

Phase-in provisions specify that parts of the new program are to be implemented only after the passage of time or some other triggering event. Eligibility may be restricted at first to low-income students, students in particular cities or school districts, or students attending failing public schools. Or the size of the voucher could be small at first and then increase gradually. Phase-in provisions have many benefits, among them:

- reducing the cost of the program during its early years by limiting the number of pupils who participate;

- pre-empting charges that the program would benefit wealthy families disproportionately or hurt minorities or low-income students; and

- giving the private sector time to accommodate new demand by starting new schools or expanding the capacity of existing schools.

Incrementalism: A Less Desirable Strategy

Incrementalism is a different strategy whereby school choice supporters endorse a very limited or modest voucher or tax credit plan containing no provisions for later expansion. Supporters then work to expand the program by introducing successive legislation, hoping the "pilot" program creates the informed awareness and support needed for passage of more ambitious programs. Examples of incrementalism include voucher programs operating in Milwaukee, Cleveland, and Florida.

Incrementalism has many of the same benefits as the phase-in strategy, and it has allowed school choice advocates in some parts of the country to clear the barriers to reform that other strategies could not. However, incrementalism can encourage the public to confuse pilot programs with real tests of the school choice concept (Merrifield 2001). A pilot voucher program limited to students from low-income families and nonreligious schools, such as the original Milwaukee program, is not a meaningful test of vouchers. Another weakness of incrementalism is that opponents of choice usually fight as hard against limited plans as against more ambitious ones.

Do Not Exclude Religious and For-Profit Schools

Regardless of the strategies they adopt, school choice advocates ought to look ahead to a school choice program that creates a genuine free market for education, free of the rules and restrictions that hobble current "pilot" programs.

Religious schools, independent nonprofit schools, and for-profit schools must be allowed to participate in school choice programs. Most private schools in the United States today are religiously affiliated because offering religious curricula and subsidies from church members are ways they compete for students against "free" public schools. For-profit schools should be allowed to participate in voucher programs because the ability or willingness of not-for-profit schools to accommodate new demand is too much in question. For-profit schools are more likely to provide innovative offerings that appeal to parents.

A New Strategy: The Parent Trigger

A new trend in school reform and education policy is a parent-powered device called the Parent Trigger (Bast *et al.* 2010). The Parent Trigger allows a majority of parents of children attending a public school to petition for one of several possible reform options. In California, where the first Parent Trigger law was adopted, those choices are (1) close the failing public school and allow parents to choose among nearby public schools; (2) convert the failing school into a charter school; or (3) implement either the "transformation" or "turn-around" strategies described in the national Race to the Top legislation.

The Parent Trigger is a promising new development for several reasons. First, it is very malleable. California's third option, which is least likely to be successful, could be replaced with vouchers, a very potent remedy for public school failure. Having charters and vouchers in the same piece of legislation brings together two groups of advocates who currently often do not agree on legislative strategies.

Unlike most reform proposals based on empowering parents, the Parent Trigger originates from activists on the political left, not from the center-right coalition. This pedigree and emphasis on grassroots empowerment create an opportunity to get support from Democrats who might otherwise oppose school choice for ideological reasons.

Elected officials like the Parent Trigger idea because it allows them to give back to parents the difficult choice of what to do about failing public schools. Legislators can vote to "let the parents decide," rather than for an overarching decree that all school districts, even very efficient ones that parents like, must offer charters or vouchers to all parents.

Most importantly, the Parent Trigger does not replace one set of interest groups – public school administrators, teachers, and politicians – with another composed of private schools, chartering organizations, and entrepreneurs. Rather, it puts the power to act in the hands of the only people who do not have a potential conflict of interest: parents.

Recommended reading: Milton Friedman, "The only solution is competition," *School Reform News*, December 1998, www.schoolreform-news.org/article/12013; Joseph L. Bast, Bruno Behrend, Ben Boychuk, and Marc Oestreich, "The Parent Trigger: A Model for Transforming Education," *Heartland Policy Brief*, The Heartland Institute, August 2010.

References

Alliance for School Choice. 2011. *Hope for America's children: School choice year book 2010-2011.*

Alt, M.N. and K. Peter. 2003. Private schools: a brief portrait. In *The condition of education 2002*. Washington, DC: U.S. Department of Education.

Arons, S. 1997. *Short route to chaos*. Amherst, MA: University of Massachusetts Press.

Arons, S. 1989-1990. In search of a theory concerning government regulation of private schools. *Educational Freedom* 23(1): 42–7.

Bast, J.L. *et al.* 2010. The parent trigger: A model for transforming education. *Heartland Policy Brief*, The Heartland Institute.

Bast, J.L. 2002a. The Heartland plan for Illinois. *Heartland Policy Study* #98, The Heartland Institute.

Bast, J.L. 2002b. Why conservatives and libertarians should support school vouchers. *Independent Review* 7(2): 265–76.

Bast, J.L. 2001. Fiscal impact of proposed tuition tax credits for the state of New Jersey. *Heartland Policy Brief*, The Heartland Institute.

Bast, J.L and H.J. Walberg. 2004 Can parents choose the best schools for their children? *Economics of Education Review* 23(4): 431–40.

Beckner, G. 2011. AAE is in for school choice in 2011. Association of American

Educators, press release, January 5. http://www.aaeteachers.org/
index.php/blog/311-aae-is-in-for-school-choice-in-2011.

Belfield, C.R. and Levin, H.M. 2001. *The effects of competition on educational
outcomes: A review of U.S. evidence*. New York, NY: National Center for the Study of
Privatization in Education, Teachers College, Columbia University.

Bethell, T. 1998. *The noblest triumph: property and prosperity through the ages*. New
York, NY: St. Martin's Griffin.

Bonsteel, A. and C. Brodt. 2000. Where is all the money going? Bureaucrats and
overhead in California's public schools part I. California Parents for Educational Choice,
December.

Borcherding, T.E. 1977. *Budgets and bureaucrats: The sources of government growth*.
Durham, NC: Duke University Press.

Brimelow, P. 2003. *The worm in the apple: How the teacher unions are destroying
American education*. New York, NY: Harper Collins.

Clowes, G.A. 2004a. Just the facts: illiteracy. *School Reform News*, June.
www.schoolreform-news.org/article/15074.

Clowes, G.A. 2004b. Polls show vouchers are popular and would be widely used. *School
Reform News*, October. www.schoolreform-news.org/article/15702.

Clowes, G.A. 2001. Soaring spending fails to lift achievement. *School Reform News*,
June. www.schoolreform-news.org/article/977.

Coons, J.E. and S.D. Sugarman. 1978, rev. 1999. Amid perplexity, who should decide?
In *Education by choice: The case for family control*. Troy, NY: Educator's International
Press, Inc. www.schoolreform-news.org/article/15845.

Coons, J.E. 1971. *Family choice in education: A model state system for vouchers*.
Berkeley, CA: Institute of Governmental Studies.

Coulson, A.J. 1999. *Market education: The unknown history*. New Brunswick, NJ:
Transaction Publishers.

DiPerna, P. 2010. Interstate survey: What do voters say about K-12 education in six
states? Foundation for Educational Choice.

Evers, W.M. and H.J. Walberg. 2003. *School accountability*. Stanford, CA: Hoover
Institution Press.

Finn, C.E. 2003. Teacher reform gone astray. In *Our schools and our future ... are we
still at risk?* edited by P.E. Peterson. Stanford, CA: Hoover Institution Press.

Figlio, D.N. and C.M.D. Hart. 2010. Competitive effects of means-tested school
vouchers, NBER Working Paper No. 16056, June.

Friedman, M. 1998. The only solution is competition. *School Reform News*, December.
www.schoolreform-news.org/article/12013.

Friedman, M. 1962. *Capitalism and freedom.* Chicago, IL: University of Chicago Press.

Friedman, M. and R. Friedman. 1980. *Free to choose.* New York, NY: Harcourt Brace Jovanovich.

Gatto, J.T. 2001. *The underground history of American education.* New York, NY: Oxford Village Press.

Green, J.P. 2001. The surprising consensus on school choice, *The Public Interest* 144: 19–35.

Greene, J.P. 1998. Civic values in public and private schools. In *Learning from school choice,* edited by P.E. Peterson and B.C. Hassel, 83–106. Washington, DC: Brookings Institution Press.

Hakim, S. *et al.,* eds. 1994. *Privatizing education and educational choice.* Westport, CT: Praeger Publishers.

Hanushek, E.A. 1998. Conclusions and controversies about the effectiveness of school resources. *Economic Policy Review,* Federal Reserve Bank of New York, March.

Hanushek, Eric A. 1996. The productivity collapse in schools. *W. Allen Wallis Institute of Political Economy Working Paper No. 8,* Rochester, NY: University of Rochester.

Hassell, B.C. 2005. *Charter school achievement: What we know.* Chapel Hill, NC: Public Impact.

Hess, F.M. 2004. *Common sense school reform.* New York, NY: Palgrave Macmillan.

Hess, F.M. 1999. *Spinning wheels: the politics of urban school reform.* Washington, DC: Brookings Institution Press.

Hoxby, C.M. 2004. Achievement in charter schools and regular public schools in the United States: Understanding the differences," December, http;//post.economics.harvard.edu/faculty/hoxby/html.

Hoxby, M.M. 2003a. School choice and competition: Evidence from the United States. *Swedish Economic Policy Review* 10.

Hoxby, C.M. 2003b. What has changed and what has not. In *Our schools and our future ... are we still at risk?* edited by P.E. Peterson. Stanford, CA: Hoover Institution Press.

Hoxby, C.M. 2002. How school choice affects the achievement of *public* school students. In *Choice with equity,* edited by P.T. Hill, 141–78. Stanford, CA: Hoover Institution Press, 2002.

Hoxby, C.M. 2001a. School choice and school productivity, or could school choice be a tide that lifts all boats? in *Economics of school choice,* edited by Caroline Hoxby. Chicago, IL: University of Chicago Press for the National Bureau of Economic Research.

Hoxby, C.M. 2001b. If families matter most. In *A primer on America's schools,* edited by T.M. Moe, 89–125. Stanford, CA: Hoover Institution Press.

Jencks, C. 1972. Education vouchers: A proposal for diversity and choice. In *Educational vouchers: concepts and controversies,* edited G.R. La Noue, 50–1. New York, NY: Teachers College Press, Columbia University.

Ladner, M. and N. Dranias. 2011. Education savings accounts: Giving parents control of their children's education. Phoenix, AZ: Goldwater Institute, January.

LeFevre, A. 2006. *Report card on American education: A state-by-state analysis.* Washington, DC: American Legislative Exchange Council.

Leisey, D.E. and C. Lavaroni. 2000. *The educational entrepreneur: making a difference.* San Rafael, CA: Edupreneur Press.

Lieberman, M. 2007. *The educational morass: Overcoming the stalemate in American education.* Lanham, MD: Rowman and Littlefield.

Lieberman, M. 1986. The due process fiasco. In *Beyond public education,* chapter 4. New York, NY: Praeger Publishers.

Lieberman, M. and C.K. Haar. 2003. *Public education as a business.* Lanham, MD: The Scarecrow Press, Inc.

Macedo, S. 2004. Crafting good citizens. *EducationNext* 4(2).

McCarthy, R., D. Oppewal, W. Peterson, and G. Spykman. 1981. *Society, state and schools: a case for structural and confessional pluralism.* Grand Rapids, MI: William B. Eerdmans Publishing Co.

Merrifield, J. 2001. *The school choice wars.* Kent, England: Scarecrow Press, Inc.

Merrifield, J. 1999. Monopsony power in the market for teachers, *Journal of Labor Research* 20(3).

Mill, J.S. 1859, reprint ed. 1947. *On liberty.* Northbrook, IL: AHM Publishing Corp.

Moe, T.M. 2001. *Schools, vouchers, and the American public.* Washington, DC: Brookings Institution Press.

National Assessment of Educational Progress (NAEP). 2007. *The nation's report card: Civics 2006.*

National Center for Educational Statistics (NCES). 2010. Public school graduates and dropouts from the common core of data: school year 2007–08, first look. http://nces.ed.gov/pubs2010/2010341.pdf.

National Center for Education Statistics. 2008. *Digest of education statistics, 2007.* http://nces.ed.gov//programs/digest/d07/.

National Commission on Excellence in Education 1983. *A nation at risk: the imperative of educational reform.* Washington, DC: U.S. Department of Education. www.ed.gov/pubs/NatAt Risk/.

Novak, M. 1996. *Business as a calling: work and the examined life.* New York, NY: Free Press.

Olsen, D.A. and M.J. Brouillette. 2000. Reclaiming our schools: increasing parental control through the universal education credit. *Cato Policy Analysis*, Cato Institute.

Olson, M. 2000. *Power and prosperity: outgrowing communist and capitalist dictatorships*. New York, NY: Basic Books Inc.

Organization for Economic Cooperation and Development (OECD). 2010. *Education at a Glance 2010.*

Organization for Economic Cooperation and Development (OECD). 2007. *Education at a Glance 2007.*

Peterson, P.E. 2006. "Thorough and efficient private and public schools," in E.J. Hanushek, ed., *Courting failure*. Stanford CA: Stanford University Education Next Press.

Peterson, P.E. 2001. Choice in American education. In *A primer on America's schools,* edited by T. Moe, 249–84. Stanford, CA: Hoover Institution Press.

Peterson, P.E. *et al.* 2001. School vouchers: results from randomized experiments. In *Economics of school choice,* edited by C.M. Hoxby. Chicago, IL: University of Chicago Press for the National Bureau of Economic Research.

Pipes, R. 1999. *Property and freedom.* New York, NY: Vintage Books.

Public Agenda. 1999. *On thin Ice: How advocates and opponents could misread the public's view on vouchers and charter schools.* Washington, DC: Public Agenda.

Reich, R.B. 2000. The case for "progressive" vouchers. *Wall Street Journal*, September 6.

Rouse, C.E. 2000. School reform in the 21st century: a look at the effect of class size and school vouchers on the academic achievement of minority students. *Working Paper* No. 440, Princeton University.

Salisbury, D.F. 2003. What does a voucher buy? A closer look at the cost of private schools. *Cato Policy Analysis*, No. 486, August 28.

Savas, E.S. 2000. *Privatization and public private partnerships.* New York, NY: Chatham House Publishers.

Seibert, P. 2004. Education entrepreneurs gather in Evanston. *School Reform News*, October. www.schoolreform-news.org/article/15706.

Schools and Staffing Survey (SASS) 2008. U.S. Department of Education, National Center for Education Statistics, http://nces.ed.gov/surveys/sass/.

Skillen, J.W., ed. 1993. *The school choice controversy: what is constitutional?* Grand Rapids, MI: Baker Book House Co.

Solmon, L.C. 2003. *Findings from the 2002 survey of parents with children in Arizona charter schools.* Santa Monica, CA: Human Resources Policy Corporation.

Sweet, M. 2003. The supply side of educational choice. *Report*. Wisconsin Policy Research Institute.

Sykes, C.J. 1995. *Dumbing down our kids*. New York, NY: St. Martin's Press.

Valente, W.D. 1985. *Education law: public and private*. St. Paul, MN: West Publishing Co.

Vedder, R.K. 2000. *Can teachers own their own schools?* Oakland, CA: The Independent Institute.

Vedder, R.K. 1996. The three Ps of American education: performance, productivity, and privatization. *Policy Study* #134, Center for the Study of American Business.

Walberg, H.J. 2010. *Advancing student achievement*. Stanford, CA: Hoover Institution Press.

Walberg, H.J. 2007. *School choice: The findings*. Washington, DC: Cato Institute.

Walberg, H.J. and J.L. Bast. 2003. *Education and capitalism*. Stanford, CA: Hoover Institution Press. www.hoover.stanford.edu/publications/books/edcap. html.

Wilson, J.Q. 1989. *Bureaucracy: what government agencies do and why they do it*. New York, NY: Basic Books.

Witte, J.F. 2000. *The market approach to education: an analysis of America's first voucher program*. Princeton, NJ: Princeton University Press.

Zuelke, D.C. 1996. *Educational private practice: your opportunities in the changing education marketplace*. Lancaster, PA: Technomic Publishing Co. Inc.

Additional Resources

- *Education & Capitalism*, by Herbert J. Walberg and Joseph L. Bast (Stanford, CA: Hoover Institution Press, 2003). Entire text is available online at www.hoover.org.

- *PolicyBot*, The Heartland Institute's free online clearinghouse for the work of other free-market think tanks, contains thousands of documents on school reform issues. Visit www.heartland.org.

- *www.schoolreform-news.org*, a Web site devoted to the latest news and commentary about school reform. Read headlines, watch videos, or participate in the conversation using Twitter and Facebook.

- *School Reform News*, a monthly publication from The Heartland Institute. Subscribe online at www.heartland.org.

Directory

The following national organizations offer additional resources about school choice.

Alliance for School Choice, www.allianceforschoolchoice.org
American Legislative Exchange Council, www.alec.org
Black Alliance for Educational Options, www.baeo.org
Cato Institute, www.cato.org
Citizens for Educational Freedom, www.educational-freedom.org
Foundation for Educational Choice, www.edchoice.org
Heartland Institute, www.heartland.org
Heritage Foundation, www.heritage.org
Hispanic CREO, www.hcreo.org
Hoover Institution, www.hoover.stanford.edu
Institute for Justice, www.ij.org
PAVE (Partners Advancing Values in Education), www.pave.org
Reason Foundation, www.reason.org
Thomas B. Fordham Foundation, www.edexcellence.net

Chapter 4
Privatization

Leonard Gilroy and Adrian Moore

---

10 Principles of Privatization Policy

1. Identify privatization opportunities.
2. Prepare a business case evaluation.
3. Create a council on efficient government.
4. Choose contractors on best value, not lowest price.
5. Use performance-based contracting.
6. Provide effective monitoring and oversight.
7. Bundle services for better value.
8. Prepare a real property inventory.
9. Divest non-core assets.
10. Make the case to the public.

Introduction

Privatization means shifting some or all aspects of service delivery from government to private-sector providers. It is a strategy to lower the costs of government and achieve higher performance and better outcomes for tax dollars spent.

A Widely Used Tool

Policymakers in many jurisdictions in the U.S. and around the world use privatization to better the lives of citizens by producing higher-quality services at lower costs, delivering greater choice, and ultimately providing more efficient and effective government (Savas 2000; Savas 2005).

In recent decades, privatization has gone from a concept viewed as radical and ideologically based to a popular and well-proven public management tool. Thousands of national, state, and local government agencies in the United States have successfully privatized scores of services (ICMA 2009). Researchers have documented the successful privatization of airports (Walsh 2007), electric and telecommunications utilities (Newbery 2001), prisons (Larason Schneider 2000), schools (Lieberman 1989), transportation (Roth 2006), and many other services (Gilroy 2009).

Why Privatize?

As this is written in 2010, a recession is causing fiscal trauma in many states. The 50 states face a combined budget gap of approximately $200 billion (McNichol and Johnson 2010). Many local governments are in desperate straits due in part to declining property tax revenues. "Creative budgeting" is no longer sufficient to hide the need to cut spending.

Government managers and concerned citizens can use privatization to achieve a number of goals:

- *Cost Savings:* A Reason Foundation review of more than 100 privatization studies found savings ranging from 20 percent to 50 percent (Hilke 1993).

- *Access to Expertise:* Contracting gives governments access on an as-needed basis to expertise they do not have in-house. It is cheaper to retain architects, engineers, and lawyers on an as-needed basis than to hire them as full-time employees.

- *Better Quality:* Competition brings out the best in competitors, whether it is in sports or in the business of providing public services. Bidders have incentives to offer the best possible combination of price and service quality to beat their rivals.

- *Improved Risk Management:* Contractors, rather than the government, are responsible for cost overruns, strikes, delays, and other risks (Lehrer and Murray 2007).

- *Innovation:* Competition to win and retain contracts spurs the discovery of new, cutting-edge solutions. Without competition, even top-notch employees may stop looking for ways to improve how they meet customers' needs.

- *Meeting Peak Demand:* The cost of providing a public service can be raised considerably by the capital and manpower needed to satisfy demand at peak periods, even though those peaks may last only for a few hours a day, a few days a week, or a few months a year. Contracting allows governments to obtain additional help when it is needed so that services are uninterrupted for residents.

- *Timeliness:* "Time is money" if you are a contractor footing the bill, or if your contract with the city or state includes penalties for delays. Contractors can recruit additional workers or provide performance bonuses to meet or beat deadlines, options that often are unavailable to in-house staff.

If badly executed, privatization like any other policy can fail. Taxpayers are no better off, and may be worse off, if a service is moved from a government agency to an incompetent or inefficient private business. But we have the experiences of governments in the United States and around the world to learn from. The ten principles of privatization that follow capture the best practices that have emerged from those experiences.

Recommended reading: Leonard Gilroy, "Local Government Privatization 101," *Policy Brief* No. 89, Reason Foundation, March 16, 2010; Leonard Gilroy, editor, *Annual Privatization Report 2009,* Reason Foundation, August 2009; E.S. Savas, *Privatization and Public-Private Partnerships* (New York, NY: Chatham House Publishers, 2000).

1. Identify privatization opportunities.

> Scores of public services have been successfully privatized by thousands of governments around the world.

Former New York Gov. Mario Cuomo once said, "It is not a government's obligation to provide services, but to see that they are provided" (Tolchin 1985). Privatization can be applied to most things government does without interfering with its legitimate obligations.

What Can Be Privatized?

The following is a partial list of services that governments in the United States and around the world have privatized successfully:

Accounting
Airports and air traffic control
Animal shelter operations and management
Bridge repair and maintenance
Building financing, operations, and maintenance
Correctional facilities
Daycare facilities
Engineering
Financial planning
Golf courses
Graphic design and printing
Human resources administration
Information technology infrastructure and network services
Legal services
Library services
Mental health services and facilities
Park operations and maintenance
Parking lots and parking meters
Planning and permitting
Risk management (claims processing, loss prevention)
Road maintenance
School construction, buses, cafeteria, driver's education

Stadium and convention center management
Street cleaning and snow removal
Swimming pools
Tollroads
Zoo operations and maintenance

Privatization is widely used by local governments. According to the International City-County Management Association (ICMA), local governments on average contract out 17 percent of all services to for-profit businesses and 16 percent to other government entities. Nonprofit organizations (such as community organizations, animal welfare groups, and churches) deliver 5 percent of public services; franchises, subsidies, and volunteers collectively account for less than 2 percent of service delivery (ICMA 2009).

How to Privatize

There are many ways to privatize public services. The four most common methods, listed in order by how much responsibility to oversee or subsidize the service the government entity typically retains (from most to least), are:

- *Contracting out:* Governments contract with private-sector service providers, either for-profit or nonprofit, to deliver public services for a fee.

- *Franchises:* Governments award private firms exclusive rights to provide public services or operate public assets, usually in return for annual lease payments or a one-time, up-front payment and subject to meeting performance expectations outlined by the government agency. This is also sometimes called leasing or concessions.

- *Vouchers:* Governments give consumers vouchers or certificates that can be redeemed for a specific service provided by a participating private business or nonprofit. Vouchers are used in several states to expand school choice (Walberg 2010).

- *Service shedding or divestiture:* Governments shed responsibility for providing a service, activity, or asset entirely, often through outright sales. Local governments routinely sell off aging or underutilized land, buildings, and equipment, returning them to private commerce where they may be more productively used.

The Yellow Pages Test

Government managers should regularly review all services and activities they engage in and classify them as either "inherently governmental" – those that should be performed only by public employees – or "commercial" – those that can be obtained from private businesses or nonprofits. Former Indianapolis mayor (now chief deputy for operations of New York City) Stephen Goldsmith calls this the "Yellow Pages test," because if a service can be found in the Yellow Pages of a phone book, then government ought to buy it rather than produce it (Goldsmith 1999).

The Yellow Pages test helps government concentrate on delivering "inherently governmental" services, such as public safety and judicial systems, while contracting with businesses and nonprofit organizations to produce other services. This has the added benefits of ending taxpayer-subsidized competition with private businesses, freeing up resources for agencies to complete their missions, and saving taxpayers money.

Leaders as diverse as Florida's former Republican governor Jeb Bush, Pennsylvania's current Democratic Gov. Ed Rendell, and Chicago's Democratic Mayor Richard Daley have embraced versions of the Yellow Pages test with great success. Bush alone achieved more than $550 million in direct savings and avoided more than $1 billion in future taxpayer costs (Gilroy 2010b).

Federal agencies are required by law to implement the Yellow Pages test. The Federal Activities Inventory Reform (FAIR) Act requires each federal agency to submit a list of activities to the Office of Management and Budget classifying federal workers into two broad categories: inherently governmental and commercial. As a result of the FAIR Act, agencies have identified more than 800,000 federal employees engaged in commercial activities – such as data collection, administrative support, and payroll services – that could be provided by the private sector (Walker 2002).

The Yellow Pages test asks, Is it really the best use of taxpayer dollars to hire and manage public employees to cut grass, change oil in cars and trucks, sweep the streets, and clean government buildings, when existing businesses already perform these tasks well and almost always less expensively than government?

Government will always cost money; it is not designed to turn a profit. Focusing resources on delivering the services government alone can and should deliver helps it achieve its highest goals while creating opportunities for entrepreneurs and businesses to provide services at lower cost to taxpayers.

Recommended reading: Stephen Goldsmith, "The Yellow Pages Test," *Nevada Journal,* Vol. 7, No. 5, Nevada Policy Research Institute, May 1999; E.S. Savas, *Privatization In The City: Successes, Failures, Lessons* (Washington, DC: CQ Press, 2005).

2. Prepare a business case evaluation.

The business case evaluation serves as a roadmap for how a project should be implemented and managed.

Competition and consumer choice in the marketplace force business managers to think very carefully about the potential costs and benefits of major resource allocations. This discipline leads companies to routinely prepare business case evaluations – analyses of the goals, costs, benefits, and impacts associated with potential sourcing options – to help managers make the right choices.

Surprisingly, this type of common-sense analysis is rare in the public sector. Requiring that business case evaluations be written and frequently revisited gives agencies, policymakers, and citizen watchdogs an opportunity to ask questions that get to the heart of the matter: What public services do we really need? Of those we really need, which must the government produce, and which could be produced by private businesses? What does the in-house option really cost? Could we achieve better performance and value through privatization?

The business case evaluation serves as a roadmap for how a project should be implemented and managed. It should be a living document that travels with the initiative through the political and management processes and is continuously updated as new data become available or as conditions change.

Key elements of a business case evaluation include:

- *Benchmarking:* Document the capital and operating costs of the service as it is currently delivered by the government. Benchmark data can be used to evaluate privatization proposals and, if adopted, their success or failure over time.

- *Rationale and justification:* State the reasons privatization is being considered. Why is the status quo undesirable? Is it because the cost is too high? Is the quality too low? Have needs and opportunities changed, making government delivery obsolete or unnecessary? What alternatives were considered? Why were they dismissed? Why can't the function be improved internally?

- *Assumptions and methodology:* List and define any assumptions associated with policy, legislation, agency direction, and market conditions that are germane to the privatization decision. Explain the methodology used to make cost comparisons and quality evaluations.

- *Success factors:* How will public administrators be able to distinguish success from failure? Success factors should be measurable and tangible and include minimum performance metrics that should be included in the final contract.

- *Transition management:* Describe how the transition in service delivery will be managed. Will a new management structure need to be created? How will stakeholders be brought into the planning process and issues related to employee transition and training and customer awareness be addressed?

- *Recommendation:* Present the privatization proposal in sufficient detail to allow comparison with the benchmark data. Identify fiscal impacts (savings, cost avoidance, income from sale of assets, and new expenses), performance standards and outcomes, new management structures, a time-line for implementation, length of contracts, and term before re-competition or renewal.

At this point, the business case evaluation could conclude that the project should not be outsourced or privatized after all. Future managers and watchdogs should be able to review past business case evaluations and decide if circumstances have changed or relevant information was overlooked and privatization should be reconsidered.

Private companies routinely perform business case evaluations before embarking on new outsourcing endeavors. Governments should do the same thing, and citizen watchdogs can help. The business case evaluation offers policymakers and administrators a powerful tool to conduct due diligence on privatization proposals.

Recommended reading: Leonard Gilroy, ed., *Annual Privatization Report 2009,* Reason Foundation, August 2009; World Bank, *The PPD Handbook: A Toolkit for Business Environment Reformers,* 2006.

3. Create a council on efficient government.

A single independent decision-making body should manage privatization and government efficiency initiatives.

Global experience with privatization shows the value of having a single independent decision-making body to manage privatization and government efficiency initiatives. Writing in 2005, Richard D. Young identified 14 such councils overseeing statewide privatization initiatives (Young 2005). At least six councils are currently active:

Arizona	Commission on Privatization and Efficiency
Florida	Council on Efficient Government
New Jersey	Privatization Task Force
Texas	Council on Competitive Government
Utah	Privatization Policy Board
Virginia	Commonwealth Competition Council

Florida's Council on Efficient Government is an excellent model for other states (Gilroy 2010c). Developed in 2004, it was a key component of a strategy that realized more than $550 million in cost savings through more than 130 privatization and competition initiatives. In 2009 alone, the council evaluated 23 new business cases for potential agency outsourcing projects with a cumulative value of more than $225 million, identifying more than $31 million in projected savings to the state (Florida Council on Efficient Government 2010).

A Council on Efficient Government should be given the responsibility and authority to:

- Develop a standardized, enterprise-wide process for identifying and implementing competitive sourcing;

- Assist agencies in developing a business case evaluation for any proposed privatization initiative – before procurement – that states the rationale for the initiative such as cost savings, service quality improvements, and changing antiquated business practices;

- Develop rules instituting performance-based contracting and business case development as requirements for state procurement;

- Disseminate lessons learned and best practices across state government;

- Conduct an annual or biannual inventory of all functions and activities performed by state government, distinguishing between inherently governmental and commercial activities;

- Create a uniform cost accounting model to facilitate "apples-to-apples" cost comparisons between public- and private-sector service provision; and

- Review and take action on complaints regarding inappropriate government competition with the private sector.

A Council on Efficient Government can facilitate regular and comprehensive reviews of state government activities with an eye toward right-sizing government through competition and privatization. At the same time, successful privatization requires a high standard of due diligence in contracting, which in turn requires a staff of experts committed to the goal of greater value to taxpayers and empowered to make decisions.

Experience in Florida, Utah, and Virginia also suggests that councils on efficient government increase the public's confidence in outsourcing and help reduce perceptions of impropriety, a common concern with privatization initiatives.

Recommended reading: Henry Garrigo, "Look Before You Leap Into Privatization: Florida's Council on Efficient Government Sets a New Standard in Transparency, Due Diligence in Privatization and Contracting Decisions," interview in Leonard Gilroy (editor), *Innovators in Action 2009,* Reason Foundation, January 2010; Florida Council on Efficient Government, *Annual Report 2009.*

4. Choose contractors on best value, not lowest price.

Rather than selecting a provider based on low cost alone, governments should choose the best combination of cost, quality, and other considerations.

Government procurement processes in the United States tend to be oriented towards "low-bid" selections in which the bidder offering the lowest bid automatically wins. Such policies were put in place primarily to prevent corruption. While this approach may make sense when buying office supplies and other simple and inexpensive goods and services, it is inadequate for outsourcing more complex services.

Best practices for government procurement and service contracting are steadily moving toward "best-value" techniques. Rather than selecting a private partner based on low cost alone, governments should choose the best combination of cost, quality, and other considerations. Such criteria may include process reinvention, financing plans, total project life-cycle costs, risk transfer, expertise and experience, and technological innovation. The more complex the service, the more important it is that a best-value selection criterion be used.

The Federal Acquisition Regulations were amended in 1996 (FAR 2.101) to allow best-value source selections in outsourcing. Federal

Acquisition Regulations define best value as "the expected outcome of an acquisition ... providing the greatest overall benefit in response to the requirement." The American Bar Association's revised Model Procurement Code also incorporates "best value" procurement as the standard.

Successful best-value contracting requires three things:

- Early determination of key parameters such as completion date, security requirements, and mobilization;

- Translation of key project outcomes into performance and output measures; and

- Development of evaluation criteria quantified either in dollars or by objective measures of technical excellence, management and financial capability, prior experience and performance, optional features offered, completion date, and risk to government.

Opening up the bid process to non-price considerations does not open the door to cronyism and other types of corruption so long as the policy is accompanied by measures ensuring accountability and transparency. Such measures can be set forth in the business case evaluation (see Principle 2) and required or enforced by the Council on Efficient Government (see Principle 3).

Some "best-value" procurement processes give preferential weight to local or in-state providers. Politicians may come under pressure from constituents and campaign donors to keep outsourced work "local," but this is almost never a valid consideration. Keeping the price of a good or service low and its quality high always should trump *who* is producing the service or *where* they might be located. Bias against out-of-state or international providers limits competition, drives up costs, and precludes the true best-value option from being properly considered.

National and international firms are increasingly bidding to provide public services at the state and local levels, bringing valuable expertise, access to capital, and often economies of scale to the task at hand. Out-of-state and international firms tend to hire the bulk of their project-level staff locally, so regardless of who wins a competition, local workers stand to benefit. Preferential treatment of local or in-state providers, therefore, should be avoided.

Recommended reading: Edward Markus, "Low bid alternatives," *American City & County,* August 1, 1997, americancityand county.com/mag/ government_low_bid_alternatives/; Adrian Moore and Geoffrey Segal, "Weighing the Watchmen: Evaluating the Costs and Benefits of Outsourcing Correctional Services – Part 1: Employing a Best Value Approach to Procurement," January 2002, Reason Foundation, reason.org/news/show/weighing-the-watchmen-evaluati.

5. Use performance-based contracting.

Performance-based contracting means focusing on *outputs* rather than *inputs* when choosing whether to privatize a service and in deciding which proposal to accept.

The use of best-value sourcing, as described in Principle 4, works hand in hand with performance-based contracting, which means focusing on *outputs* rather than *inputs* when choosing whether to privatize a service and which proposal should be accepted.

Government managers often think of their own programs in terms of the management and budget restraints they face: procedures, processes, wages to be paid, cost of materials and supplies, and the amount or type of equipment needed. When they think about outsourcing a service, they may frame the contract in those same terms, specifying how much manpower and equipment must be allocated to do the job. But forcing contractors to emulate in-house procedures eliminates many of the reasons to privatize.

Performance-based contracts specify outcomes and results rather than inputs. Performance-based contracting systems typically have three key components:

- *Identify the real objectives:* The U.S. Air Force used to require a janitorial service to strip and rewax floors once a week. Then it realized that it didn't matter how often the floors were stripped and waxed so long as they are kept clean, free of scuff marks, and have a glossy finish. When the Air Force modified its statement of work in the contract, the contractor was able to achieve the real objective in a more cost-effective way, which led to a 50 percent savings for the Air Force (OMB 1998). Similarly, state departments of transportation in Florida and Virginia switched to performance-based contracts for statewide highway maintenance and reported savings ranging from 6 percent to 20 percent (Segal and Montague 2004).

- *Quantify the required outputs:* Once the objective is identified, it becomes possible for the manager to focus on how success or failure can be objectively measured. The Indiana Toll Road lease, for example, is governed by a detailed 263-page concession agreement designed to protect the public's interests (Segal 2006). The contract requires the concessionaire to clear dead animals in the roadway within eight hours and to fill potholes within 24 hours. Many of the standards in the contract exceed the standards applied to roads under the control of the Indiana Department of Transportation.

- *Financial incentives and penalties:* Keeping employees accountable and productive requires close and effective personnel management. Outsourcing a service to a private contractor means the government sheds that management role and in its place uses incentives and penalties to ensure the contractor produces the required outcomes. The concession agreement in the Indiana Toll Road lease, for example, sets the conditions for the state to cancel the contract and resume operations of the road should the contractor fail to perform as required. Other contracts specify payments that correspond with reaching certain performance thresholds such as productivity, costs, and timeliness.

Performance-based contracts often make payments and contract extension or renewal dependent on the contractor achieving certain performance targets. This shifts the risk of failure, delay, or price overruns from taxpayers to the provider. Contracts should be written to hold providers accountable for failure as well as success, which means avoiding taxpayer bailouts or guarantees and applying real penalties for failure to meet performance goals.

Using performance-based contracts can be challenging. Officials must choose services suitable to performance-based contracts and devise ways to tie payment to performance and performance to the results the public expects of the agency. Performance contracting can be done well or poorly. The key to using performance-based contracting to serve the public good is the practical matter of understanding what has worked and what has not.

Recommended reading: Adrian Moore and Wade Hudson, "The Evolution of Privatization Practices and Strategies," in Robin Johnson and Norman Walzer, eds., *Local Government Innovation: Issues and Trends in Privatization and Managed Competition* (Westport, CT: Quorum Books, 2000); Robert D. Behn and Peter A. Kant, "Strategies for Avoiding the Pitfalls of Performance Contracting," *Public Productivity and Management Review,* Vol. 22, No. 4 (1999), pp. 470-89.

6. Effective monitoring and oversight.

Effective monitoring pays for itself by improving the quality, transparency, and accountability of services.

Once a privatization proposal has been selected and put into effect, the role of the public sector shifts from planning to monitoring and oversight. Except in cases involving the outright sale of an asset or shedding responsibility for delivering a service (see Principle 9), the public entity should never sign a contract and simply walk away.

Importance of Monitoring

Strong reporting, evaluation, and auditing components must be put in place to monitor the providers' performance. Effective monitoring pays for itself by improving the quality, transparency, and accountability of services.

While monitoring and oversight systems are becoming more refined, governments still have a ways to go. According to New York University economics professor Jonas Prager, "Public sector decision makers have yet to learn from the private sector the significance of managing outsourcing. ... Efficient monitoring, though costly, pays for itself by preventing overcharges and poor quality performance in the first place, by recouping inappropriate outlays, and by disallowing payment for inadequate performance" (Prager 1994, 182).

Government managers should think about how they will monitor providers *before* they issue a request for proposal or sign the contract. "The design of the deal can make an enormous difference in the future success of monitoring the contractor," according to Tom Olsen, former director of enterprise development for the City of Indianapolis. "Strategic thinking on monitoring needs to begin at the time a deal is structured, not after" (quoted by Eggers 1997, 22).

A well-designed monitoring plan, sometimes called a Quality Assurance Plan (QAP), defines precisely what a government must do to guarantee that the contractor's performance meets the contract performance standards. The monitoring plan should include specific reporting requirements on quantified outputs, regular meetings with minutes, complaint procedures, and access to contractor's records on request. The plan should focus on monitoring and evaluating the major outputs of the contract so monitors don't have to waste too much time and resources on mundane and routine tasks that aren't central to the contract.

The Right People

Effective privatization requires having the right people with the right training in positions to oversee the letting and execution of contracts. As contracting grows, the management of contracts becomes a more important part of how agencies accomplish their goals. The Council on Efficient Government (see Principle 3) should help agencies and departments develop and train their staff.

Different services require different types and levels of monitoring. For highly visible services that directly affect citizens, such as snow removal and garbage pickup, poor service will be exposed through citizen complaints. For highly complex or technical services, it may make sense to hire a third party to monitor the contractor. Where the consequences of even minor problems are large – aircraft maintenance, for example – high-cost and high-control preventive monitoring techniques may be necessary.

Public Employee Transition

There are typically very few layoffs in association with privatization. Instead, the bulk of public employees are hired by the contractor (at least on a provisional basis), are re-assigned to another government position, or take early retirement. Regardless, it is important that management communicate early and often with employees and unions regarding privatization initiatives and develop a plan to manage public employee transitions.

Employee transition plans often focus on developing job placement policies for affected employees, such as requiring that each affected employee be interviewed and considered for job placement within the vendor company, severance compensation, and early retirement incentive packages. Officials also should consider developing re-employment and retraining assistance plans for employees not retained or employed by the contractor and offer Critical Employee Retention salary increases to retain those individuals identified as critical to successful transitions.

Recommended reading: William D. Eggers, *Performance Based Contracting: Designing State of the Art Contract Administration and Monitoring Systems,* Reason Foundation, May 1997; Jonas Prager, "Contracting Out Government Services: Lessons from the Private Sector," *Public Administration Review,* March/April 1994, Vol. 54, No. 2.

7. Bundle services for better value.

Service bundling across divisions and departments can drive down costs.

Public administrators may find greater economies of scale, cost savings, and value for money by bundling several – or even all – of the services delivered by a department or subdivision into a single outsourcing initiative, rather than treat individual services or functions separately.

Administrative Support
Because many governments and private companies outsource payroll, information technology, mail, risk management, and other support functions, there are robust and competitive markets of providers for these services. Service bundling across divisions and departments can drive down costs by eliminating redundancy and expanding the pool of potential providers.

Bundling can occur among cities and counties, among departments of state government, and even among states. In January 2009, Minnesota Gov. Tim Pawlenty and Wisconsin Gov. Jim Doyle each signed executive orders calling for department heads to identify activities, programs, and services on which the two states could cooperate to save costs (Pawlenty 2009).

Contract Cities

Since 2005, five cities serving more than 200,000 residents incorporated in metropolitan Atlanta, Georgia as "contract cities." These newly incorporated cities contract with private businesses to deliver nearly all of their non-safety-related public services, dramatically reducing costs and improving services along the way (Gilroy 2009b).

Sandy Springs, Georgia was the first of the contract cities (Gilroy 2010b). Fed up with high taxes, poor service delivery and a perceived lack of local land use control, residents voted to incorporate as an independent city. Instead of creating a new municipal bureaucracy, the city opted to contract out for nearly all government services except police and fire services, which are required under the state constitution to be provided by public-sector entities.

The city's successful launch was facilitated by a $32 million contract with CH2M-Hill OMI, an international firm (with an unusual name!) that oversees and manages day-to-day municipal operations. The contract value was just above half what the city traditionally was charged in taxes by Fulton County, saving the new city's citizens millions of dollars a year.

Sandy Springs maintains ownership of assets and budget control by setting priorities and service levels. The contractor is responsible for staffing and all operations and services. According to Sandy Springs Mayor Eva Galambos, the city's relationship with the contractor "has been exemplary. We are thrilled with the way the contractors are performing. The speed with which public works problems are addressed is remarkable" (Gilroy 2010b).

On a smaller scale, Centennial, Colorado privatized all of its public works functions in 2008. Similarly, Bonita Springs, Florida privatized all of its community development services (planning, zoning, permitting, inspections, and code enforcement) that same year. Pembroke Pines, Florida privatized its entire building and planning department in June 2009.

Facility Maintenance in Georgia

Georgia's Department of Juvenile Justice began outsourcing facility maintenance at 30 of its 35 facilities in 2001, marking the first successful state correctional system maintenance outsourcing to a private firm (Gilroy, Summers, Randazzo, and Kenny 2010). The partnership was structured to provide long-term, performance-based maintenance without increasing the budget.

For the first six months of the contract, corrective maintenance work orders outnumbered preventive maintenance work orders as long-standing maintenance needs were addressed. After two years, preventive maintenance work orders were almost double the corrective work orders, but the *cost* of preventive maintenance remained at 2000 labor costs (before maintenance was outsourced).   Recognizing the success of this approach, Georgia officials initiated a similar large-scale outsourcing contract for the management and maintenance of numerous other secure-site facilities.

Recommended reading: Oliver Porter, "Public-Private Partnerships for Local Governments: The Sandy Springs Model," interview in Leonard Gilroy (editor), *Innovators in Action 2009,* Reason Foundation, January 2010; Leonard C. Gilroy, Adam B. Summers, Anthony Randazzo, and Harris Kenny, *Public-Private Partnerships for Corrections in California: Bridging the Gap Between Crisis and Reform,* Reason Foundation, April 2010.

8. Prepare a real property inventory.

A government that knows what it owns and what those assets are worth gets more out of its assets and stops wasting unused ones.

How much land and other property does your local, county, or state government own? It is an important question that taxpayers should ask. Nearly half of state and local governments in the United States do not have the property and asset inventories needed to answer this question. Many of those that do are not putting the information to use by productively managing what they own.

How to Prepare an RPI

A real property inventory (RPI) is a written record of real property assets, which typically are immovable property such as office buildings, warehouses, heavy equipment, and bridges. Governments also can track additional property, such as vehicles, in a comprehensive inventory.

The cost of establishing an RPI is not trivial, but it reaps significant benefits. A government that knows what it owns, what it is worth, and if it is using all that it owns, is in a better position to get the most out of its assets and to stop wasting unused ones. A good RPI identifies the property and its location, condition, value, best use, and lease information, if any.

Geographic information systems (GIS) are increasingly used by governments to identify their land and asset holdings, map parcels, and build digital databases in order to create an RPI. In a GIS survey, aerial photography, property deeds, lists of property history, and historical information are collected to complete the inventory process.

Using an RPI

After developing an inventory, officials can use computerized maintenance management system (CMMS) software, such as ARCHIBUS (archibus.com), to reallocate resources to their best possible use. This increases fiscal responsibility, as state agencies can determine if there are two or more offices in proximity to each other that could be combined. This financial management also helps the budgeting process by finding assets to sell, increasing the revenue stream, and potentially decreasing lease and maintenance costs through space consolidation.

The process of creating an RPI can suggest additional ways to save money. While using a GIS auditing process to map its real property in the late 1990s, for example, the state of Wyoming found approximately 250,000 parcels that were not listed on tax rolls. Similarly, the Cincinnati Metropolitan Sewer District used GIS to find parcels with sewer connections that were not being billed. The district generated thousands of dollars in missing revenue, more than enough to pay for its GIS unit.

Case Study: Georgia

Using the state's Building, Land & Lease Inventory of Property (BLLIP), Georgia officials identified several properties that were not being put to their full use (Gilroy 2010b). In one case, three state agencies agreed to co-locate in a single building to offer "one-stop shopping" for their clients.

This project resulted in maintenance and security cost savings totaling $150,000 annually, an additional 18,000 square feet of office space, $22 million in new revenue to the state by selling surplus property, and $1.1 million saved in 2006 through renegotiation and consolidation of leases that will project into a total savings of $20.5 million through 2012.

BLLIP also identified two properties in close proximity to each other that could be consolidated, saving Georgia $102 million in a 10-year time-frame. The fiscal benefits Georgia attained did not come from passive management, but intentional pursuit of efficiency.

Recommended reading: New York Office of the State Comptroller, *Capital Planning and Budgeting: A Tutorial for Local Government Officials, Conducting a Capital Assets Inventory,* n.d.; Fernando Fernholz and Rosemary Fernholz, *A Toolkit for Municipal Asset Management,* submitted to the Municipal Finance Task Force by RTI International, March 2007; John Palatiello, *What's in the Government's Attic?* Reason Foundation, December 2004.

9. Divest non-core government assets.

The experience of state and local governments shows the huge potential of asset divestiture.

In the business world, financially stressed firms often find it good practice to divest non-core, non-essential assets. Divisions or subsidiaries that are poorly run by a large conglomerate often receive a new lease on life under new, leaner management. The one-time windfall from the sale permits the seller to pay down debt or obtain capital for other needed investments without having to raise prices or engage in new borrowing.

The same practices can be used by governments facing budgetary challenges. Asset sales (the outright sale of government land or assets) and asset leases (long-term leases of public assets to private-sector investor-operators) are no longer a new or radical proposition:

- More than 100 airports have been sold or privatized throughout the world, including Buenos Aires, Frankfurt, Johannesburg, London, Madrid, Melbourne, Paris, and Rome.

- Water supply and distribution systems have been privatized in many countries, including Argentina, France, Great Britain, and, to a lesser extent, the United States.

- Electric and gas utilities have been privatized in a number of countries.

- Toll roads and private highways have been built in dozens of Asian, European, and Latin American countries. Since 2005, government-run toll roads have been privatized in Colorado (Northwest Parkway), Illinois (Chicago Skyway), Indiana (Indiana Toll Road), and Virginia (Pocahontas Parkway).

- Indianapolis, Las Vegas, Los Angeles, Pittsburgh, and other cities are considering leasing parking assets after witnessing Chicago's groundbreaking $1.15 billion lease of its downtown parking meter system in 2009 and its previous $563 million lease of four downtown parking garages.

The recent experience of state and local governments demonstrates the huge potential of asset divestiture initiatives. For example, the Arizona Land Department generated $51.2 million in June 2003 through the sale of two parcels of land, even though the properties had been appraised for only $27.9 million. Orange County, California raised more than $300 million through asset sales and sale-leasebacks over the course of 18 months to help recover from the county's collapse into bankruptcy in 1995.

In New York, the Empire State Development Corporation generated hundreds of millions of dollars in revenues through sales and leasebacks of state-owned properties including the New York Coliseum, state mental health campuses, parking lots, armories, and state-owned golf courses. In one of its first sales, New York divested a state-owned golf course for more than $3 million.

The initial windfall to government is generally the most dramatic financial impact of privatizing an infrastructure facility, but these initiatives also can generate new ongoing revenue streams. Most state and municipal enterprises are exempt from all taxation, so converting an airport or highway or water system into an investor-owned business converts it also into a tax-paying business. Airports, for example, are often the largest single land use in a city or county, yet they are generally not part of the property tax base.

In the case of asset leases, public administrators not only realize the benefits of upfront payments, but also professional asset management, greater operating efficiency, lower operating and maintenance costs, better customer service, less political patronage, access to equity markets for capital, shareholders who will hold management accountable, and many other benefits.

Agreements to sell or lease assets should make clear that the government entity will not be liable for debts or liabilities if the new owner is unsuccessful. The promise, even implicit, that government will bailout the private company can undermine incentives to be efficient and thus the rationale for privatization.

Recommended reading: Adrian Moore, Geoffrey Segal, and John McCormally, "Infrastructure Outsourcing: Leveraging Concrete, Steel, and Asphalt with Public-Private Partnerships," *Policy Study* No. 272, Reason Foundation, September 2000; Gene Saffold, "Chicago's Parking Meter Lease: A Win-Win-Win for Motorists, Taxpayers and the City," interview in Leonard Gilroy (editor), *Innovators in Action 2009,* Reason Foundation, January 2010.

10. Make the case to the public.

Policymakers should lay out the pros and cons to the public to ensure informed debate and to rally support for the decision.

People rightly want to know how privatization might affect their everyday lives. Policymakers should lay out the pros and cons to the public right away to ensure a full debate and to rally public support behind the right decisions. Some key steps in making the case to the public include:

- Commit early on to an open and transparent process;

- Invite the news media, bloggers, and taxpayer advocates;

- Know who the possible private-sector partners are;

- Develop a communications strategy;

- Involve public employees and other interested parties who might be predisposed to oppose privatization as early as possible; and

- Be ready to compromise.

The introduction and initial discussions of privatization will set the tone and define the terms of debate for the rest of the process. Naming a blue-ribbon task force of citizens and public- and private-sector representatives to study the options and issue a report is often a good way to collect and present factual information and set possible time-lines without politicizing the issue.

Meetings of the task force should be public and potential critics should be invited and treated well. Questions that ought to be anticipated include: Why can't the government provide the services as efficiently as the private sector? Why not a two-year contract instead of a ten-year deal? Will the government lose control over the services? Who will citizens call if the service is not provided properly?

A communications strategy should include public meetings that have formal notices, agenda, and minutes; a schedule of meetings with stakeholders, editorial boards, bloggers, and civic and business leaders; presentations to government entities and local service organizations; preparation and submission of letters to the editor and editorials; participation in online discussions, and availability of spokespersons to reporters, bloggers, and talk radio show hosts.

All these elements must be organized and coordinated early in the process and should continue after a proposal has been accepted and implemented. The purpose for planning the campaign is not to "orchestrate public opinion" or "control the message," but to avoid simple mistakes that unintentionally offend key stakeholders or lead to erroneous claims or promises being made.

It is sometimes necessary for proponents to compromise certain elements of the proposal to gain the required votes. For example, a 20-year contract proposal could be pared back to a ten-year deal with a ten-year option for renewal. An initial contract proposal involving public employees moving to private employment can be scaled back to a management contract involving private management while the employees stay employed with the public entity. It is wise for proponents to consider these strategies during their initial discussions.

Ultimately a clear communications and public relations strategy is crucial to getting buy-in for a privatization initiative. Credible community leaders, the media, and active citizens have to understand the initiative and its expected outcomes. This helps to avert failure of privatization by building support up front and getting clarity on expectations. It also helps to tailor the privatization to the things people really care about, making it more likely the outcome will align with what citizens want.

Recommended reading: Daniele Calabrese, "Strategic Communication for Privatization, Public-Private Partnerships, and Private Participation in Infrastructure," World Bank, 2007; Robin A. Johnson, *How to Navigate the Politics of Privatization,* Reason Foundation, July 2002; Cecilia Cabañero-Verzosa and Paul Mitchell, *Communicating Economic Reform,* World Bank, 2002.

References

Behn, Robert D. and Peter A. Kant. 1999. Strategies for avoiding the pitfalls of performance contracting. *Public Productivity and Management Review* 22 (4): 470-89.

Cabañero-Verzosa, Cecilia, and Paul Mitchell. 2002. Communicating economic reform. World Bank.

Calabrese, Daniele. 2007. Strategic communication for privatization, public-private partnerships, and private participation in infrastructure. World Bank.

Eggers, William D. 1997. Performance based contracting: designing state of the art contract administration and monitoring systems. Reason Foundation, May.

Fernholz, Fernando, and Rosemary Fernholz. 2007. A toolkit for municipal asset management. Submitted to the Municipal Finance Task Force by RTI International, March.

Florida Council on Efficient Government. 2010. *Annual report 2009.*

Garrigo, Henry. 2010. Look before you leap into privatization: Florida's council on efficient government sets a new standard in transparency, due diligence in privatization and contracting decisions. Interview in *Innovators in action 2009,* ed. Leonard Gilroy. Reason Foundation, January.

Gilroy, Leonard. 2010a. Local government privatization 101. *Policy Brief,* No. 89, Reason Foundation.

Gilroy, Leonard. 2010b. What Hoosiers can learn from sandy springs, Georgia." *Indiana Policy Review* 20 (1): 23-6.

Gilroy, Leonard. 2010c. State competitive government commission: a tool for "right-sizing" Kansas government. Testimony to the Kansas House Appropriations Committee, January 27.

Gilroy, Leonard, ed. 2009. *Annual privatization report 2009.* Reason Foundation, August.

Gilroy, Leonard C., Adam B. Summers, Anthony Randazzo, and Harris Kenny. 2010. *Public-private partnerships for corrections in California: bridging the gap between crisis and reform.* Reason Foundation, April.

Goldsmith, Stephen. 1999. The yellow pages test. *Nevada Journal* 7 (5), Nevada Policy Research Institute, May.

Hilke, John. 1993. Cost savings from privatization: a compilation of findings. Reason Foundation, March.

ICMA. 2009. Profile of local government service delivery choices, 2007. Washington, DC: International City-County Management Association.

Johnson, Robin A. 2002. How to navigate the politics of privatization. Reason Foundation, July.

Larason Schneider, Anne. 2000. Public-private partnerships in the U.S. prison system. In *Public private policy partnerships*, ed. Pauline Vaillancourt Rosenau. Cambridge, MA: The MIT Press.

Lehrer, Eli and Iain Murray. 2007. The continuing value of privatization. *CEI on point,* Competitive Enterprise Institute, October 25.

Lieberman, Myron. 1989. *Privatization and educational choice.* New York, NY: St. Martin's Press.

Markus, Edward. 1997. Low bid alternatives. *American City & County,* August 1.

McNichol, Elizabeth and Nicholas Johnson. 2010. Recession continues to batter state budgets; state responses could slow recovery. Center on Budget and Policy Priorities, May 27.

Moore, Adrian and Geoffrey Segal. 2002. Weighing the watchmen: evaluating the costs and benefits of outsourcing correctional services – part 1: employing a best value approach to procurement. Reason Foundation, January.

Moore, Adrian, Geoffrey Segal, and John McCormally. 2000. Infrastructure outsourcing: leveraging concrete, steel, and asphalt with public-private partnerships. *Policy Study,* No. 272, Reason Foundation, September.

Moore, Adrian and Wade Hudson. 2000. The evolution of privatization practices and strategies. In *Local government innovation: issues and trends in privatization and managed competition*, eds. Robin Johnson and Norman Walzer. Westport, CT: Quorum Books.

Newbery, David M. 2001. *Privatization, restructuring, and regulation of network utilities.* Cambridge, MA: The MIT Press.

NY Office of the State Comptroller. n.d. Capital planning and budgeting: a tutorial for local government officials, conducting a capital assets inventory.

Office of Management and Budget (OMB). 1998. A guide to best practices for performance-based service contracting. Office of Federal Procurement Policy, October.

Palatiello, John. 2004. What's in the government's attic? Reason Foundation, December.

Pawlenty, Tim. 2009. Minnesota and Wisconsin governors sign groundbreaking executive orders to explore shared state services. Office of the Governor, news release, January 13.

Porter, Oliver. 2010. Public-private partnerships for local governments: the Sandy Springs model. Interview in *Innovators in action 2009,* ed. Leonard Gilroy. Reason Foundation, January.

Prager, Jonas. 1994. Contracting out government services: lessons from the private sector. *Public Administration Review* 54(2).

Roth, Gabriel, ed. 2006. *Street smart: competition, entrepreneurship, and the future of roads.* San Francisco, CA: Independent Institute.

Saffold, Gene. 2010. Chicago's parking meter lease: a win-win-win for motorists, taxpayers and the city. Interview in *Innovators in action 2009*, ed. Leonard Gilroy. Reason Foundation, January.

Savas, E.S. 2000. *Privatization and public-private partnerships.* New York, NY: Chatham House Publishers.

Savas, E.S. 2005. *Privatization in the city: successes, failures, lessons.* Washington, DC: CQ Press.

Segal, Geoffrey, Adam Summers, Leonard Gilroy, and W. Erik Bruvold. 2007. *Streamlining San Diego: achieving taxpayer savings and government reforms through managed competition.* Reason Foundation and San Diego Institute for Policy Research, September.

Segal, Geoffrey. 2006. Bottom-line on Indiana toll road deal. *Indiana Policy Review,* July 10.

Segal, Geoffrey and Eric Montague. 2004. Competitive contracting for highway maintenance: lessons learned from national experience. Washington Policy Center, January.

Tolchin, Martin. 1985. More cities paying industry to provide public services. *New York Times,* May 28.

Walberg, Herbert. 2010. *Advancing student achievement.* Stanford, CA: Hoover Institution.

Walker, David M. 2002. Improving the sourcing decisions of the federal government. Testimony before the Subcommittee on Military Readiness, Committee on Armed Services, House of Representatives, United States General Accounting Office, June 26.

Walsh, Tom. 2007. Global experience in privatizing airports. *Asian Airlines & Aerospace*, July.

World Bank. 2006. *The PPD handbook: a toolkit for business environment reformers.*

Young, Richard D. 2005. On privatization – competitive sourcing in state government. Columbia, SC: USC, Institute for Public Service and Policy Research, May.

Additional Resources

- *PolicyBot*, The Heartland Institute's free online clearinghouse for the work of other free-market think tanks, contains hundreds of documents on privatization. It is on Heartland's Web site at www.heartland.org.

- *www.budgetandtax-news.org*, a Web site devoted to the latest news and commentary about budget and tax issues, often addresses privatization. Read headlines, watch videos, or participate in the conversation using Twitter or Facebook.

- *Budget and Tax News*, a monthly publication from The Heartland Institute. Subscribe online at www.heartland.org.

Directory

The following national organizations are reliable sources of information on privatization.

American Legislative Exchange Council, www.alec.org
American Road and Transportation Builders Association, www.artba.org
Americans for Tax Reform, www.atr.org
AquaFed - The International Federation of Private Water Operators,
    www.aquafed.org
Business Coalition for Fair Competition,
    www.governmentcompetition.org
Cato Institute, www.cato.org
Heartland Institute, www.heartland.org
Heritage Foundation, www.heritage.org
Mercatus Center at George Mason University, www.mercatus.org
Michigan Privatization Report, www.mackinac.org/pubs/mpr/
National Association of Water Companies, www.nawc.org
National Council for Public-Private Partnerships, www.ncppp.org
NCPA Idea House: Privatization, www.ncpa.org/pd/private/priv.html
Professional Services Council, www.pscouncil.org
Public Works Financing, www.pwfinance.com
Reason Foundation: Privatization Center,
    www.reason.org/privatization/index.shtml
Serco Institute, www.serco.com/institute/index.asp
State Budget Solutions, www.statebudgetsolutions.org

Chapter 5
Business Climate

Joseph L. Bast

---

10 Principles of a Good Business Climate

1. Keep total tax burden low.
2. Keep taxes on businesses low.
3. Avoid corporate welfare.
4. Remove privileges enjoyed by labor unions.
5. Lower or eliminate minimum wages.
6. Reduce workers compensation costs.
7. Keep housing affordable.
8. Reduce regulatory burdens.
9. Discourage lawsuit abuse.
10. Attract members of the creative class.

Introduction

The "business climate" of a nation, state, or city refers to the combined effect on businesses of public policies, natural endowments, and other assets that affect business start-ups and profitability. A good business climate encourages existing businesses to grow, people to start new businesses, and national and international businesses to invest in an area. A poor business climate does the opposite.

Maintaining a good business climate has never been more important. Thanks to the Internet, the collapse of communism around the world, and advances in shipping and logistics, capital and labor are much more mobile than in the past. Businesses must bid for customers and workers not only from local competitors but from businesses in other communities, in other states, and even in other countries. Small changes in taxes, regulations, and other cost-drivers can lead to businesses losing customers and possibly failing or relocating.

There is no single list of factors or recipe for a good business climate. At least four business magazines – *Forbes*, *Site Selection*, *CEO Magazine*, and *Directorship Magazine* – regularly rank the states using a mix of publicly available data and the judgement of their reporters. *Forbes,* for example, describes its methodology as follows:

> First, we look at projections of job, income and gross state product growth. We also examine venture capital money going into an area as well as new businesses that have cropped up in the past three years. Another addition is the role that government plays on the business climate in terms of environmental and labor laws, as well as taxes and incentives. These factors play out on the state level instead of on the local level. Overall, we examine 32 criteria to assemble the list (Badenhausen 2007).

Forbes bundles those 32 criteria into six categories: business costs, labor, regulatory environment, economic climate, growth prospects, and quality of life.

Independent think tanks also produce business climate rankings that have the virtue of being more objective and data-driven, although no two indices present the same combination of factors or sources of data or give each variable the same weight. They include the American Legislative Exchange Council (ALEC), Beacon Hill Institute, Cato Institute, Council on State Taxation (COST), Heritage Foundation, Small Business & Entrepreneurship Council (SBEC), and Tax Foundation. The latest rankings are available on the Web sites of these organizations.

The SBEC combines 16 rankings of tax rates into a Business Tax Index (Keating 2010). The 16 taxes are listed in the box below.

These examples of business climate indices suggest some agreement on the factors most likely to affect a state or nation's competitiveness. The ten principles of a good business climate that follow draw from these and other sources.

Small Business & Entrepreneurship Council
Business Climate Index

1. Top personal income tax rate
2. Top individual capital gains tax rate
3. Top corporate income tax rate
4. Top corporate capital gains tax rate
5. Any added income tax on S-Corporations
6. Whether or not the state imposes an alternative minimum tax on individuals
7. Whether or not the state imposes an alternative minimum tax on corporations
8. Whether or not the state's personal income tax brackets are indexed for inflation
9. Property tax rates
10. Consumption-based tax rates (i.e., sales, gross receipts, and excise taxes)
11. Whether or not the state imposes a death tax
12. Unemployment tax rates
13. Whether or not the state has a tax limitation mechanism
14. Whether or not the state imposes an Internet access tax
15. Gas tax rate
16. Diesel tax rate

Recommended reading: Raymond Keating, "Business Tax Index 2010: Best to Worst State Tax Systems for Entrepreneurship and Small Business," Small Business & Entrepreneurship Council, 2010, www.sbecouncil.org/uploads/BTI2010_2.pdf; Kail Padgitt, "2010 State Business Tax Climate Index (Seventh Edition)," Tax Foundation, *Background Paper* No. 59, September 22, 2009, www.taxfoundation.org/research/show/22658.html.

1. Keep total tax burden low.

Researchers agree that keeping total tax burden low is more important than any single tax rate.

Politicians sometimes propose to raise taxes on some goods and services while lowering taxes on other goods and services, with the goal of a more "fair" or "efficient" tax code. Often, these "tax swaps" result in a net increase in tax revenues. While there may be some benefit to lowering an individual tax rate that is high compared to those in neighboring and competing states, it is a mistake to lose sight of total tax burden and the simple truth that *what* is taxed or *how* it is taxed is less important than *total tax burden.*

A dollar in tax revenue is a dollar less that consumers can spend on goods and services and that business owners can invest in hiring employees to make and sell those products. It doesn't matter if the tax is imposed on cigarettes or property, Internet purchases, or income. What matters is the total tax burden. Keeping the total burden low is the first principle of a good business climate.

Most analyses published during the late 1970s and early 1980s found state taxes had little impact on economic growth because tax differences among the states were dwarfed by differences in transportation, labor, and energy costs. More recent research, however, has changed the consensus. Zsolt Becsi, an economist with the Atlanta Federal Reserve Bank, wrote in 1996, "[U]nder certain conditions, taxes may have permanent effects on growth, and convergence is not automatic. Because policies can affect long-term growth, economists are again taking this research seriously" (Becsi 1996).

In 1994, Timothy Bartik, a senior economist with the Upjohn Institute, conducted a literature review and estimated that for every 1 percent decrease in taxes, there is a 0.3 percent increase in economic activity. Tax increases, he found, produce a similar opposite effect (Bartik 1994).

Economist Richard Vedder, a distinguished professor of economics at Ohio University, examined several dozen measures of taxes and spending in the years 1957, 1977, and 1997. In 2001 he reported, "In every single case, without exception, the results are consistent: High or rising taxes are associated with lower amounts of economic growth. The use of more sophisticated statistical models produces the same sort of result: higher taxes, lower growth" (Vedder 2001, 9).

In 2006, economist J. Scott Moody at the Maine Heritage Policy Center, a nonpartisan research institute, reported the impact of total tax burden on population growth, personal income growth, and employment growth for all 50 states from 1994 to 2004 (Moody 2006). Low-tax states had population growth rates nearly three times greater than high-tax states (17.5 percent versus 6.4 percent), personal income growth 32 percent greater (75.6 percent versus 57.3 percent), and employment growth 78 percent greater (23.3 percent versus 13.0 percent).

A similar report released in 2006 by the Tax Foundation looked at differences in economic growth rates between 2000 and 2005 for the ten best and ten worst states as ranked by the foundation's Business Tax Climate Index, which is a sum of scores for taxes on corporate and individual income, sales, and property, and unemployment insurance premiums. It found the ten states with the lowest taxes experienced personal income growth that was 44 percent faster than in the ten states with the highest taxes from 2000 to 2005. Employment in the low-tax states grew twice as fast, economic output 52 percent faster, and population 164 percent faster (Stanek 2006).

"Taxes are an important cost to business, as important as the cost of labor and raw materials," says Tax Foundation President Scott A. Hodge. "Nearly all of the best states raise sufficient revenue without imposing at least one of the three major state taxes: sales taxes, personal income taxes, and corporate income taxes" (quoted in Stanek 2006).

Recommended reading: J. Scott Moody, "Higher Taxes Lower Economic Performance," *Maine Issue Brief,* Maine Heritage Policy Center, September 19, 2006; Steve Stanek, "Lowest Business Tax States Have Best Economies: Study," *Budget & Tax News*, December 2006; Richard Vedder, "Taxes and Economic Growth," Taxpayers Network Inc., September 2001, p. 9.

2. Keep taxes on businesses low.

Keep taxes paid directly by businesses simple and low to encourage entrepreneurship and investment.

Second in importance only to keeping overall tax burdens low is keeping the tax burden on corporations low. Few people understand how many taxes businesses have to pay and how those taxes affect their decisions, or how taxes impose costly accounting and reporting burdens. With a top federal rate of 35 percent, American companies pay one of the highest corporate tax rates of any of the industrialized countries (Chen and Mintz 2010). State taxes add to this burden, making it even more difficult to compete with competitors in India, China, and other economic powerhouses.

The Small Business & Entrepreneurship Council identifies the following taxes borne by businesses as especially harmful to a state's business climate. The quotations are from the SBEC's 2010 Business Tax Index, written by Raymond Keating, and used with permission:

Capital Gains Taxes – "One of the biggest obstacles that start-ups or expanding businesses face is access to capital. State capital gains taxes, therefore, affect the economy by directly impacting the rate of return on investment and entrepreneurship. Indeed, capital gains taxes are direct levies on risk taking, or the sources of growth in the economy. High capital gains taxes restrict access to capital, and help to restrain or redirect risk taking."

Personal Income Tax – "State personal income tax rates affect individual economic decisionmaking in important ways. A high personal income tax rate raises the costs of working, saving, investing, and risk taking. ... [M]ore than 90 percent of businesses file taxes as individuals (e.g., sole proprietorship, partnerships and S-Corps.), and therefore pay personal income taxes rather than corporate income taxes."

Income Tax on S-Corporations – "Subchapter S-Corporations let certain businesses adopt the benefits of a corporation, while allowing income to pass through to be taxed at the individual level. Most states recognize S-Corporations, but a few either tax such businesses like other corporations or impose some kind of added tax."

Individual Alternative Minimum Tax – "The individual alternative minimum tax (AMT) imposes a minimum tax rate that must be paid by individuals, regardless the tax credits or deductions taken. The AMT diminishes the effectiveness of potentially positive, pro-growth tax relief measures, while also raising the costs of tax compliance."

Corporate Alternative Minimum Tax – "The corporate alternative minimum tax (AMT) imposes a minimum tax rate that must be paid by corporations, regardless of the available tax credits or deductions taken. Again, the AMT diminishes the effectiveness of potentially positive, pro-growth tax relief measures, and hikes compliance costs, in particular by forcing firms to effectively calculate their taxes under two tax codes."

Unemployment Tax Rates – "The unemployment tax on wages is another burden on entrepreneurs and business. High state unemployment tax rates increase the relative cost of labor versus capital, and provide incentives for labor-intensive businesses to flee from high-tax states to low-tax states."

Death Taxes – "High state death taxes offer incentives to move investment and business ventures to less taxing climates; foster wasteful expenditures on tax avoidance, estate planning and insurance; and force many businesses to be sold, borrowed against or closed down."

Internet Taxes – "The Internet serves as a tremendous boost to economic growth and a great expansion of economic opportunity. For small businesses, the Internet allows for greater access to information and markets. Indeed, the Internet gives smaller enterprises access to global markets that they might not have had in the past. Unfortunately, some states have chosen to impose sales taxes on Internet access."

Concerning the final tax in the SBEC's list, extending state sales taxes to purchases made over the Internet is viewed by many politicians as a way to increase revenues and "level the playing field" between retailers with bricks-and-mortar stores on Main Street and big and distant corporations. But this rhetoric overlooks a number of important facts.

The Constitution correctly limits the states to taxing only businesses with a physical presence in their jurisdictions, giving taxpayers the right to vote on whether or not they should be taxed. Online retailers use fewer public services that state and local taxes pay for, and so can be properly relieved of their burden. Millions of small businesses on Main Street are using the Internet to find customers and expand their sales, blurring any distinction that could be made between bricks-and-mortar and online retailers. State taxes on Internet sales add to the total tax burden and would make it less attractive for businesses and consumers to move to or stay in the state.

Once again it is important to keep *total tax burden* in mind as the most important element of a business climate. Creating new taxes is almost never the way to *lower* total tax burden.

Recommended reading: Raymond Keating, "Business Tax Index 2010: Best to Worst State Tax Systems for Entrepreneurship and Small Business," Small Business & Entrepreneurship Council, 2010, www.sbecouncil.org/uploads/BTI2010_2.pdf; Adam D. Thierer and Veronique de Rugy, "The Internet Tax Solution: Tax Competition, Not Tax Collusion," *Policy Analysis* No. 494, Cato Institute, October 23, 2003.

3. Avoid corporate welfare.

A poor business climate cannot be improved by offering subsidies or tax abatements to politically favored businesses.

Can the destructive effects of high tax rates be offset by selectively lowering taxes on some businesses or offering them subsidies to stay in the state? Many politicians think they can, but research on the actual results of business tax incentive programs finds they do not create jobs or promote economic growth.

A 1999 review of state economic performance found "the states that spent the most on economic development programs were more likely to experience slow job and/or income growth than states with the lowest economic development expenditures" (Gulibon 1999, 9). A 2001 review of more than 300 scholarly papers on economic development programs found, "studies of specific taxes are split over whether incentives are effective, although most report negative results" (Buss 2001, 99).

An examination of the effect of state economic development incentives on 366 Ohio businesses that began large expansions between 1993 and 1995, published in 2002, found the incentives had little or no impact on expected employment growth, and the possible small impact was negative (Gabe and Kraybill 2002). A 2004 survey article by University of Iowa economists Peter Fisher and Alan Peters concluded:

> The upshot of all of this is that on this most basic question of all – whether incentives induce significant new investment or jobs – we simply do not know the answer. Since these programs probably cost state and local governments about $40-$50 billion a year, one would expect some clear and undisputed evidence of their success. This is not the case. In fact, there are very good reasons – theoretical, empirical, and practical – to believe that economic development incentives have little or no impact on firm location and investment decisions (Peters and Fisher 2004).

Separate from the question of whether tax incentives and subsidies have a positive impact on state and local economies is whether they are cost-effective; that is, if they are worthwhile. Even if robust evidence of a positive effect of targeted fiscal incentives were to be found, it would not tell us if the tax dollars given away would have produced better returns if put toward new roads, schools, crime prevention ... or left in the pockets of taxpayers.

If the only problem with selective tax abatement programs were that they frequently do not produce positive results, their use could nonetheless be tolerable, perhaps as evidence of good-faith efforts by politicians to "do something" about an economic crisis. But selective tax abatements actually harm a state's economy (Beck 1987). Private firms are encouraged to allocate their resources to lobbying efforts rather than to market analysis or productive efforts. Location decisions are distorted because private firms are locating on the basis of subsidy rather than markets, meaning inefficient enterprises are subsidized at the expense of efficient ones. Finally, economically valid business investments are discouraged by the higher taxes that must be paid to subsidize the politically selected investments, resulting in a negative final impact on economic growth. As the John Locke Foundation notes,

Unlike the maintenance of low across-the-board tax rates or the provision of core public services such as education, highways, and public safety, corporate welfare doesn't benefit everyone. It requires public officials to intervene in private markets to decide which businesses or regions are worthy of support. This sets the stage for increased special-interest lobbying, strings-attached campaign contributions, and unethical behavior in public office (John Locke Foundation 2006, 30).

For all these reasons, state policymakers would be well advised to avoid economic development programs that award tax abatements to selected firms.

Recommended reading: John Locke Foundation, *Agenda 2006,* Raleigh, NC: John Locke Foundation, 2006; Grant Gulibon, "Growing Pennsylvania's Economy: Tax Cuts vs. Economic Development Programs," March 1999, The Commonwealth Foundation, www.heartland.org/article/3071.

4. Remove privileges enjoyed by labor unions.

Free businesses and workers from unwanted unions by removing privileges that labor unions have received.

Unions in 2009 represented 12.3 percent of wage and salaried workers in the U.S., down from 20.1 percent in 1983 (BLS 2010). Nevertheless, through their power to strike and disrupt a business's activities, unions continue to raise wages in some industries above levels that would otherwise prevail. In an age where labor and capital are highly mobile, raising wages significantly above levels justified by workers' productivity can damage both the business and its workers.

Wise union leaders make sure their demands do not outpace increases in worker productivity. But union leaders who are more concerned with gaining immediate benefits for workers irrespective of their productivity force businesses to do one of three things: substitute machines and technology for some workers and thereby raise worker productivity to justify higher compensation for the remaining workers; relocate operations to places (including foreign countries) where worker compensation is in line with worker productivity; or close down operations and cease to exist.

Many states intentionally or unintentionally extend privileges to unions that make it easier for them to organize, threaten to strike, or steer government contracts to union shops. Removing those privileges can improve a state's business climate by freeing businesses and workers from unwanted unions and allowing less-expensive nonunion shops to bid on government projects. The following recommendations appear in the *2007 Index of Worker Freedom: A National Report Card*, by Brian M. Johnson, published by the Alliance for Worker Freedom in 2007 (Johnson 2007).

Right to Work Laws

Right to Work laws are statutes prohibiting companies from making membership in unions and payment of union dues a condition of employment either before or after an employee is hired. While the Taft-Hartley Act of 1947 banned closed shops, it left the door open to union shops, where unions and employers could lawfully require new employees to join unions as part of collective bargaining agreements and only if the contract allows the worker at least thirty days after the date of hire or the effective date of the contract to join the union. Right to Work laws forbid this practice.

The impact of Right to Work laws on economic growth has been extensively studied. Though the conclusions remain controversial, there is general agreement that Right to Work laws lead to lower union membership levels relative to states without such laws and higher economic growth rates (Moore 1998). Anecdotal evidence in support of this conclusion is easy to come by: The National Institute for Labor Relations Research reported in April 2008 that private-sector jobs in Right to Work states increased by a net 17.7 percent between 1997 and 2002, more than twice the rate of increase in states without Right to Work laws (NILRR 2008). In sum, just as in the case of selective treatment of businesses, laws giving advantages to labor unions impair the general prosperity of states and the nation as a whole.

Paycheck Protection

"Paycheck protection" refers to laws prohibiting public employee labor organizations from using public employee dues or fees for expenditures unrelated to collective bargaining – such as electioneering, lobbying, and public relations – without each member's consent. The laws put the burden on unions to secure affirmative written consent to spend dues money on politics or other extraneous purposes, rather than assume permission is granted unless an employee files an objection to such expenditures (NAWER 2008).

Paycheck protection laws advance worker freedom. – and therefore make a state a better place to work and start a business – by protecting workers from union intimidation and ensuring that dollars taken from workers in the form of union dues are spent representing workers before management, and not on politics and other activities unrelated to what should be the core purpose of labor unions. Paycheck protection is popular with conservatives and business groups because it limits the funds unions can devote to politics, which go overwhelmingly to some Democratic candidates for office. But it also should be popular with civil libertarians and workers' rights advocates, since the current system is rife with abuse. Seven states have some form of paycheck protection, six by legislation and one by executive order.

Prevailing Wage Laws

The federal Davis-Bacon Act requires contractors and subcontractors working on federal or District of Columbia construction contracts, or federally assisted contracts in excess of $2,000, to pay workers no less than the currently "prevailing wage" paid in the area in which the construction project is carried out. The federal government and many state governments use various voluntary surveys to determine the wage that "prevails" in the field of construction.

Unionized contractors and construction crews have a strong incentive to respond to wage surveys, while nonunion contractors have little reason to do so. As a result, the prevailing wage is most often equal to the union wage, even though only a small share of construction workers are union members. This drives up the cost of public construction projects. The additional cost to public works projects attributable to the prevailing wage has been estimated to be 22 percent of the cost of labor and 9.91 percent of overall construction costs, for an annual cost to taxpayers of $8.6 billion a year (Glassman, Head, Tuerck, and Bachman 2008).

Repeal or reform of prevailing wage laws ought to be strongly supported by liberals, since one of the effects of the laws is to limit competition from small or recently formed businesses willing to under-bid unionized incumbent firms. Since the new competitors are more likely to be minority-owned or to hire nonunion workers, the effect of prevailing wage laws is to freeze minorities out of the construction industry. Indeed, this was the original purpose of the Davis-Bacon Act, a shameful legacy of the Jim Crow era (Frantz 1994).

Thirty-two states have prevailing wage laws that extend the requirement beyond federal construction projects.

Recommended reading: Brian M. Johnson, *2007 Index of Worker Freedom: A National Report Card*, Alliance for Worker Freedom, 2007; John Frantz, "Davis-Bacon: Jim Crow's Last Stand," *The Freeman: Ideas on Liberty*, Vol. 44, No. 2 (February 1994).

5. Lower or eliminate minimum wages.

High minimum wages destroy job opportunities for young people, increase demand for welfare, and place a drag on economic growth.

Minimum wage is the lowest hourly wage employers may legally pay employees. With passage of the Fair Minimum Wage Act of 2007, the federal minimum wage was raised from $5.15 an hour to $7.25 an hour by 2010. Nearly all states have laws setting the minimum wage at least as high as the federal minimum.

Most support for a minimum wage comes from a sense of compassion for the poor and unskilled, a fine sentiment. But supporters fail to understand how markets set wages, who actually works for the minimum wage in today's economy, and how employers react to minimum wages that are higher than the productivity of some workers.

A worker's compensation is largely determined by his or her productivity. A worker who produces significantly more value to a company than he or she is being paid has a strong incentive to work for a company willing to pay more, and other companies will see the opportunity to profit by hiring that worker. The rising level of job mobility in the U.S. economy is evidence that employees and employers are very aware of the wages being paid by competitors, and both parties are willing to negotiate. Most wages are higher than the minimum wage, not because a government law requires them to be, but because businesses compete vigorously for workers.

The typical person who earns the minimum wage is a teenager or someone just entering the workforce for other reasons, such as previous drug use or imprisonment. According to economist Walter Williams, "Workers earning the minimum wage or less tend to be young, single workers between the ages of 16 and 25. Only about 2 percent of workers over 25 years of age earn minimum wages" (Williams 2006). Most people who earn the minimum wage are members of households where others make substantially higher wages. According to Williams, "only 5.3 percent of minimum wage earners are from households below the official poverty line; 40 percent of minimum wage earners live in households with incomes $60,000 and higher; and, over 82 percent of minimum wage earners do not have dependents" (*Ibid.*).

What happens to young people or people with few skills whose value to a company is less than the minimum wage? A worker who produces less value to a company than he or she is being paid is a burden on the company's profitability. Over time, assuming the worker's lack of productivity is observed by management, the worker's productivity has to rise, his or her compensation has to fall, or the worker has to be terminated by management. When governments intervene in this process by setting a minimum wage, they do nothing to increase a worker's productivity, and they prohibit a decrease in compensation. This leaves only one option for the employer: termination.

High minimum wages in fact have been shown to have a negative effect on job creation (Balis 2007). With the Great Recession driving unemployment rates to double digits in many cities, high minimum wages are creating a climate where young people and others entering the workforce have fewer job opportunities, creating greater demand for welfare and other social services and hindering economic growth.

Recommended reading: Milton Friedman, "Social Welfare Measures," Chapter 11 of *Capitalism and Freedom,* Chicago: University of Chicago

Press, 1962, pp. 177-89; Ryan Balis, "Employment: Do Minimum Wage Increases Benefit Workers and the Economy?" National Center for Public Policy Research, January 2, 2007.

6. Reduce workers compensation costs.

The high cost of workers compensation discourages the launch of new businesses and discourages job creation.

Workers compensation statutes ensure that workers injured or disabled on the job are provided with fixed monetary awards. Typically, the funds used to provide employees with workers compensation are paid out by an employer on a monthly or yearly basis.

The workers compensation system developed as a compromise. Workers seeking financial relief from the cost of injuries incurred while at work did not want to have to go to court to sue for that relief. Employers wanted to find a way to reduce the costs of defending against such lawsuits. The deal was a "win-win" in the sense that it at least temporarily reduced legal costs, allowing more of the money paid by employers to reach injured workers. But over time, the deal has produced some undesirable unintended consequences.

The most obvious problem has been the rapid rise in workers compensation premiums over time. N. Michael Helvacian, in a report for the National Center for Policy Analysis, identified several reasons for the rising costs (Helvacian 2006). First, state regulators often fail to adequately risk-adjust premiums, resulting in most employers paying high premiums to subsidize a few industries with poor safety records. Second, states typically require employers to buy workers compensation insurance separate from the health insurance plans they have for their employees, meaning it often doesn't provide the cost savings of managed care or HSAs.

Third, workers compensation policies encourage workers to report injuries that may not be work-related because benefits under the workers compensation policy are better than under their regular health insurance policy. Finally, excessive regulation of premiums in the workers compensation insurance market results in relatively uncompetitive insurance markets.

A less-obvious, but no less important, cost of workers compensation laws, but no less important, is the loss of worker freedom that comes from a system that prohibits choosing insurance coverage or contracting directly with employers to substitute some insurance coverage for higher pay. The high cost of the system takes money out of workers' pockets and lowers the profits of their employers; both lower productivity and hinder economic growth.

Reforms that would make workers compensation less expensive include adjusting premiums according to the experience of individual firms rather than occupational or industry risk ratings; combining employee health plans and workers compensation medical coverage so employees could use the same provider networks and employers could pay the same negotiated fees; and creating Workers Compensation Accounts (WCAs) that would give workers more flexibility in how to spend the money allocated for their benefit.

Recommended reading: Michael N. Helvacian, "Workers' Compensation: Rx for Policy Reform," *NCPA Policy Report* No. 287, National Center for Policy Analysis, September 2006.

7. Keep housing affordable.

Public policies have made housing overly expensive, prompting workers to seek employment where housing is affordable.

Affordable housing is an important part of a good business climate, since workers take into account the cost of housing when negotiating wages or salaries. An inadequate supply of housing can drive up prices and encourage people to seek employment in areas where housing is cheaper and more plentiful.

Proposals to increase regulation of the real estate industry were popular in 2009-10 thanks to record foreclosures, a collapsing credit market, spiraling losses for some of the nation's largest financial institutions, and government agencies racing to find short-term solutions to stop the bleeding. However, many of these problems are the result of regulations already in place that unnecessarily raise housing costs, limit competition, and expose taxpayers to risk. Restoring order to housing markets requires the following public policy reforms:

No bailouts – Underwriting by mortgage brokers and mortgage bankers became increasingly careless during the housing boom, resulting in unprecedented numbers of foreclosures. Letting the lenders get into trouble and possibly go bankrupt or be acquired by other firms is the best way to solve the problem. Holding lenders and borrowers accountable to the terms of their contracts is the only way to "solve" the home mortgage crisis. Those who bought houses they could not afford should not be insulated from the consequences of their decisions; this is what gave rise to the housing bubble in the first place. In short, the government should not use responsible taxpayers' funds to bail out irresponsible buyers and lenders.

Privatize government-supported enterprises – Government-supported enterprises such as Fannie Mae, Freddie Mac, and the Federal Home Loan Bank pose significant systemic risk to the nation's overall financial system (DeHaven 2009). Although activities they perform may be valuable, they should be performed by the private sector without any promise, implicit or explicit, that taxpayers will come to the rescue when they fail. Likewise, the Federal Housing Administration, insofar as it exists at all, should uphold standards that reduce its chance of becoming a burden on taxpayers.

Repeal "smart growth" laws – Zoning ordinances, building codes, and smart growth policies all tend to increase the cost of home ownership and contributed to the housing bubble and subsequent collapse. Home values skyrocketed in cities with smart growth policies and strict building codes, and these cities experienced the highest rates of subprime lending, the biggest crashes in home values, and consequently the highest rates of foreclosure (Cox 2008). Repealing these policies and regulations would go a long way toward solving the affordable housing problem.

Vouchers for the poor – Public housing for low-income individuals and families continues to be an unfilled promise. Federal and local governments finally began privatizing public housing in the 1990s by subsidizing new construction that is privately owned, privately financed, and leased to former public housing tenants in a mixed-income format. More privatization and expanded use of housing vouchers is necessary (Higginson 2008).

Sound housing policy for the twenty-first century requires government be much less involved in the private housing market than was common in the twentieth century. The history and economics of housing give ample testimony to the fact that government involvement brings more government regulations, unsustainable investment levels, and higher housing costs.

Recommended reading: Tad DeHaven, "Three Decades of Politics and Failed Policies at HUD," *Policy Analysis* No. 655, Cato Institute, November 2009; Wendell Cox, "How Smart Growth Exacerbated the International Financial Crisis," *WebMemo,* The Heritage Foundation, April 29, 2008; William Higginson, "Housing Policy for the 21st Century," *Policy Study* No. 121, The Heartland Institute, July 2008.

8. Reduce the burden of regulations.

Regulations impose heavy burdens on businesses and individuals, yet frequently produce few if any social benefits.

Government regulations have a major effect on business climate. Along with cutting taxes, deregulation is one of the principal levers policymakers can move to improve their business climates.

Regulation and Economic Growth

Evidence of the negative effects of regulation on economic growth was found at the international level in a recent analysis showing "a strong causal link between regulatory quality and economic performance" (Jaliliana, Kirkpatrick, and Parker 2007; see also Nicoletti and Scarpetta 2003). Annual rankings of countries by their "economic freedom" also find close correlations between economic growth and indices of freedom, with regulations being an important part of the indices (Heritage Foundation and Wall Street Journal 2008).

The cost of regulations at all levels in the U.S. is estimated to be more than $1.5 trillion per year (ATRF 2008). Studies of regulations at the national level in the U.S. have found many regulations impose costs much greater than the benefits they create (Hahn 2005). Money spent complying with regulations reduces business and household incomes, giving rise to health and accident risks that must be taken into account when measuring the net benefit of the regulations. Economists estimate that every $15 million in additional regulatory compliance costs induces one fatality due to lost income (Lutter *et al.* 1999).

An analysis of the relation between federal regulation – measured by the number of pages in the *Federal Register* – and output per unit of capital, economic growth, and productivity showed that every 1 percentage point increase of the ratio of regulation to capital correlates with a .24 percentage point decrease in capital productivity (Dawson 2007).

Why Regulate?

If regulation is so expensive and often counterproductive, why regulate at all? At first (and even second) glance, it is difficult to understand why some industries are regulated and others are not. For example, until recently prices for many utilities (electricity, telephone, natural gas, water, and sewer services) were nearly universally regulated while prices for food, housing, and personal computers seldom were. Some industries such as railroads, airlines, and trucking have been or are being deregulated.

Either the demand to be regulated varies from industry to industry and over time, or the supply – the willingness of policymakers to approve regulation – is determined by something more than "the public interest" or even campaign contributions. During the 1990s, economist James L. Johnston offered a theory of regulation that solved this riddle (Johnston 1996a, 1996b). He observed that regulation often emerges when three conditions are present: the product or service is subject to substantial shifts in supply and demand, supply reliability cannot be achieved through precautionary stocks or other market techniques, and substantial social costs are incurred when supplies are interrupted or demand suddenly increases. The intended effect of regulation in such cases is to improve the stability of supply by encouraging extra investment in reliability.

Johnston's theory explains why electric utilities and the supply of doctors, for example, are so widely regulated – electricity is difficult to store, and the social costs of a power blackout or a natural disaster causing thousands or millions of people to need medical care would be huge. It also explains why the emergence of new financial instruments (such as mutual funds and futures and options markets) and institutions (such as

Underwriters Laboratories and J.D. Powers and Associates) can make regulation less necessary.

The Johnston Test

Johnston's theory of regulation provides a measurable objective for regulation: Reducing the social costs caused by interruptions to the supply of or demand for key goods or services. This in turn provides a new way to discover deregulation opportunities and increase the odds that deregulation initiatives are successful (Bast 2010).

Policymakers should begin by asking if current regulations are justified by the Johnston Test: Does the industry they pertain to exhibit all three traits of an industry that requires regulation? If not, then that industry is a candidate for deregulation.

If an industry has one or two but not all three of the traits of an industry that should be regulated, then a deregulation effort should be tailored to address the one or two areas where markets might not be expected to succeed without high social costs. For example, the high social cost of hurricanes and other extreme weather events could be addressed through insurance programs or nonprofit programs that reward voluntary efforts to preserve fragile shorelines.

Even industries that pass the Johnston Test can be candidates for deregulation. The test directs our attention to how new technologies or market institutions can emerge that stabilize prices without government's help. For example, the creation of derivative markets for oil and natural gas made government price controls unnecessary. New financial markets can similarly reduce risk in other areas, making deregulation possible.

Unnecessary regulations cause waste and lost productivity. Hundreds of billions of dollars a year could be saved by asking if current and proposed regulations are justified by the Johnston's Test, and by then repealing those that fail the test. Deregulation is a proven way to improve business climates while benefitting consumers.

Recommended reading: James L. Johnston, "Which Industries Are Regulated?" The Heartland Institute, December 10, 1996; Joseph L. Bast, "Why Regulate? New Applications of the Johnston Test," *Policy Brief,* The Heartland Institute, August 2010; Robert W. Hahn, *In Defense of the Economic Analysis of Regulation* (Washington, DC: AEI-Brookings Joint Center for Regulatory Studies, 2005).

9. Discourage lawsuit abuse.

Lawsuit abuse imposes billions of dollars of unnecessary costs on businesses and citizens every year.

A state and nation's legal system plays a major role in enforcing contracts and upholding the Rule of Law, which in turn affects the business climate. A state's tort system – the subset of laws governing questions of liability in the event of injury – helps protect the safety of the state's residents and visitors, while its cost influences the competitiveness of businesses operating within its borders.

In an increasingly globalized economy, U.S. firms must compete with businesses in other countries that operate under different tort systems. "European courts," writes Northwestern University law professor Stephen Presser, "are much less likely to hand out unpredictable and disproportionate damage judgments – unlike American courts, where ruinous verdicts are a potential in too many lawsuits" (Presser 2002, 1).

Good and Bad Tort Systems
A good tort system compensates victims fully, in a timely fashion, and without excessive costs to either the parties or taxpayers. A bad tort system produces unpredictable awards, requires months or years of litigation before awards are made, and consumes a significant portion of monies in lawyer fees and court costs. A good tort system sends clear signals to potential litigants about their duties and obligations, which leads to behavior that minimizes unnecessary conflicts and social costs.

Unfortunately, the U.S. tort system has become increasingly dysfunctional over time. The Pacific Research Institute noted in March 2010:

> There is growing evidence that tort costs in the United States are far greater than in other countries, and that much of the difference is due to lawsuit abuse. Lawsuit abuse and the accompanying excessive litigation and damage awards act as a destructive "excess tort tax," which drags down the economy of a state and the country. Excessive tort burdens divert resources to the lawsuit industry and away from more productive activities such as R&D or expanding access to health care. There is growing evidence that today's U.S.

tort system is a net cost to society at the margin (McQuillan and Abramyan 2010, 17).

The authors of another report from the Pacific Research Institute, titled *Jackpot Justice,* found the total annual cost of the U.S. tort liability system in 2007 was $865 billion (McQuillan, Abramyan, and Archie 2007). Alarmingly, less than 15 cents of every dollar reached injured people, with the rest consumed by lawyers' fee, court costs, and other legal expenses.

A Tort Reform Agenda

During the 1980s and 1990s, many states reformed their tort systems to discourage lawsuit abuse. Ten states adopted reforms in the past two years: Arizona, California, Florida, Georgia, Indiana, Louisiana, Oklahoma, Rhode Island, Tennessee, and West Virginia. Of this group, Oklahoma was the most successful, adopting reforms in 16 different areas of tort law (ATRA 2009). Though reform opportunities vary from state to state, the following have proven beneficial in states where they have been adopted:

Limit non-economic tort damages – Claims for non-economic tort damages, such as pain and suffering and loss of conjugal affection, are a major source of lawsuit abuse. Such claims are impossible to objectively quantify, and jurors are in a poor position to make good judgments about conflicting claims. States that have capped non-economic tort damages have seen the amount of litigation and average awards drop significantly, along with malpractice premiums that raise costs for firms and consumers.

Cap or ban punitive damages – Punitive damages are awarded by juries above the amount necessary to make the victim whole in order to punish a defendant and/or deter future bad behavior. Like non-economic damages, this is an area of frequent abuse that is usually beyond the proper role and competence of a jury. Such damages are is also a windfall for trial lawyers.

Limit contingent fees – Contingent fee lawyers typically receive about one-third of the total verdict amount they recover. This can result in a windfall for lawyers in cases where the recovery amount is high but the time invested by lawyers is low, while plaintiffs watch much of their awards go into their lawyers' pockets. A strong case can be made that lawyers, as fiduciaries for their clients, have a legal duty to turn over to their clients any fees in excess of amounts that are reasonable and risk-based (Horowitz 2001).

Pass a "loser pays" law – Under the "American rule" of litigation, each side bears its own legal fees, win or lose. Outside the U.S., most other countries use what is called the "English rule," under which the loser pays the other side's legal fees. Many scholars over the years have called for the U.S. to adopt the "English rule" as a way to discourage frivolous claims and give litigants an incentive to arrive at settlements more quickly.

Adopt an FDA defense law – Compliance by drug companies with the labeling and warning requirements imposed by the Food and Drug Administration (FDA) ought to preempt legal challenges alleging failure to communicate a drug's proper use or warn of possible side-effects. Drugs approved by the FDA have gone through a grueling process of testing that takes an average of ten years and costs nearly $1 billion. State legislatures can adopt legislation affirming the use of an "FDA defense" by drug companies.

Enact stiffer sanctions on frivolous claims – In most states, the prevailing parties in cases found to have been frivolous can recover their legal fees. State legislatures can give judges the authority to levy additional monetary sanctions on parties, lawyers, and law firms that file frivolous claims.

Recommended reading: Lawrence J. McQuillan and Hovannes Abramyan, *U.S. Tort Liability Index 2010,* Pacific Research Institute, March 2010; Lawrence J. McQuillan, Hovannes Abramyan, and Anthony P. Archie, *Jackpot Justice: The True Cost of America's Tort System*, Pacific Research Institute, 2007; Michael Horowitz, "Can Tort Law Be Ethical? A Proposal to Curb Ill-Gotten Gains," *The Weekly Standard*, March 19, 2001, pp. 18-20.

10. Attract members of the creative class.

Highly creative people can be attracted to a city or state by keeping their needs and preferences in mind.

A final component of a good business climate is adopting policies that make cities and communities attractive to scientists, engineers, entrepreneurs, and other members of the so-called "creative class." These individuals are sought after by companies, with the result that businesses will move to cities and regions where such individuals congregate.

The Rising Creative Class

Richard Florida, at the time a professor of economic development at Carnegie Mellon University and now at the University of Toronto, in his 2001 book *The Rise of the Creative Class,* contended that "regional economic growth is driven by the location choices of creative people – the holders of creative capital – who prefer places that are diverse, tolerant, and open to new ideas" (Florida 2002, 223). His "Creativity Index" found two major trends – "the first is a new geographic sorting along class lines," the second is "that the centers of the Creative Class are more likely to be economic winners" (*Ibid.*, 235).

Some of Florida's bigger claims appear to have been overblown (Malanga 2004), but underneath the hype are some facts that anyone interested in improving a city's, state's, or nation's business climate ought to keep in mind. For example, the number of scientists and engineers, according to Florida, "increased from 42,000 in 1900 to 625,000 in 1950, before expanding to 5 million by 1999 – an eightfold increase since midcentury. ... In 1900 there were just 55 scientists and engineers for every 100,000 people in the United States. That figure increased to 400 by 1950 and to more than 1,000 in 1980. By 1999 there were more than 1,800 scientists and engineers per 100,000 people" (*Ibid.*, 45).

Florida reports a similarly dramatic rise in the number of professional artists, writers, and performers, growing from 200,000 in 1900 to 525,000 in 1950 and 2.5 million in 1999, or from 250 for every 100,000 Americans in 1900 to 350 by 1950, 500 in 1980, and 900 in 1999 (*Ibid.*, 46).

Lifestyle Demands

The lifestyle demands of members of the creative class and the effects they have on the nations, states, and cities that attract them have been described by Florida as well as several other authors including Daniel Pink (Pink 2001), Joel Kotkin (Kotkin 2000), David Brooks (Brooks 2001) and George Gilder (Gilder 2000). Three that stand out are:

- Members of the creative class are younger than the average worker and seek cities with amenities that suit their lifestyles.

- They change jobs frequently and consequently prefer to live in cities with lots of job opportunities to avoid having to relocate.

- Creative people spend more time on outdoor recreation and view their cities the way tourists do, as a collection of places to visit to have fun.

A group of people who should be considered members of the "creative class," but who don't receive enough attention from policymakers, are entrepreneurs. Entrepreneurs, as wealth creators, ought to be recruited by any city or state trying to improve its business climate. They are extremely sensitive to income tax rates since most of their business income is reported as personal income and subject to individual income taxes (Merrill 2007). They need flexible labor policies in order to assemble new labor forces or change existing ones, meaning policies that favor labor unions are unfavorable to entrepreneurship.

Excessive regulation, the threat of frivolous litigation, and the other obstacles to businesses mentioned earlier in this chapter apply with extra weight to entrepreneurs since they often lack the experience and resources to surmount these obstacles. Entrepreneurs are less likely than established businesses to engage in lobbying for subsidies, tax abatements, or other kinds of favoritism, so such programs tend to work to their disadvantage.

One way states can find out how they stand in the competition for entrepreneurs is to check the "State New Economy Index" created by the Information Technology and Innovation Foundation and the Ewing Marion Kauffman Foundation (Atkinson 2008). The index is based on 29 indicators grouped into five categories: knowledge jobs, globalization, economic dynamism, transformation to a digital economy, and technological innovation capacity.

Recommended reading: Chris Edwards, "Taxes and Small Business Job

Creation," statement before the Senate Committee on Finance, Cato Institute, February 23, 2010; Richard Florida, *The Rise of the Creative Class*, New York, NY: Basic Books, 2002; Steven Malanga, "The Curse of the Creative Class," *City Journal,* Manhattan Institute, Winter 2004.

References

Atkinson, Robert D. 2008. *2008 state new economy index.* Information Technology and Innovation Foundation and the Ewing Marion Kauffman Foundation, February.

ATRA. 2009. State tort reform enactments. American Tort Reform Association.

ATRF. 2008. Cost of government day: 2008 report. Americans for Tax Reform Foundation, www.atr.org/content/pdf/2008/July/071508ot-cogdreport.pdf.

Badenhausen, Kurt. 2007. Special report: the best states for business. Forbes.com, July 11. www.forbes.com/2007/07/10/washington-virginia-utah-biz-cz_kb_0711bizstates.html.

Balis, Ryan. 2007. Employment: do minimum wage increases benefit workers and the economy? National Center for Public Policy Research, January 2.

Bartik, Timothy. 1994. Jobs, productivity, and local economic development: what implications does economic research have for the role of government? *National Tax Journal* 47: 847–62.

Bast, Joseph. 2010. Why regulate? New applications of the "Johnston test." *Policy Brief,* The Heartland Institute, August.

Beck, John H. 1987. Selective tax abatements: do they work? *Policy Study* No. 14, The Heartland Institute, March.

Becsi, Zsolt. 1996. Do state and local taxes affect relative state growth? *Economic Review,* Federal Reserve Bank of Atlanta, March.

BLS. 2010. Union members 2009. Bureau of Labor Statistics, January 22.

Brooks, David. 2001. *Bobos in paradise: the new upper class and how they got there.* New York, NY: Simon and Schuster.

Chen, Duanjie and Jack Mintz. 2010. U.S. effective corporate tax rate on new investments: highest in the OECD. *Tax & Budget Bulletin* No. 62, Cato Institute, May 5.

Cox, Wendell. 2008. How smart growth exacerbated the international financial crisis. *WebMemo,* The Heritage Foundation, April 29.

Dawson, John W. 2007. Regulation and the macroeconomy. *Kyklos* 60 (1): 15–36.

DeHaven, Tad. 2009. Three decades of politics and failed policies at HUD. *Policy Analysis* No. 655, Cato Institute, November.

Edwards, Chris. 2010. Taxes and small business job creation. Statement before the Senate Committee on Finance, Cato Institute, February 23.

Florida, Richard. 2002. *The rise of the creative class.* New York, NY: Basic Books.

Frantz, John. 1994. Davis-Bacon: Jim Crow's last stand. *The Freeman: Ideas on Liberty* 44 (2).

Friedman, Milton. 1962. "Social Welfare Measures," Chapter 11 of *Capitalism and Freedom,* Chicago: University of Chicago Press.

Gabe, Todd and David S. Kraybill. 2002. The effect of state economic development incentives on employment growth of establishments. *Journal of Regional Science* 42 (4).

Gilder, George. 2000. *Telecosm: how infinite bandwidth will revolutionize our world.* New York, NY: The Free Press.

Glassman, Sarah, Michael Head, David G. Tuerck, and Paul Bachman. 2008. *The federal Davis-Bacon Act: the prevailing mis-measure of wages.* Beacon Hill Institute at Suffolk University, February.

Gulibon, G. 1999. Growing Pennsylvania's economy: tax cuts vs. economic development programs. The Commonwealth Foundation, March. www.heartland.org/article/3071.

Hahn, Robert W. 2005. *In defense of the economic analysis of regulation.* Washington, DC: AEI-Brookings Joint Center for Regulatory Studies, pp. 41ff.

Helvacian, N. Michael. 2006. Workers' compensation: Rx for policy reform. *NCPA Policy Report* No. 287, National Center for Policy Analysis, September.

Heritage Foundation and Wall Street Journal. 2008. *2008 index of economic freedom,* www.heritage.org/Index/.

Higginson, William. 2008. Housing policy for the 21st century. *Policy Study* No. 121, The Heartland Institute, July.

Horowitz, Michael. 2001. Can tort law be ethical? a proposal to curb ill-gotten gains. *The Weekly Standard,* March 19, pp. 18-20.

Jaliliana, Hossein, Colin Kirkpatrick, and David Parker. 2007. The impact of regulation on economic growth in developing countries: a cross-country analysis. *World Development* 35 (1): 87-103.

John Locke Foundation. 2006. *Agenda 2006.* Raleigh, NC: John Locke Foundation.

Johnson, Brian M. 2007. *2007 index of worker freedom: a national report card.* Alliance for Worker Freedom.

Johnston, James L. 1996a. A general theory of regulation and deregulation. In *Deregulation of energy: intersecting business, economics and policy,* Conference Proceedings, 17th Annual North American Conference, U.S. Association for Energy Economists, October, pp. 145-154.

Johnston, James L. 1996b. Which industries are regulated? The Heartland Institute, December 10. www.heartland.org/article/11789.

Keating, Raymond. 2010. Business tax index 2010: best to worst state tax systems for entrepreneurship and small business. Small Business & Entrepreneurship Council. www.sbecouncil.org/uploads/BTI2010_2.pdf.

Kotkin, Joel. 2000. *The new geography: how the digital revolution is reshaping the American landscape.* New York, NY: Random House.

Lutter, Randall *et al.* 1999. The cost-per-life-saved cutoff for safety-enhancing regulations. *Economic inquiry* 37 (599): 608.

Malanga, Steven. 2004. The curse of the creative class. *City Journal,* Manhattan Institute, Winter.

McQuillan, Lawrence J. and Hovannes Abramyan. 2010. *U.S. tort liability index 2010.* San Francisco, CA: Pacific Research Institute, March.

McQuillan, Lawrence J., Hovannes Abramyan, and Anthony P. Archie. 2007. *Jackpot justice: the true cost of America's tort system.* San Francisco, CA: Pacific Research Institute.

Merrill, Peter. 2007. The corporate tax conundrum. *Tax Notes,* TaxAnalysts.com, October 8.

Michigan Chamber of Commerce. 2007. Legal reform in Michigan: past, present and future.

Moody, J. Scott. 2006. Higher taxes lower economic performance. *Maine Issue Brief,* Maine Heritage Policy Center, September 19.

Moore, William J. 1998. The determinants and effects of right-to-work laws: a review of the recent literature. *Journal of Labor Research* 19 (3): 449-69.

NAWER. 2008. Paycheck protection. *Issue Brief,* National Alliance for Worker and Employer Rights. www.freeworkplace.org/legislativeupdate/pp.php, accessed on August 18, 2008.

Nicoletti, Giuseppe and Stefano Scarpetta. 2003. *Regulation, productivity, and growth: OECD evidence.* Policy research working paper. The World Bank, January.

NILRR. 2008. Right to work states' lead in job growth consistent over time. News release, National Institute for Labor Relations Research, April 15.

Padgitt, Kail. 2009. 2010 state business tax climate index (seventh edition). *Background Paper* No. 59, Tax Foundation, September 22. www.taxfoundation.org/research/show/22658.html.

Peters, Alan and Peter Fisher. 2004. The failures of economic development incentives. *Journal of the American Planning Association* 70: 27-37.

Pink, Daniel. 2001. *Free agent nation: how America's new independent workers are transforming the way we live.* New York, NY: Warner Books.

Presser, Stephen B. 2002. How should the law of products liability be harmonized? what Americans can learn from Europeans. *Global liability issues.* Center for Legal Policy, Manhattan Institute, February.

Stanek, Steve. 2006. Lowest business tax states have best economies: study. *Budget & Tax News,* December.

Vedder, Richard. 2001. Taxes and economic growth. Taxpayers Network Inc., September.

Williams, Walter 2006. Minimum wage, maximum folly. Townhall.com, April 26.

Additional Resources

- *PolicyBot*, The Heartland Institute's free online clearinghouse for the work of other free-market think tanks, contains hundreds of documents on business climate issues. It is on Heartland's Web site at www.heartland.org.

- *www.budgetandtax-news.org*, a Web site devoted to the latest news and commentary about budget and tax issues, often addresses business climate issues. Read headlines, watch videos, or join the conversation by using Twitter or Facebook.

- *Budget and Tax News*, a monthly publication from The Heartland Institute. Subscribe online at www.heartland.org.

Directory

The following national organizations are reliable sources of information on business climate issues.

Alliance for Worker Freedom, www.workerfreedom.org
Americans for Tax Reform Foundation, www.atr.org
American Legislative Exchange Council (ALEC), www.alec.org
Beacon Hill Institute, www.beaconhill.org
Cato Institute, www.cato.org
Council on State Taxation (COST), www.cost.org

Heartland Institute, www.heartland.org
Heritage Foundation, www.heritage.org
John Locke Foundation, www.johnlocke.org
Manhattan Institute, www.manhattan-institute.org
National Alliance for Worker and Employer Rights,
    www.freeworkplace.org
National Institute for Labor Relations Research, www.nilrr.org
Pacific Research Institute, www.pacificresearch.org
Small Business & Entrepreneurship Council (SBEC),
    www.sbecouncil.org/
Tax Foundation, www.taxfoundation.org

Chapter 6
Telecommunications

Hance Haney and George Gilder

---

10 Principles of Telecommunications Policy

1. Encourage new investment in telecom services.
2. Repeal discriminatory taxes and fees.
3. Oppose "network neutrality" regulations.
4. Reduce intrastate access charges on telephone calls.
5. End requirements that telcos file tariffs.
6. Give providers greater freedom to set prices.
7. Exempt competitive services from utility commission jurisdiction.
8. End or reform carrier-of-last-resort and build-out obligations.
9. Minimize government's role in broadband deployment.
10. Give a single agency responsibility for consumer protection.

Introduction

Since the Great Depression, the telecom industry has been subject to comprehensive regulation, with the Federal Communications Commission (FCC) in charge of interstate services and state public utility commissions overseeing intrastate services. This regulatory regime sufficed in the days of copper wires and mechanical switches but is anachronistic in an era of fiber optics, routers, cell phones, and Internet "teleputers."

Today, telephone companies compete with wireless phone and cable companies using Voice over Internet Protocol (VoIP) to deliver phone service. "Cable's digital phone service is now available to over 97 million U.S. homes and more than 13.5 million homes are now subscribing, with that number growing by more than one million per quarter in recent quarters" (NCTA 2009). Comcast had 5.6 million voice customers in August 2008, making it the fourth-largest landline phone provider behind AT&T, Verizon, and Qwest (Fernandez 2008).

Wireline phone companies also face significant competition from cell phones. There were 163.2 million wirelines and 238.2 million cell phones in service at the end of June 2007 (FCC 2008b), and a growing number of cell phone customers are "wireless-only" or "mostly wireless." More than one-third of the nation's households fell into one of those two categories in 2007 (Blumberg and Luke 2008).

Cell phones will become more reliable and less costly in the future and they are beginning to feature television, location services based on global positioning systems, and Internet access. Wireless providers already have 35 million broadband subscribers (more than either the cable or phone companies), even though wireless broadband services are currently slow compared to DSL and cable modem services (FCC 2008b).

Cell phone companies and others are gearing up to add more speed. For example, a consortium that includes Google, Intel, Comcast, Time Warner, Clearwire, and Sprint Nextel plans to build a wireless broadband network based on WiMAX technology that will rival DSL and cable modem services in speed and is much cheaper to deploy than DSL, cable modem service, or the 3G networks Verizon Wireless and AT&T are deploying. The consortium is determined to beat Verizon and AT&T to the market. Meanwhile, AT&T reported its 3G network, currently rated the fastest, would be available in 350 leading U.S. markets by the end of 2008 (AT&T 2008).

Even the largest firms are not immune to competition. AT&T lost 1.2 million landlines nationwide in the first quarter of 2008 (Cheng and Lavallee 2008) and more than 1.5 million more in the second quarter (AP 2008). One industry analyst estimates Verizon and AT&T are losing residential phone lines at a rate of about 10 percent per year (Savitz 2008). Another analyst projects that by 2012 the market share of incumbent telephone companies will have dwindled to 51 percent, with potent competition from a variety of innovators using VoIP (SNL Kagan 2008).

The traditional rationale for utility regulation – that telephone and cable services are natural monopolies – is gone. Continued utility regulation – except as may be necessary for ensuring interconnectivity and number portability – is unnecessary and distorts competition in ways that harm consumers. So far, few states have faced up to this challenge.

The question is frequently asked whether it is necessary to remove all regulation, or whether consumers would benefit more from a combination of regulation and competition. The answer is that competition and regulation are incompatible. As Robert W. Crandall of the Brookings Institution pointed out:

> The economic lesson from the history of regulation is that regulation and competition are a bad emulsion. Once the conditions for competition exist, it is best for regulators to abandon the field altogether. This is particularly true in a sector that is undergoing rapid technological change and therefore requires new entry and new capital. The politics of regulation favor maintaining the status quo, not triggering creative destruction (Crandall 2005, 166).

Distinguished economist and former federal regulator Alfred Kahn agrees:

> The [telecommunications] industry is obviously no longer a natural monopoly, and wherever there is effective competition – typically and most powerfully, between competing platforms, landline telephony, cable and wireless – regulation of the historical variety is both unnecessary and likely to be anti-competitive ... (Kahn 2007).

Congress didn't act to deregulate the railroads until 1979, after President Jimmy Carter stated in a message to Congress that deregulation was necessary to avert an industry crisis. Without regulatory reform, telephone companies could face the same predicament, since current telephone regulation is modeled after former railroad regulation (Huber *et al.* 1999, 214-220). Among other things, the regime forces the regulated entities to set some prices below cost (for example, residential and rural services) – forcing them to operate at a loss and discouraging competitive entry that would produce more choices for consumers; and set other prices well above cost – creating magnets for competition and eroding subsidies to support the services priced below cost. Eventually the system implodes.

Regulatory reform of wireline phone service is lagging behind wireless and cable, both of which were largely deregulated at the federal level during the Clinton administration when they faced much less actual competition than phone companies do now. Preemption of state regulation of wireless services in 1993 coincided with the auctioning of additional spectrum, because Congress assumed competitors would materialize. The elimination of cable rate regulation in 1996 occurred while cable operators still retained 91 percent of all subscribers, because Congress saw that new entrants such as direct broadcast satellite service providers were attracting many customers.

A few states, in particular Indiana, have taken the lead in regulatory reform. In March 2006, Indiana Gov. Mitch Daniels signed into law measures eliminating hidden subsidies in intrastate access charges, ending tariff filing requirements, permitting pricing flexibility, taking away from the state utility commission jurisdiction to regulate competitive services, streamlining provider-of-last-resort regulation, and assigning responsibility for consumer protection and broadband deployment to other state agencies.

These reforms may seem radical to anyone who remembers the days when incumbent phone companies were monopolies. But the monopoly era is over. The reforms enacted in Indiana are an appropriate and necessary response to the surge of competition that has transformed the telecommunications industry.

This chapter describes the beneficial results of what Indiana and other innovation leaders have done and how other states can follow their lead to reap the rewards of new investment in telecommunications services.

Recommended reading: Robert W. Crandall, *Competition and Chaos* (Washington, DC: Brookings Institution, 2005); George Gilder, *Telecosm: How Infinite Bandwidth Will Revolutionize Our World* (New York, NY: The Free Press, 2000).

1. Encourage new investment in telecom services.

New investment in telecom services produces wide-reaching economic benefits.

The main reason policymakers should undertake regulatory reform is to attract new investment to the telecom sector so phone, cable, and Internet consumers can receive the services they want at competitive prices. New investment in telecom is necessary to deliver this result, and the states that attract it will also reap the added rewards of job creation and economic growth.

The U.S. Internet of 2015 will be at least 50 times larger than it was in 2006 (Swanson and Gilder 2008). Internet growth at these levels will require a dramatic expansion of bandwidth, storage, and traffic management in core, edge, metro, and access networks. Building the infrastructure needed to cope with this exaflood[1] will be very expensive, likely requiring some $137 billion in global new investment and $50 billion in the U.S. over the next two years.

The good news is that this investment will be a powerful generator of new jobs and economic growth. A study by the Brookings Institution found "for every one percentage point increase in broadband penetration in a state, employment is projected to increase by 0.2 to 0.3 percent per year. For the entire U.S. private non-farm economy, this suggests an increase of about 300,000 jobs ..." (Crandall, Lehr, and Litan 2007). The authors call broadband "an important basic infrastructure that is expected to produce spillover and wide-reaching benefits across the economy."

A study by Carnegie Mellon University and MIT's Communications Futures Program, conducted for the U.S. Department of Commerce, found "between 1998 and 2002, communities in which mass-market broadband was available by December 1999 experienced more rapid growth in employment, the number of businesses overall, and businesses in IT-intensive sectors, relative to comparable communities without broadband

---

[1] An exabyte is one-quintillion byte units of information or computer storage. "Exaflood" refers to the massive growth in Web site traffic underway, rising from around 20 exabytes in 2006 to an expected 1,000 exabytes by 2015.

at that time" (Gillett, Lehr, Osorio, and Sirbu 2006).

The Brookings Institution's Robert Litan has measured the social benefits of broadband deployment and use resulting from lower medical costs and costs of institutionalized living and more seniors and individuals with disabilities being able to participate in the labor force. "Considered together, these three benefits are estimated to accumulate to at least $927 billion in 2005 dollars ... This amount is equivalent to half of what the United States currently spends annually for medical care for all its citizens ($1.8 trillion)" (Litan 2005).

Those states that are leading the way in removing regulatory barriers to telecom investment have seen significant new investment in new services. According to a 2008 report by Ball State University researchers, during the 18 months following passage of HEA 1279, Indiana's reform legislation, telephone companies reported investing more than $516 million and creating more than 2,200 jobs in Indiana (Ball State University 2008). The study goes on to report:

- "According to FCC data, from July 1 to December 31 of 2006, nearly 400,000 new high-speed technology lines were installed in Indiana, a 33 percent increase from the previous six-month period. As of December 31, 2006, Indiana had 1.5 million high-speed technology lines, a 72 percent increase over 2005."

- "Competing video service is now available from AT&T (U-verse) in select areas of Anderson, Bloomington, Indianapolis, Kokomo, [and] Muncie. Verizon is offering fiber to the household Internet TV service (FiOS) in Fort Wayne, New Haven and Huntertown."

- "Washington, Indiana became the third city in the nation and the first in the state of Indiana to launch next-generation WiMAX wireless service in September 2007, reaching more than 6,000 homes and businesses. Other Indiana markets scheduled for WiMAX deployment during the first quarter 2008 will provide new, high-bandwidth Internet services to roughly 35,000 households in both underserved and rural areas."

Recommended reading: Ball State University, Digital Policy Institute, "An Interim Report on the Economic Impact of Telecommunications Reform in

Indiana: A White Paper," February 15, 2008; Sharon E. Gillett, William H. Lehr, Carlos A. Osorio, and Marvin A. Sirbu, "Measuring the Economic Impact of Broadband Deployment, Final Report," Carnegie Mellon University and MIT's Communications Futures Program, February 28, 2006.

2. Repeal discriminatory taxes and fees on telecom services.[2]

Phone calls and cable services are taxed at two times the rate as clothing, sporting goods, and other household products.

The first thing elected officials should consider doing to encourage investment in telecom services is repeal discriminatory taxes and fees on telecom services. Taxes and fees on cable TV and telephone subscribers average 13.40 percent, twice as high as the national average retail sales tax of 6.61 percent (Tuerck *et al.* 2007). In other words, phone calls and cable services are taxed at two times the rate as clothing, sporting goods, and other household products.

The national annual burden on cable TV and telephone customers is approximately $37 billion. Taxes reduce consumer demand for cable television by between 17.5 percent and 35 percent and for wireless telephone services by between 13.3 and 15.3 percent. Taxes and fees cause an annual "deadweight loss" to society of more than $11 billion (Brito and Ellig 2006; Ellig and Taylor 2006).

Taxes also vary from one communication service to another and according to the technology used to deliver otherwise-similar services. A typical phone call placed with a wireline phone is taxed at 16.87 percent, while a call placed over a cell phone and billed at the same rate is taxed at 11.78 percent. If placed using a VoIP service like Vonage, the call in most states isn't taxed at all.

---

[2] Unless otherwise indicated, the statistics in this section are taken from David Tuerck, Paul Bachman, Steven Titch, and John Rutledge, "Taxes and Fees on Communication Services," *Heartland Policy Study* No. 113, The Heartland Institute, May 2007 rev. June 2007.

A typical pay-per-view movie ordered through a cable TV box is taxed at 11.69 percent, while the same movie downloaded over the Internet using a service such as iTunes is not taxed. The new video services being offered by wireline phone companies will probably be taxed at 5 or 6 percent.

Communications taxes and fees are regressive with respect to income: Their rate as a percent of household income declines as household income rises. Poor households pay 10 times as much, as a percentage of their income, in taxes and fees on cable TV and telephone services as do affluent families (about 1 percent versus 0.1 percent). Public officials seeking to close the so-called "digital divide" can lower the price of communication services by repealing discriminatory taxes and fees.

High and discriminatory taxes and fees are legacies of an era when cable and telephone companies had near-monopolies and could pass the cost of taxes and fees along to their then-captive ratepayers. Today, competition allows consumers to choose less-taxed alternatives, causing taxes and fees to distort buying and investment decisions. Policymakers should bring public policy up-to-date with the following changes:

■ Local governments can reduce cable franchise fees, making sure they do not exceed the true economic cost of using public rights-of-way (Speta 2002). Regulations that impose costs on cable companies and their new competitors from the phone and wireless sectors should be avoided or repealed.

■ States can adopt legislation that lowers and streamlines communication taxes, as Virginia and Ohio have done. States also can preempt local franchise laws that impose excessive fees or restrict new entry by competitors, following the example of such states as Indiana, Ohio, and Wisconsin. As this is done, it's important to allow cable companies to operate under the same franchise agreements as their competitors.

■ The federal government recently phased out a 3 percent national excise tax on all wireless and on wireline long-distance calls, a positive and long-overdue step. The federal government can go further by adopting legislation prohibiting states and cities from adopting discriminatory sales, use, or business taxes on communication services.

Recommended reading: David Tuerck, Paul Bachman, Steven Titch, and John Rutledge, "Taxes and Fees on Communication Services," *Heartland Policy Study* No. 113, The Heartland Institute, May 2007 rev. June 2007; Scott Mackey, "The Excessive State and Local Tax Burden On Wireless Telecommunications Service," *State Tax Notes,* July 2004, pp. 181-94; Council on State Taxation, "2004 State Study and Report on Telecommunications Taxation," Telecommunications Tax Task Force, March 2005.

3. Oppose "network neutrality" regulations.

Attempts to legislate network neutrality risk a repeat of the disaster that was caused by the Telecom Act of 1996.

"Network neutrality" is a somewhat-flexible label given to ideas concerning the rights of Internet users to control the service they receive from Internet service providers (ISPs). It comes to the attention of policymakers when its advocates call for regulations that would prevent network providers from offering deals to one content provider unless they offer the same deal to all providers (Lessig and McChesney 2006). It is also often evoked as a free speech principle that network providers should not discriminate among messages based on their content.

In 2005, the FCC endorsed four principles of network neutrality that are widely supported by ISPs and their customers: (1) consumers are entitled to access the lawful Internet content of their choice; (2) consumers are entitled to run applications and services of their choice, subject to the needs of law enforcement; (3) consumers are entitled to connect their choice of legal devices that do not harm the network; and (4) consumers are entitled to competition among network providers, application and service providers, and content providers (FCC 2005).

"Although the Commission did not adopt rules in this regard," the FCC statement read, "it will incorporate these principles into its ongoing policymaking activities. All of these principles are subject to reasonable network management." This is essentially where federal policy remains today, despite efforts to codify the principles into federal law.

Should the FCC or state regulators do more to enforce network neutrality? Most surely not. While the principles themselves may be sound, giving the FCC authority to turn them into a regulatory code and then to enforce it risks a repeat of the disaster that was caused by the Telecom Act of 1996, when thousands of pages of new regulations and years of litigation slowed innovation to a crawl and helped cause the telecom crash of 2000-2003.

Turning the principles of network neutrality into regulations would expand the FCC's regulatory power over ISPs, preventing them from "throttling" service to heavy users or providing tiered service, where customers pay different amounts for different levels of access. This is the opposite of the pricing flexibility and freedom to innovate that is required to encourage and reward new investment in telecom services and infrastructure (Costin 2008).

For years, some network neutrality advocates have predicted that broadband providers would contrive integrated content-conduit plays enabling them to reap profits from broadband content and destroy competition and innovation. This hasn't happened because content and conduit are naturally separate: If you have the best content, you want it on everyone's conduit, and if you have the best conduit, you want everyone's content on it. There are no synergies between creating attractive and original content and building powerful and available broadband networks. Consequently, the most profitable product in cable is not TV but open Internet service. The market will continue to push phone and cable companies to provide consumers with more choice, not less (Lee 2008).

Several prominent telecom experts sent an open letter to U.S. Representatives Joe Barton and John Dingell in 1996 that said in part, "By deterring product differentiation, net neutrality regulation could easily have the perverse effect of limiting or even destroying competition. Homogeneity imposed by regulation, in other words, could lead us back to monopoly" (Arrison *et al.* 2006).

Calls for network neutrality regulations are especially ill-timed because of the exploding demand for broadband services described in Principle 1. Billions of dollars need to be raised from investors and invested quickly to keep up with the demand for speed and bandwidth. Adoption of new regulations to enforce the vague principles of network neutrality would persuade many investors to stay on the sidelines, as occurred in the cable industry following re-regulation in 1992 and the phone industry following passage of the regulation-laden 1996 Telecommunications Act. In both cases, telecom investment crashed when investors saw that new rules would undermine expected returns on new investments. Investors returned to the cable industry in 1996, following repeal of price controls, and to the phone industry beginning in 2004 when the FCC scaled back network-sharing rules.

Advocates of network neutrality regulations disregard the need for a regulatory environment that protects and rewards the new investments needed in broadband infrastructure.

Recommended reading: Bret Swanson and George Gilder, "Estimating the Exaflood," Discovery Institute, January 29, 2008, www.discovery.org/a/4428; Timothy B. Lee, "The Durable Internet: Preserving Network Neutrality without Regulation," *Policy Analysis* No. 626, Cato Institute, November 12, 2008.

4. Reduce intrastate access charges on telephone calls.

Reform voice call termination rates so there is parity and technological neutrality.

A principal aim of legislators and regulators in regulating telecom service providers is to ensure that high-quality phone service is available and affordable everywhere. But there are dramatic variations in the cost of providing traditional (analog) phone service depending on population density. This type of phone service would not be affordable in many rural areas and would be more expensive in residential areas if rates were set according to cost.

A number of direct and indirect subsidy mechanisms provide support for rural and residential phone services. One of the indirect subsidies at the state level is intrastate access charges that long-distance and wireless providers pay to smaller rural local phone providers and new entrants who originate or terminate calls for them. Phone companies historically over-charged long-distance and business customers, and in some cases still do, so they can offer lower prices for rural and residential phone service and still recover their total costs.

Such cross-subsidies cannot be maintained in a competitive market if competitors can choose to serve profitable customers and ignore everyone else. Since competitors are free to choose their customers, cross-subsidies discourage competitive entry in high-cost areas when the incumbent is charging a lower price than a competitor would need to charge to cover its costs plus earn a reasonable profit. In the low-cost areas, competitive entry is extremely profitable when the incumbent's services are priced high enough to subsidize other customers. Competitors can profitably under-price the incumbent in low-cost areas while the incumbent is helpless to match the price decreases.

Consumers suffer the consequences. High-cost consumers are deprived both of competitive choices and ultimately of the heavily subsidized service they need. Low-cost consumers also are harmed – even if they have a choice of providers – because the inflated price charged by the incumbent acts as an umbrella that guarantees competitors also can maintain a high price without fear that the incumbent could cut its prices below theirs. Reforming voice call termination rates and removing the remaining implicit subsidies from intrastate access charges would spread the benefits of competition in both urban and rural areas.

In Indiana, the cost of intrastate access does not exceed the cost of interstate access. This policy of "parity" makes sense, because interstate access charges are fully compensatory and a telephone company does not incur a separate set of costs when it provides intrastate versus interstate access.

Reducing intrastate access charges does not necessarily mean forcing rural and residential consumers to pay higher prices for basic service. Indirect subsidization through intrastate access charges can be replaced with an explicit funding mechanism into which all competitors must contribute equitably and out of which any competitor who wishes to serve a high-cost area may receive adequate funding.

In some cases, reducing access charges would spur the deployment of broadband in rural areas without sacrificing consumer choice. Access charges were originally set to reflect the cost of analog phone service, which is more expensive to deliver than wireless or VoIP phone services. Smaller rural providers are still under "rate-of-return" or "cost-plus" regulation entitling them to recover their costs plus earn a reasonable return of approximately 10 to 15 percent. Since the return is defined as a percentage of the costs they incur, as costs go up so do profits. Moreover, since VoIP often deprives smaller rural providers and new entrants of access charges, current policies discourage rural phone companies from marketing VoIP services.

States therefore should consider reducing intrastate access charges for smaller rural providers and new entrants to remove a disincentive to market less-expensive phone services such as wireless and VoIP. It is not possible to preserve the status quo, nor is it desirable to postpone reform. If wireline and wireless phone companies are forced to charge or pay inflated call termination rates, they will lose customers to lower-priced VoIP offerings. If they are required to reduce intrastate access charges at least to the same level as interstate access charges, they can provide a more competitive offering.

Policymakers could reduce intrastate long-distance rates for most consumers and promote the availability of flat-rate long-distance plans by reducing intrastate access charges. Ideally, the current system of high intrastate access charges and low interstate access charges ought to be replaced with parity and technology neutrality in call termination fees generally.

5. End requirements that telcos file tariff notices.

Incumbent telephone companies shouldn't have to give advance notice of their price and service decisions to competitors.

The requirement put on telephone companies to file tariffs[3] in advance of their plans to alter rates, terms, and conditions is intended to prevent a common carrier from discriminating. This type of disclosure sounds harmless and pro-consumer, but it is often anti-competitive and harms

---

[3] Tariffs are filings containing the rates, terms, and conditions of certain services provided by telecommunications carriers. Incumbent Local Exchange Carriers (ILECs) file tariffs with the FCC for interstate local access service and with state utility commissions for local and intrastate service. Long-distance service and many broadband services have been detariffed. Tariffs are optional for Competitive Local Exchange Carriers (CLECs).

consumers.

Many states allow tariffs to go into effect at the conclusion of a notice period unless the state utility commission chooses to conduct a hearing. In Illinois, for example, changes in the rates or terms of phone service go into effect after 45 days' notice to the state commission and to the public. Meanwhile, competitors (primarily cable companies using VoIP and wireless companies) are free to inspect the tariff and beat the incumbent to market with a competitive offering of their own.

In a competitive market, rivals take advantage of advance filing of tariffs to benchmark their prices and service conditions to what the incumbents plan to offer. Rivals can wait until they receive formal notice of an incumbent's plans before they change the price or quality of their product or service as necessary to avoid losing sales. This cat-and-mouse game reduces the incentives for both the incumbent and the rivals to innovate.

The FCC concluded in 1996 that it would be pro-competitive to neither require *nor allow* long-distance carriers to file tariffs because it would increase incentives for innovation, make it easier to offer discounts and customized service arrangements, and reduce the possibility of tacit coordination in price-setting (FCC 1996).

Tariffs may have been appropriate in a monopoly environment where there was no need to worry about information-sharing because there were no competitors. This situation no longer exists in intrastate phone markets. There should be no formal notification requirements.

6. Give providers greater freedom to set prices.

Competition, not regulation, is the way to ensure that prices are as low as possible.

Deregulation opened the long-distance market to competitors in the early 1980s and subsequently reformed vestiges of utility regulation that inhibited full competition such as implicit subsidies, tariffs, and price ceilings and floors. The results were innovation, improved service quality, greater choice of providers, and lower prices. Average revenue per minute of long-distance calling dropped from 15 cents in 1992 to 6 cents in 2006, a decrease of 60 percent. During 2007, the price of interstate toll service rose 2.4 percent compared to a 4.1 percent increase in the overall consumer price index (FCC 2008a, iv).

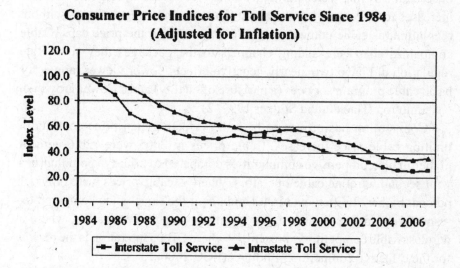

Consumer Price Indices for Toll Service Since 1984 (Adjusted for Inflation)

Wireless was completely deregulated early in the Clinton administration, and the average cost per minute of cell phone use has fallen 85 percent, from 47 cents in 1994 to 7 cents in 2006 (FCC 2008c, 8). Minutes of cell phone use are significantly less expensive in the U.S. than in Western Europe (where revenue per minute averaged 20 cents in the last quarter of 2006) and Japan (26 cents) (*Ibid.*, 10). Price regulation in other countries has had the unintended effect of preserving higher prices (Littlechild 2006).

Full pricing flexibility also could bring more innovation, improved service quality, choice of providers, and lower prices for local voice, video, and advanced data services. Capping rates discourages competition by making it highly profitable to serve some customers and unprofitable to serve others. High-cost consumers are deprived both of competitive choices and ultimately of the heavily subsidized service they need as low-cost customers take advantage of competitive offerings. Meanwhile, the competition for low-cost customers is illusory: Competitors are free to charge unreasonably high prices because the incumbent is helpless to cut its prices selectively.

The story on pricing flexibility for cable services is somewhat different from voice. Federal price controls on cable television were lifted by the Cable Communications Policy Act of 1984 but then reimposed in the Cable Television Consumer Protection and Competition Act of 1992, and lifted once again by the Telecommunications Act of 1996. The rate of price increases for cable service was about the same under regulation as without regulation, as cable companies found ways around the price caps. Cable companies also were adding channels to the packages they sold. Rate regulation did have two clearly negative effects: lower viewer ratings for basic cable program services (a measure of quality) and a slower growth in consumption (Hazlett and Spitzer 1997, 2).

Competition has proven to be more effective than price controls in limiting cable price increases. Cable prices in 2005 were "20.6 percent higher in noncompetitive communities compared to prices in communities with second wireline cable operators, whereas cable prices were only 7.1 percent higher, 1.4 percent higher and about the same when compared to, respectively, prices in communities with low cable penetration, where a wireless cable competitor is present, or where DBS penetration is the reason for the effective competition finding" (FCC 2006, 5).

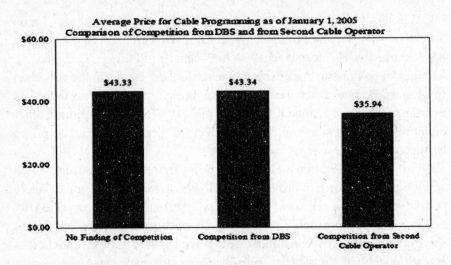

Those states that have removed restrictive video franchise requirements have seen new investment, more competition, and lower cable prices. "Consumers have enjoyed greater choice and a range of new services, including on-demand video and 'a la carte' content selection, at lower cost.

Legacy cable providers have responded to new competition by lowering costs and improving service" (Titch 2007).

In January 2009, "intense competition for cable and satellite customers between AT&T U-verse and Verizon FiOS high-speed fiber providers has driven down rates for Internet, phone, and TV service and is likely the reason that companies allow these savings to continue past the promotional period. In the past year, bundles of the three services have dropped in price by up to 20 percent, to as low as $80 a month" (Consumer Report 2009).

There is scant dissent that telecom services should be deregulated when markets are competitive, but wide differences of opinion as to when there is sufficient competition to warrant regulatory reform. Opponents of deregulation have proposed that a market is competitive only when every consumer has a choice of providers or the incumbent loses significant market share. The FCC has rejected both of these ideas (FCC 1999).

As to waiting until every consumer has a choice of providers, the FCC concluded this approach might allow competitors to "game the system" in that they could prevent an incumbent from obtaining pricing flexibility indefinitely by choosing not to serve certain customers. Moreover, the FCC expressed the view that it isn't administratively possible to determine the exact moment relief should be granted under this type of test.

Experience shows that a market is competitive anytime there are no barriers to entry, such as exclusive franchises or prohibitive investment costs, and where actual and/or potential competitors can offer reasonable substitute products or services (Baumol and Sidak 1994). This describes the telecom market, since phone companies, wireless providers, and cable VoIP operators provide services that large numbers of consumers consider substitutes in many circumstances. Technological change and regulatory reform have reduced barriers to entry, allowing dissatisfied consumers to take their business elsewhere. Competition, not regulation, is keeping prices low and consumers satisfied.

Recommended reading: Thomas W. Hazlett and Matthew L. Spitzer, *Public Policy Toward Cable Television: The Economics of Rate Controls* (Cambridge, MA: The MIT Press and The AEI Press, 1997); William J. Baumol and Gregory J. Sidak, *Toward Competition in Local Telephony* (Cambridge, MA: The MIT Press and The AEI Press, 1994).

7. Exempt competitive services from utility commission jurisdiction.

There is no reason for a utility commission to retain jurisdiction to intervene in a marketplace that has become competitive.

One way to reform regulation of competitive communications services is for the legislature to direct the agency with jurisdiction to use its best judgment in determining when regulation is no longer necessary. This was the approach Congress took with the 1996 Telecommunications Act. It didn't work.

Instead of deregulating telecom, Congress and the FCC re-regulated it. They imposed new layers of price controls and sharing requirements on high-speed access lines. They gave new powers to ever-eager utility commissions in the 50 states. They micromanaged negotiations between competitors. And the million-word law became a playground for lawyers and bonanza for bureaucrats. The 1996 act's failure to deregulate was a primary cause of the telecom and technology crash of 2000-2003 (Gilder and Swanson 2002).

Congress even included a provision in the 1996 law authorizing regulated entities to petition for regulatory relief, and provided that the petition would be deemed granted if the FCC failed to issue an appealable written decision within 15 months explaining why it was denying the petition. Ten years later, this provision has had only limited success.

Indiana took a better approach by prohibiting its state commission from exercising jurisdiction over communications services. Non-basic telecommunications service, commercial mobile service, advanced and broadband services, information services, and Internet Protocol-enabled communications services were all placed outside the state commission's jurisdiction by the 2006 law. Basic telecommunications service followed on June 30, 2009.

As wireless and VoIP offerings have begun to steal significant market share from the incumbent wireline providers, it has been argued that those services should not be permitted to escape regulation just because they rely on different technology. Others argue regulation of the incumbent phone companies could be threatened unless regulation is expanded to cover their competitors.

The latter argument at least recognizes the fact that regulation imposes burdens such as subsidy obligations. If the same burdens apply to all competitors, regulation-based competitive advantages and disadvantages will not distort competition. But if such regulation is unnecessary, then it imposes an unnecessary cost on providers and consumers and serves only to discourage investment in the industry. The best way to "level the playing field" among competitors is to eliminate, not add, regulations.

There is no reason for a utility commission to retain jurisdiction to intervene in a marketplace that has become competitive, because the market will take care of most regulatory objectives. Partial regulation is unsustainable (see Robert Crandall's observation, quoted in the Introduction), so the solution can only be to phase out current regulations. If competitive services are not expressly exempted from utility regulation, a state commission becomes a target for commercial rivals seeking a regulatory advantage, activists seeking to promote a policy agenda, or even a formerly regulated entity seeking protection.

Utility commissions in California and a few other states retain authority to regulate wireless services to the extent permitted under federal law. In Illinois the legislature authorized the utility commission to exclude wireless services from "active regulatory oversight," which it did. Florida, Indiana, Michigan, New York, Texas, and most other states have statutes expressly exempting wireless services from state commission jurisdiction.

VoIP services are expressly exempted from state commission jurisdiction in Florida, Indiana, Michigan, North Carolina, Ohio and a few other states. The FCC is currently considering whether VoIP is a telecommunications or an information service. If the former, it is subject to legacy telephone regulation unless the FCC elects to forbear from applying regulation (in which case the states would be preempted); if the latter, it is unregulated. The FCC already has ruled that certain VoIP services are interstate and therefore may not be subject to utility-type regulation by the states (FCC 2004).

Companies find it easier to plan massive investments in network upgrades when laws expressly provide that competitive communications services are not subject to the jurisdiction of an agency that practices utility regulation. Commission decisions do less to reduce regulatory uncertainty than statutes since agency decisions are subject to litigation and FCC review, and the commission itself can change its decision anytime it wants or merely threaten to change it when the commission wants something. Investment flows to the arena not only with the least regulation but also with the lowest threat of re-regulation.

The wisest approach from the standpoint of minimizing unnecessary risk and uncertainty is for states to remove all competitive services (including wireless, VoIP, and basic and non-basic wireline services) from state utility commission jurisdiction.

8. End or reform carrier-of-last-resort and build-out obligations.

In competitive markets, carrier-of-last-resort and build-out requirements can be replaced with competitively neutral subsidies.

A now-obsolete way to provide high-quality, affordable telecommunication services to all consumers in a monopoly environment was to award an exclusive franchise to one service provider and require it to extend service to all consumers at similar rates. The monopoly made it easy for the service provider to subsidize high-cost customers through rate averaging.

Exclusive franchises are now prohibited as a result of the 1996 Telecommunications Act, but the obligation remains on incumbent telephone companies to be carriers of last resort (COLR), providing service throughout the existing service territory at similar rates with their losses covered by federal and state high-cost funds. Similarly, even though cable markets are now competitive in virtually all markets, many cities still impose build-out requirements on new entrants, requiring them to submit plans to serve the entire community by some deadline.

The problem with both COLR and build-out requirements is that low-cost customers no longer can be forced to subsidize high-cost customers. Low-cost customers can now sign up with a competing service provider able to offer lower rates by choosing to serve only low-cost customers. The incumbent is still required to serve everyone else. But there are fewer low-cost customers to generate a subsidy for the high-cost customers, so an incumbent either has to be able to recover its costs from the remaining customers through rate increases, or policymakers need to find ways to distribute the cost of providing subsidized service to high-cost customers equitably among the competing providers.

The telephone rate-averaging requirement should be eliminated. It can be replaced with a competitively neutral subsidy mechanism in which all providers participate, and retail prices in rural areas should be set no lower than prices in urban areas.

Next, an incumbent phone company should not be required to act as a carrier of last resort where the market is competitive and consumers can choose among multiple providers. In a competitive market rivals sometimes sign exclusive deals with property developers or landlords. If the incumbent has a COLR obligation, it may be required to build costly facilities to serve a single customer in an office park, shopping mall, or housing development. The revenue may be inadequate to cover the cost without rate averaging. Regulation that imposes costs on some carriers but not others is anti-competitive.

The Indiana law addresses this problem in part by protecting an incumbent from having to provide communications service to occupants of multi-tenant nonresidential real estate if the owner, operator, or developer of the property does any of the following to benefit another provider: (1) permits only one provider to install communications facilities or equipment on the premises, (2) accepts incentives from a provider in exchange for allowing the provider the exclusive right to provide service to the premises, (3) collects charges from occupants for communications service, or (4) enters into a prohibited agreement with a provider.

Florida ended all carrier-of-last-resort obligations on phone companies effective January 1, 2009. It previously automatically relieved a carrier of last resort of its obligation to provide basic local telecommunications service to any customer in a multi-tenant business or residential property when an owner or developer permits only one communications service provider to install its facilities or equipment and under other circumstances. That approach was more comprehensive than, and superior to, Indiana's.

The case of cable service is similar. Incumbent cable companies often operate under mandates in their franchise agreements to provide universal service to the community. A "level playing field" could require that competitors be subject to the same requirement – that they "build out" their network to cover the entire community by some deadline. But there is no social purpose served by requiring that every customer be served before a single customer is given a second, third, or even fourth choice of cable provider. The "level playing field" goal can better be met by relieving both the incumbent and new competitors from build-out requirements (Skorburg, Speta, and Titch 2007, 17-19).

In high-cost areas where a carrier of last resort is necessary to deliver basic service, the provider should be allowed to choose the most efficient technology, such as VoIP or wireless. Indiana takes this approach to telephone service, relieving the carrier of having to offer costly service using outmoded network facilities and then find a way to subsidize it.

Finally, competitors should be given the opportunity to become providers of last resort. Any provider ought to be allowed to bid for contracts to provide essential telecommunication service in high-cost areas and receive adequate and equitable support from an explicit funding mechanism, if it wins the contract. Incumbent providers that currently provide subsidized service should not be under any legal obligation to continue to serve areas where other providers have won the contracts.

9. Minimize government's role in broadband deployment.

Most broadband initiatives by municipalities have been costly financial failures.

There has been debate for years over government's role in building and operating broadband systems and whether current subsidies for traditional phone service should be expanded to cover advanced services such as broadband. Given the economic benefits of broadband, should governments use taxpayers' money to subsidize its more rapid or widespread deployment?

Municipalities around the country have experimented with building and operating their own broadband systems. Despite high hopes and often significant investments of taxpayer dollars, most of these systems have been financial failures. University of Denver finance professor Ronald Rizzuto audited the three largest and longest-running municipal communications systems in Iowa, often cited as successes by advocates of municipal broadband, and found the reality was quite different:

- "Cedar Falls' municipal communications system had a negative annual free cash flow to equity in nine of its ten years of existence. Its internal rate of return is -7.24 percent, meaning it has been a poor investment for taxpayers and ratepayers.

- "Muscatine's municipal system increased its total debt from $20.30 million in 1998 to $36.49 million in 2004. It is $25,554,984 below its payback point after seven years of operation, and its internal rate of return is -84.7 percent.

- "Spencer's communications utility appeared to achieve positive annual free cash flow to equity in 2003 and 2004 after four years of deficits, but it has received large subsidies from Spencer's electric utility. Adjusting for these subsidies eliminates Spencer's surplus. The combined investment by the two utilities is $18,286,703 below its payback, and its internal rate of return is -45.79 percent" (Rizzuto 2005).

Telecom policy analyst Steven Titch's study of BVU OptiNet, a municipal fiber-to-the-home system in Bristol, Virginia, found a net operating loss and higher-than-expected marketing, interest, and programming costs (Titch 2005). "Even municipal broadband operations regarded as successful, such as BVU OptiNet, are still millions of dollars short of breaking even," Titch concluded.

The failure of most municipal broadband initiatives is partly the result of competition from private broadband networks that have been deployed without public subsidies. While there are some areas where broadband service remains uneconomical with today's technology, those areas are continuing to shrink.

Connected Nation, a nonprofit organization, was formed to foster the creation of other partnerships between the public and private sectors to promote private investment in broadband. In Kentucky, for example, a Connected Nation project helped to increase the percentage of households with access to broadband from 60 percent to 95 percent. (Boulard 2008). The percentage of people actually using broadband jumped from 22 to 44 percent. Minnesota, Ohio, Tennessee, and West Virginia also have implemented Connected Nation models (Connected Nation 2009).

If lawmakers want to subsidize broadband, subsidies should be limited to unserved or underserved areas and employ an explicit and competitively neutral funding mechanism. But beware. The Universal Service Fund (USF) administered by the FCC, which subsidizes basic phone service, has been criticized for years as wasteful and inefficient (Vasquez 2006; McTigue and Ellig 2005). State programs are often no better.

A recent report by the U.S. Government Accountability Office (GAO) notes Congress, when it created the USF, anticipated that competition and new technologies would eliminate the need for universal service support mechanisms, but the explicit fund grew nearly 153 percent between 1998 and 2007 (GAO June 2008). Reform of the subsidy mechanisms has been seriously considered on many occasions but has proven to be politically impossible every time.

The best ways to promote investment in broadband appear in previous principles of this chapter: cut taxes and fees on telecom services and remove regulatory barriers to competition and consumer choices. Direct government subsidies or investment in broadband is unnecessary.

Recommended reading: Joseph Bast, "Municipally Owned Broadband Networks: A Critical Evaluation (Revised Edition), *Heartland Policy Study* No. 105, October 2004; Gary Boulard, "High Speed to the Hinterlands," *State Legislatures*, January 2008; Connected Nation, www.connectednation.org, last visited January 9, 2009.

10. Give a single agency responsibility for consumer protection.

Utility commissions rarely have expertise in enforcing consumer protection laws.

Identity theft, noncompliance with the do-not-call registry, fraud, loss of privacy, spamming, telemarketing scams, and unauthorized charges are examples of real problems consumers face in cyberspace. Although utility regulation and consumer protection are related, a utility commission is seldom better-suited than a state attorney general to protect consumers.

The lack of consumer protection expertise at the FCC was on display recently when the GAO found that although the FCC received 454,000 complaints between 2003 and 2006, it closed about 83 percent without taking any enforcement action (GAO 2008b). The agency has not set measurable enforcement goals, developed a well-defined enforcement strategy, or established performance measures linked to the enforcement goals. The GAO also found the Federal Trade Commission (FTC), which has primary responsibility for consumer protection throughout the economy as a whole, has specific goals and performance measures that allow it to target its enforcement activities and efficiently use its limited resources (GAO 2008a).

Indiana withdrew from the state utility commission jurisdiction to regulate telephone services, but it allows the commission to continue to require service providers – other than commercial mobile service providers – to report annually on service quality. The commission will not have jurisdiction over quality of service aside from mandating reports, however.

States should give a single agency responsibility for enforcing consumer protection laws to ensure uniform treatment of all commercial entities. The advent of robust competition in telecommunications makes it counterproductive to maintain redundant jurisdiction for telephone companies by increasing the risk of uneven enforcement, which could distort competition.

Recommended reading: GAO, "FCC Needs to Improve Performance, Management and Strengthen Oversight of the High-Cost Program," GAO-08-633, June 2008; GAO, "FCC Has Made Some Progress in the Management of Its Enforcement Program but Faces Limitations, and Additional Actions Are Needed," GAO 08-125, February 2008.

Conclusion

States discourage phone and cable companies from offering more competitive services and generating new jobs and economic growth by imposing taxes and regulations that are no longer appropriate for a highly competitive and fast-growing industry. Laws requiring cross-subsidies, utility regulation of competitive services, pricing inflexibility, tariff filing requirements, and consumer protection oversight in the hands of government staff whose specialty is regulation are not in the public interest. All serve chiefly as obstacles to investment that reduce asset values of all telecom suppliers.

Legacy regulation restricts service strategy flexibility and the creativity needed for real competition in the Internet age, even when pursued in the name of "competition." By embracing regulatory reform, legislators can expand customer choice, decrease prices, and ignite the broadband expansion necessary to economic growth and technological progress.

The favorite argument of opponents of regulatory reform is that the time is not right because some consumers have fewer competitive choices than others. But the falling prices of long-distance telephone service and "triple-play" packages being marketed by cable and telephone companies show the competition that exists today is fully sufficient to protect consumers. If incumbent phone companies attempt to exploit consumers by unreasonably raising prices or degrading service, there is sufficient competitive pressure from VoIP and wireless services that they will face swift punishment in the marketplace. Incumbent cable companies face similar pressure from phone companies and wireless competitors. Today consumers are virtual regulators.

It would be wrong to withhold regulatory relief until competitors are in a position to serve every consumer or the incumbent loses a particular market share. These tests are inherently arbitrary, can be exploited by competitors, and are nearly impossible to administer.

This is a golden opportunity for states facing new challenges for jobs and economic growth. By removing the cobwebs of regulations that afflict telecom, policymakers can open up new technological opportunities and economic efficiencies that promise a direct economic stimulus. With simple reforms of outmoded laws, they can ignite innovation and a revival based on technologies tapping into new worldwide webs of glass, light, and air.

References

Arrison, Sonia, Wayne Brough, Jeffrey A. Eisenach, Hance Haney, Thomas Hazlett, Thomas M. Lenard, and John Rutledge. 2006. *Experts oppose net neutrality.* Discovery Institute, May 9. www.discovery.org/a/3500.

Associated Press. 2008. *Earnings rose at AT&T, but revenue misses forecast.* July 24.

AT&T. 2008. *AT&T offers nation's fastest 3G network.* News release.

Ball State University, Digital Policy Institute. 2008. *An interim report on the economic impact of telecommunications reform in Indiana: a white paper.* February 15. www.bsu.edu/digitalpolicy/media/pdf/V2_DPI_Final_Master.pdf

Bast, Joseph. 2004. Municipally owned broadband networks: a critical evaluation (revised edition). *Heartland Policy Study* No. 105, The Heartland Institute, October. www.heartland.org/article/15842.

Baumol, William J. and Gregory J. Sidak. 1994. *Toward competition in local telephony.* Cambridge, MA: The MIT Press and The AEI Press.

Blumberg, Stephen J. and Julian V. Luke. 2008. *Wireless substitution: early release of estimates from the national health interview survey, January-June 2008.* Division of Health Interview Statistics, National Center for Health Statistics, December 17.

Boulard, Gary. 2008. High speed to the hinterlands. *State Legislatures*, January.

Brito, Jerry and Jerry Ellig. 2006. Video killed the franchise star: the consumer cost of cable franchising and proposed policy alternatives. *Journal of Telecommunications and High Technology Law* 5.

Cheng, Roger and Andrew Lavallee. 2008. AT&T gets wireless, data lift. *The Wall Street Journal,* April 23.

Connected Nation. www.connectednation.org. (accessed January 9, 2009).

Consumer Report. 2009. Fiber-optic providers are leading choices for internet, television, and telephone service. News release, January 5.

Costin, Brian. 2008. Net neutrality. *Research & Commentary*, The Heartland Institute, March. www.heartland.org/article/23001.

Council on State Taxation. 2005. *2004 state study and report on telecommunications taxation.* Washington, DC: Telecommunications Tax Task Force, March.

Crandall, Robert W. 2005. *Competition and chaos.* Washington, DC: Brookings Institution.

Crandall, Robert, William Lehr, and Robert Litan. 2007. *The effects of broadband deployment on output and employment: a cross-sectional analysis of U.S. data.* Washington, DC: Brookings Institution.

Ellig, Jerry and James M. Taylor. 2006. The irony of transparency: unintended consequences of wireless truth-in-billing. *Loyola Consumer Law Review* 9.

FCC. 2008a. *Reference book of rates, price indices, and household expenditures for telephone service.* Industry Analysis and Technology Division, Wireline Competition Bureau. hraunfoss.fcc.gov/edocs_public/attachmatch/DOC-284934A1.pdf

FCC. 2008b. *High-speed services for internet access: status as of June 30, 2007.* Industry Analysis and Technology Division, Wireline Competition Bureau, March.

FCC. 2008c. *Annual report and analysis of competitive market conditions with respect to commercial mobile services.* February 4. hraunfoss.fcc.gov/edocs_public/attachmatch/FCC-08-28A1.pdf

FCC. 2006. *Report on cable industry prices.* FCC 06-179. December 27.
hraunfoss.fcc.gov/edocs_public/attachmatch/FCC-06-179A1.pdf

FCC. 2004. *In the matter of Vonage Holdings Corporation petition for declaratory ruling concerning an order of the Minnesota Public Utilities Commission.* WC Docket No. 03-211, Memorandum Opinion and Order, November 12.

FCC. 1999. *Fifth report and order and further notice of proposed rulemaking.* FCC 99-206, August 27. www.fcc.gov/Bureaus/Common_Carrier/Orders/1999/ fcc99206.pdf

FCC. 1996. *In the matter of policy and rules concerning the interstate, interexchange marketplace, second report and order.* paragraph 53, October 31.
www.fcc.gov/Bureaus/Common_Carrier/Orders/1996/fcc96424.txt

Fernandez, Bob. 2008. Comcast's on the line. *Philadelphia Inquirer,* August 24.

GAO. 2008a. *FCC needs to improve performance, management and strengthen oversight of the high-cost program.* GAO-08-633, June.

GAO. 2008b. *FCC has made some progress in the management of its enforcement program but faces limitations, and additional actions are needed.* GAO 08-125, February.

Gilder, George. 2000. *Telecosm: how infinite bandwidth will revolutionize our world.* New York, NY: The Free Press.

Gilder, George and Bret Swanson. 2002. Unleash broadband. *The Wall Street Journal,* July 8.

Gillett, Sharon E., William H. Lehr, Carlos A. Osorio, and Marvin A. Sirbu. 2006. *Measuring the economic impact of broadband deployment, final report.* Carnegie Mellon University and MIT's Communications Futures Program. February 28,
www.eda.gov/ImageCache/EDAPublic/documents/pdfdocs2006/mitcmubbimpactreport_2epdf/v1/mitcmubbimpactreport.pdf

Haney, Hance and George Gilder. 2008. *More broadband, increased choice and lower prices begin with regulatory reform.* Discovery Institute, August.
www.discovery.org/a/7371

Hazlett, Thomas W. and Matthew L. Spitzer. 1997. *Public policy toward cable television: the economics of rate controls.* Cambridge, MA: The MIT Press and The AEI Press.

Huber, Peter W., Michael K. Kellogg, and John Thorne. 1999. *Federal telecommunications law* (2nd ed.). New York, NY: Aspen Publishers.

Kahn, Alfred E. 2007. FTC workshop on broadband connectivity competition policy. February 13. www.ftc.gov/opp/workshops/broadband/presentations/kahn.pdf

Lee, Timothy B. 2008. The durable internet: preserving network neutrality without regulation. *Policy Analysis* No. 626, Cato Institute, November 12.
cato.org/pub_display.php?pub_id=9775

Lessig, Lawrence and Robert W. McChesney. 2006. No tolls on the internet. *Washington Post*, June 8, p. A23.

Litan, Robert E. 2005. *Great expectations: potential economic benefits to the nation from accelerated broadband deployment to older Americans and Americans with disabilities.* New Millennium Research Council, December.

Littlechild, Stephen. 2006. Lessons from America on pricing mobile calls. *Financial Times,* May 21.

Mackey, Scott. 2004. The excessive state and local tax burden on wireless telecommunications service. *State Tax Notes,* July, pp. 181-194.

McTigue, Maurice and Jerry Ellig. 2005. *Performance measures for FCC universal service programs.* Mercatus Center, October 17.

NCTA. 2009. *Digital phone/cable telephony (VoIP – Voice over Internet Protocol).* Issue paper, National Cable and Telecommunications Association. www.ncta.com/IssueBrief.aspx?contentId=3023. (accessed January 20, 2009).

Rizzuto, Ronald J. 2005. Iowa municipal communications systems: the financial track record. *Heartland Policy Study* No. 110, The Heartland Institute, September.

Savitz, Eric. 2008. Who needs wirelines? Bernstein says Verizon, AT&T seeing accelerating residential line losses. *Tech Trader Daily,* February 7.

Skorburg, John, James Speta, and Steven Titch. 2007. The consumer benefits of video franchise reform in Illinois. *Heartland Policy Study* No. 112, The Heartland Institute, April. www.heartland.org/article/20871.

SNL Kagan. 2008. *SNL Kagan forecasts rapid shift in composition of residential phone service.* Press release, April 28.

Speta, James B. 2002. Competitive neutrality in right of way regulation: a case study in the consequences of convergence. *Connecticut Law Review* 2 (35): 808-13.

Swanson, Bret and George Gilder. 2008. *Estimating the exaflood.* Discovery Institute, January 29. www.discovery.org/a/4428

Titch, Steven. 2007. *Better prices and better services for more people: assessing the outcomes of video franchise reform.* Reason Foundation, January. www.reason.org/ps355.pdf.

Titch, Steven. 2005. Municipal broadband: optimistic plan, disappointing reality. *Heartland Policy Study* No. 108, The Heartland Institute, June.

Tuerck, David, Paul Bachman, Steven Titch, and John Rutledge. 2007. Taxes and fees on communication services. *Heartland Policy Study* No. 113, The Heartland Institute, May rev. June.

Vasquez, Vince. 2006. *Digital welfare: the failure of the universal service system.* Pacific Research Institute, February.

Additional Resources

Additional information about information technology and telecom issues is available from The Heartland Institute.

■ *PolicyBot*, The Heartland Institute's free online clearinghouse for the work of other free-market think tanks, contains thousands of documents on information technology and telecommunications issues. It is on Heartland's Web site at www.heartland.org.

■ *www.infotech-news.org*, a Web site devoted to the latest news and commentary about infotech and telecom issues. Read headlines, watch videos, or join the conversation by using Twitter or Facebook.

■ *InfoTech & Telecom News*, a monthly publication from The Heartland Institute. Subscribe online at www.heartland.org.

Directory

The following national organizations support sound telecom policies.

American Enterprise Institute, www.aei.org
American Legislative Exchange Council, www.alec.org
Association for Competitive Technology, www.actonline.org
Beacon Hill Institute, www.beaconhill.org
Cato Institute, www.cato.org
Competitive Enterprise Institute, www.cei.org
The Discovery Institute, www.discovery.org
Heartland Institute, www.heartland.org
Heritage Foundation, www.heritage.org
Hudson Institute, www.hudson.org
Institute for Policy Innovation, www.ipi.org
Mercatus Center, www.mercatus.org
Pacific Research Institute, www.pacificresearch.org
Progress and Freedom Foundation, www.pff.org
Reason Foundation, www.reason.org

Chapter 7
State Fiscal Policy

Steve Stanek and Richard Vedder

---

10 Principles of State Fiscal Policy

1. Above all else: Keep taxes low.
2. Don't penalize earnings and investment.
3. Avoid "sin" taxes.
4. Create a transparent and accountable budget.
5. Privatize public services.
6. Avoid corporate welfare.
7. Cap taxes and expenditures.
8. Fund students, not schools.
9. Reform Medicaid programs.
10. Protect state employees from politics.

Introduction

Legislators must balance the conflicting demands of taxpayers, beneficiaries of public services, and interest groups inside and outside government. The work of state elected officials, always difficult and important, has been made even more so by the rapid growth of state government in recent years. Consider, for example, the following measures of state government growth:

- From 1991 through 2001, total state spending grew by about $556 billion, an 88 percent increase over 1991 spending. The average annual spending growth rate for the period was 6.57 percent, more than double the combined average annual increase of 2.2 percent in prices for government purchases and 1 percent in population.

■ State revenues, including taxes and fees and federal grants, grew from 4.63 percent of Gross Domestic Product (GDP) in 1961 to 8.58 percent in 2001.

■ Per-capita state spending in current dollars climbed 25-fold, from $131 in 1961 to $3,282 in 2001 (Snell, Eckl, and Williams 2003).

With the spread of term limits, more elected officials are new to the job than at any time in recent memory. But they have many sources of advice, starting with the professional staff of every legislature and including such membership organizations as the American Legislative Exchange Council (ALEC), National Conference of State Legislatures (NCSL), and Council of State Governments (CSG). "Think tanks" such as the Tax Foundation, Reason Foundation, and The Heartland Institute also publish research and analysis, much of it available on their Web sites.

Faced with a steady stream of reports and studies from government agencies and nongovernment advocacy groups, elected officials can easily lose sight of the principles and lessons that should form the foundation of what they were sent to the state capital to accomplish or protect. These principles are rooted in the American experience and attract broad bipartisan support among thoughtful elected officials.

This chapter presents ten such fundamental principles addressing the tax and budget aspects of state government. These principles do not address matters of social policy, such as abortion and pornography, or regulatory matters such as environmental protection, smoking bans, or telecommunications regulation. Nor do they amount to a political philosophy or ideology.

The ten principles in this chapter *do* provide the reader with an authoritative guide to the following fiscal policy issues facing policymakers in every state:

■ *Taxes:* How high or low should they be, what should be taxed, and what are the consequences of changing tax policy?

- *Budgets:* When should states outsource the production of services to private providers? How does the budget process affect spending levels and how can it be improved?

- *Economic Development:* What policies should states pursue to encourage maximum economic growth?

- *Schools, Health Care, and Public Employees:* What policies have other states pursued to control spending and achieve high performance in education, health care, and public-sector employee policy?

Sound principles of fiscal policy can promote economic growth, protect citizens from uncertainty and excessive taxation, and help lawmakers deal with conflicting demands. These principles also can help legislators stay focused on the core responsibilities of state government, rather than straying into less-necessary areas whenever extra funds are available.

Recommended reading: R.K. Snell, C. Eckl, and G. Williams, "State Spending in the 1990s," 2003, www.ncsl.org/programs/fiscal/stspend90s.htm; Evergreen Freedom Foundation, "State Expenditure and Tax Limit Model Language," 2005, www.effwa.org/pdfs/tel.pdf.

1. Above all else: Keep taxes low.

The evidence is clear and has been for many years: High taxes hinder economic growth and prosperity.

Low Taxes Are an American Tradition

"An unlimited power to tax involves, necessarily, a power to destroy." So said Daniel Webster in a case heard by the U.S. Supreme Court in 1819. This view goes to the heart of why the nation's Founders believed keeping taxes low is a key fiscal principle for all levels of government.

The Founders waged the War of Independence largely in response to Britain's excessive taxes on the colonies without their representation in Parliament. They were immigrants from European countries where high and discriminatory taxes had prevented economic growth and were used to penalize politically unpopular groups and raise funds to reward popular groups.

Adam Smith, the great English philosopher and economist whose works the Founders studied, taught that "taxes should be levied only to support a limited government and should satisfy four maxims: equity, transparency, convenience, and efficiency. According to Smith, nations that maintain free markets and limited taxes will maximize their wealth" (Walton 2003).

Except in times of war, the effective tax rate imposed by all levels of government in the U.S. seldom rose above 5 percent prior to 1916 (Rabushka 2002). During the past century, unfortunately, the U.S. has moved far away from the low-tax views of the Founders. Today, total tax burden stands at 31.6 percent of personal income, with the national government imposing a tax burden of 21.0 percent and state and local governments imposing an additional 10.6 percent (Dubay and Hodge 2006). The typical taxpayer must work 116 days a year just to pay his taxes (*Ibid.*).

High Taxes Cause Slower Economic Growth

High taxes (relative to other countries and states) have a profoundly negative effect on economic growth (Vedder 2001). Nations with lower effective tax rates tend to grow faster than those with higher taxes, accounting for much of the dramatic differences in prosperity between the U.S. and Europe and among European countries (Miles *et al.* 2006).

Similarly, states with high taxes grow more slowly than states with lower taxes, after controlling for other factors (Bast and Beck 1990). A ranking of the 50 states by their overall tax burden from 1980 to 2000 shows real personal income grew an average of 96 percent in the ten states with the lowest state and local taxes as a percent of income. New Hampshire had the lowest state tax burden and a 117 percent real income growth. Real personal income grew just 52 percent in the ten states with the highest tax burdens (Edwards, Moore, and Kerpen 2003). Moreover, low-tax states that raise their taxes relative to other states experience slower economic growth, even if their total tax burden remains lower than their neighbors (Genetski and Skorburg 1991).

Cutting Taxes Spurs Economic Growth

The history of tax changes at the federal level shows how cutting taxes can spur economic growth. The Economic Recovery Tax Act of 1981, which included a 25 percent across-the-board tax cut, helped real annual economic growth average 3.2 percent during the 1980s. It had been 2.8 percent during the mid- and late 1970s and fell to 2.1 percent during the 1990s, a decade that saw tax hikes from Republican and Democratic presidents alike (Mitchell 1996). Similarly, federal marginal tax rate cuts in 2002 and 2003 caused investment in equipment and software to increase almost at once, causing investment, employment, and wage growth to be strong throughout 2004 (Entin 2006, 10-11).

Tax cuts at the state level also have led to more rapid economic growth. From 1964 to 1999, Tennessee's rate of economic growth was approximately 20 percent higher than its northern neighbor, Kentucky. Tennessee maintained low taxes and was one of nine states that had a falling tax burden relative to other states over that period. Kentucky's tax burden, on the other hand, rose sharply (Vedder 1995).

Colorado, with a falling tax burden, outgrew neighboring Nebraska, Wyoming, and New Mexico, all with rising taxes. New York's tax burden increased more than in neighboring Pennsylvania, New Jersey, and Massachusetts, and it grew more slowly than any of them (*Ibid.*).

America's low-tax heritage and the negative economic effects of high taxes show the first principle of fiscal policy ought to be to keep taxes as low as possible.

Recommended reading: Daniel J. Mitchell, "The Historical Lessons of Lower Tax Rates," *Heritage Foundation Backgrounder* #1086, The Heritage Foundation, 1996, www.heritage.org/Research/ Taxes/BG1086.cfm; Richard K. Vedder, "Taxes and Economic Growth," Taxpayers Network, Inc., 2001, www.heartland.org/article/8714.

2. Don't penalize earnings and investment.

Taxes on earnings and investment income are particularly harmful to economic growth.

Income taxes have a large negative effect on economic growth. Between 1957 and 1997, real personal income growth was more than twice as high in the states that did not raise their income taxes (or increased them only minimally), compared to states with the biggest increases in income taxes (Vedder 2001). In the 1990s, nearly three million native-born Americans left the 41 states with general income taxes for the nine states without income taxes. People were voting with their feet to avoid income taxes (Vedder 2005).

Despite much "soak the rich" rhetoric, progressive income taxes have just the opposite effect. Between 1957 and 1997, the tax share paid by those in the top 10 percent of reported income was inversely related to the after-tax income share of the other 90 percent. "In other words, when tax share of the top 10 percent goes up, the after-tax income share of the other 90 percent goes down" (Hartman 2002).

Similarly, taxes on investment earnings slow economic growth by discouraging the business investments that make job creation and economic growth possible. Taxes on investment also discourage saving for future consumption, and they shift current consumption from nondurable to durable goods, such as houses, cars, and boats (Cai and Gokhale 1997; Kotlikoff 1993).

"When a tax is imposed on capital, the quantity of capital employed falls until the rate of return rises to cover the tax, leaving the after-tax return about where it was before the tax. The tax is largely shifted to users of capital and those who work with it" (Entin 2006, 14). Reducing taxes on capital by one percentage point increases private-sector GDP by about 1.5 percent, with about two-thirds going to labor income and about one-third going to capital income (*Ibid.*).

States that want more economic growth should lower or eliminate their taxes on earnings and investment.

Recommended reading: Richard K. Vedder and Lowell E. Gallaway, "Tax Reduction and Economic Welfare," Joint Economic Committee of Congress, April 1999, www.house.gov/jec/fiscal/tax/reduce. htm.

3. Avoid "sin" taxes.

Taxes on specific goods and services are often unfair, unreliable, and regressive.

Excise taxes often are attractive to elected officials because they are not paid by a majority of their constituents and are less visible than broad-based taxes. But they are a poor source of state revenue.

Excise taxes often are imposed unfairly on unpopular products without regard to the costs their users impose on the rest of society. For example, federal excise taxes on beer were raised in 1990 along with taxes on "luxury" items including expensive cars, fur coats, jewelry, yachts, and private airplanes. Yet, when the taxes on the "luxury" goods were rolled back 15 years later, the higher tax on beer remained (Stanek 2005).

High excise taxes often lead to evasion – such as purchasing cigarettes and even telephone service over the Internet – and if the tax rate is sufficiently high, to underground markets and counterfeiting. Black markets create opportunities for organized crime and can threaten people's health by leading to the circulation of products that have not been approved or inspected for safety.

Excise taxes are an unreliable revenue source. They require regular rate increases to keep pace with inflation, whereas income, sales, and property taxes all rise with inflation or economic growth. Because of their narrow bases, excise taxes require relatively high rates to raise funds. High rates, in turn, cause changes in economic behavior that create social costs but no social benefits.

Excise taxes are regressive. For example, people with low incomes not only pay a higher percentage of their incomes on cigarette taxes than do wealthier people, they even pay more in absolute terms. Persons earning less than $10,000 paid an average of $81 a year in tobacco taxes, versus $49 for those who make $50,000 or more (Bartlett 1998).

Excise taxes originated centuries ago when government's revenue needs were smaller, interstate commerce was rare, and enforcement was often easier. A strong case can be made that excise taxes are obsolete (Wagner 2005).

Recommended reading: R. Wagner,"State Excise Taxation: Horse-and-Buggy Taxes in an Electronic Age," *Background Paper* No. 48, Tax Foundation, 2005, www.taxfoundation.org; Robert A. Sirico, "Sin Taxes: Inferior Revenue Sources," *Budget & Tax News*, July 2004, www.heartland.org/article/15293.

4. Create a transparent and accountable budget.

> Focus attention and resources on providing those services that are the core functions of state government.

The sole purpose of collecting taxes is to finance the core functions of state government. But few states have budget processes in place that enable legislators to identify those functions and measure the performance of state agencies.

Key elements of a transparent and accountable budget process include the following (Evergreen Freedom Foundation 2005):

■ Adopt a meaningful tax and spending limit to frame the budget debate;

■ Enact a non-partisan revenue forecast process to project budget revenue;

■ Utilize performance-based budgeting to make "build or buy" decisions; and

■ Utilize independent and comprehensive performance audits with results reported directly to the public.

States can create commissions to determine what their core functions should be. In 1996 the Arkansas Murphy Commission decided the core functions of Arkansas government were to ensure safety, facilitate the "rule of law" and a system of justice, assure proper help is provided to individuals who legitimately cannot meet their own basic human needs, assure educational opportunity exists for all citizens, and act as a responsible steward of public property and the environment (Murphy Report 1999).

Similarly, California's Governor's Council on Information Technology said in its 1995 report, "Just as California's families focus on essentials when their budgets are tight, we want our government doing only what it should do, not what it might do. We do not want government to make a function more efficient if it should not be performing that function at all" (Governor's Council on Information Technology 1995, Sp. 11).

Recommended reading: B. Williams and L. Harsh, "The Stewardship Project," Evergreen Freedom Foundation, 2003, www.effwa.org/pdfs/ CoreFunctions.pdf; Murphy Report, "Summary of Key Recommendations," 1999, www. reformarkansas.org.

5. Privatize public services.

> Privatization is a proven way to reduce government spending while preserving or improving the quality of core public services.

Once a state's core functions are identified, elected officials must decide whether to rely on government or the private sector to produce goods and services. Privatization is the practice of moving the production and delivery of public goods and services from the public sector to the private sector. Common methods include contracting out, vouchers, public-private partnerships, and load-shedding (Savas 2005).

Costs are often unnecessarily high in the public sector because the discipline of the market is missing. Whereas greater productivity in the private sector is usually rewarded with higher sales, profits, salaries, and stock prices, in the public sector it often means a smaller budget in future years, along with less income and authority for government officials. Rules and regulations designed to hold government employees accountable are no substitute for the feedback private-sector companies get from competition and profit-and-loss statements (Wilson 1989).

Privatization is a bona fide "megatrend" in the U.S. and worldwide (Wolf 1990). Private companies build highways, prisons, water treatment plants, hospitals, airports, and nearly every other facility governments own. They haul garbage, manage public employee pension funds, clean parks, provide security services, and perform other public services. Extensive research shows private vendors save taxpayers money while improving the quality of services (Hilke 1993).

In 2005, Florida became the first state to fully privatize its child welfare programs. That same year, Indiana contracted out food service at state prisons, expecting to save $12 million a year, and Chicago took in $1.8 billion by leasing the Chicago Skyway, an eight-mile stretch of toll road, to a consortium of investors.

How-to manuals and expert advice on privatization are available from the Reason Foundation (www.reason.org), Deloitte Research (www.deloitte.com), and other organizations and consulting firms. See Chapter 4 for more information about privatization.

Recommended reading: Geoffrey Segal, *Annual Privatization Report*, Reason Foundation, 2005, www.reason.org/apr2005; Adrian Moore, "Making Privatization Work for State Government," *ALEC Policy Forum*, American Legislative Exchange Council, September 2002, www.alec.org/meSWFiles/pdf/0222.pdf.

6. Avoid corporate subsidies.

Subsidies to corporations and selective tax abatement are questionable politics and bad economics.

Subsidies, tax abatements, low-interest loans, and special worker training are often offered to corporations. Such assistance is unnecessary if general taxes are kept low and uniform. If taxes are high and unequal, a legislator's time is better spent working to change the system. As the John Locke Foundation notes,

> Unlike the maintenance of low across-the-board tax rates or the provision of core public services such as education, highways, and public safety, corporate welfare doesn't benefit everyone. It requires public officials to intervene in private markets to decide which businesses or regions are worthy of support. This sets the stage for increased special-interest lobbying, strings-attached

campaign contributions, and unethical behavior in public office (John Locke Foundation 2006, p. 30).

Corporate subsidies are also bad economics. Even the wisest public officials cannot allocate resources as fairly or effectively as capital markets, which efficiently set the prices of debt or equity securities issued by companies. Public officials try to pick winners and avoid losers, but experience shows they seldom succeed.

A 1999 review of state economic performance found "the states that spent the most on economic development programs were more likely to experience slow job and/or income growth than states with the lowest economic development expenditures" (Gulibon 1999, p. 9).

It is better to leave money in taxpayers' hands than to give it to a few politically chosen individuals and businesses in hopes they will make the best investment decisions. Lower tax rates benefit the economy as a whole. See Chapter 5 for a longer discussion of corporate subsidies and tax abatements.

Recommended reading: John Locke Foundation, *Agenda 2006*; Grant Gulibon, "Growing Pennsylvania's Economy: Tax Cuts vs. Economic Development Programs," The Commonwealth Foundation, March 1999, www.heartland.org/article/3071.

7. Cap taxes and expenditures.

A tax and expenditure limitation (TEL) protects elected officials from public pressure to spend surplus tax revenues during good economic times.

Politics causes government spending to rise beyond the level that most people, even most elected officials, believe is ideal. During good economic times, elected officials come under enormous pressure to spend every available tax dollar. During bad economic times, the beneficiaries of new programs oppose any spending cuts. It is a recipe for inefficient government growth, fiscal crises, and tax increases.

Incentives to spend too much exist even without the surplus–deficit cycle. Government's powers to tax and regulate can be used to concentrate benefits on a small number of beneficiaries while spreading the cost across large numbers of taxpayers, none of whom pays so much as to justify spending time or money opposing the transfer (Olson 1971). "Logrolling" – the practice of trading votes for favorite projects – also results in more spending being approved than any individual elected official might otherwise support (Buchanan and Tullock 1962).

Counteracting these incentives requires constitutional limits on the power to tax and spend. Elected officials cannot be forced to spend money they cannot constitutionally collect or spend.

Restoring correct incentives to government can be done in a number of ways. One approach is to require super-majority votes for tax increases. A better way is to adopt a tax and expenditure limitation (TEL) limiting the growth of taxes or spending to the sum of inflation and population growth, so that government grows no faster than the private sector. Any revenue collected above this limit is either saved in a rainy day fund or returned to taxpayers. Colorado's Taxpayer's Bill of Rights (TABOR) offers one model for such limitation.

The best TELs are constitutional because statutory limitations are often evaded. TELs can allow voters to override the limit in a special election. TELs also should apply to local governments to avoid cost-shifting from the states to local governments.

Recommended reading: Barry Poulson, "Tax and Spending Limits: Theory, Analysis, and Policy," Independence Institute, 2004, www.i2i.org/article.aspx?ID=975; Lewis K. Uhler and Barry Poulson, "How to Limit Taxes and Spending," Oklahoma Council of Public Affairs, 2003, www.ocpathink.org/ViewPerspectiveStory.asp?ID=48.

8. Fund students, not schools.

States and cities that have experimented with school choice have seen gains in academic achievement.

Free and universal K-12 education is generally agreed to be one of the core functions of state government. But by international and historical standards, public schools in the U.S. are costly and yield poor achievement results (Walberg 2001). According to education economist Caroline Hoxby, the productivity of public schools in the U.S. (measured by dividing a measure of student achievement by per-pupil spending in inflation-adjusted dollars) has fallen more than 50 percent in the past 30 years (Hoxby 2001).

Many of the school districts with the highest per-capita spending – in Chicago, New York, Washington, D.C., and other major cities – report the worst academic performance. Clearly, more money is not the answer (Hanushek 1995).

However, a small number of cities (Milwaukee and Cleveland) and states (Arizona, Florida, Pennsylvania) are experimenting with school choice, and they have seen achievement gains (Holland 2005; Bast and Walberg 2004b).

School choice means parents are free to choose which schools their children attend and public funding follows the student. Some types of choice are severely limited – public school choice programs, for example, give parents a choice only of nearby public schools. Charter schools are free from some of the regulations imposed on regular public schools but still are public schools.

Voucher programs, which pay for tuition even if parents choose private schools for their children, create the most choice and competition and consequently hold the most promise for improving public education. School choice allows parents to play a much bigger role in their children's education – something experts agree leads to higher academic achievement – and gives schools a powerful incentive to set and reach higher standards.

States that are serious about improving the quality of K-12 education and getting more value for taxpayers must expand parental choice in education. See Chapter 3 for more information about improving public schools.

Recommended reading: Herbert J. Walberg and Joseph L. Bast, *Education and Capitalism* (Stanford, CA: Hoover Institution Press, 2003), www.hoover.stanford.edu/publications/books/fulltext/edcap/253.pdf; Joseph L. Bast and Herbert J. Bast, *Let's Put Parents Back in Charge!* (Chicago, IL: The Heartland Institute, 2004).

9. Reform Medicaid programs.

Spending on Medicaid can be brought under control without lowering the quality of care received by Medicaid patients.

Next to education, Medicaid is the largest single expense in most state budgets. Costs are rising at double-digit rates in many states, while fraud and abuse take an alarming share of every dollar spent (Herrick 2005a).

States have many tools they can use to rein in spending on Medicaid while improving the quality of medical services provided to its beneficiaries (Arnett 1999). Reforms include:

■ Enroll people with preexisting medical conditions in high-risk pools offering subsidized private health insurance (Meier 1999);

■ Reduce the price of private insurance by removing unnecessary price controls and coverage mandates, which increase health care costs by forcing consumers to buy insurance coverage for services they don't need (Matthews 2005);

■ Limit Medicaid eligibility to the truly poor and limit coverage to those services mandated under federal law;

■ Implement disease management programs, which reduce unnecessary drug expenditures while protecting patients with multiple prescriptions from potentially deadly drug interactions (Konig 2005a); and

■ Empower state employees and Medicaid recipients with HSAs, already popular in the private sector (Guppy 2005).

Florida is a pioneer in redesigning Medicaid to be more patient-friendly and less costly. The state allows private-sector health care provider networks to create benefit packages customized to meet the needs of Medicaid patients, who are permitted by the law to opt out of Medicaid plans and use their state-paid premiums to purchase private insurance (Konig 2005b).

See Chapter 1 for more information about health care reform.

Recommended reading: John McClaughry, Greg Blankenship, and Michael Van Winkle, "A Health Care Reform Agenda for Illinois," Illinois Policy Institute, 2004; John McClaughry, "A Health Care Reform Agenda," State Policy Network, 2001.

10. Pay government workers a market wage and protect them from politics.

Many government workers are overpaid, and their union dues are used to influence elections.

Many government employees are over-paid and have benefits that are much more generous than their private-sector counterparts. This is inseparable from the rise of public-sector unions and their improper influence on elections. The tenth and final principle of state fiscal policy is that government workers should be paid market wages and the dues they pay to unions should not be used to influence elections.

Generous Compensation and Benefits

State and local government employees in 2010 earned average total compensation of $39.60 an hour, compared to $27.42 an hour for private industry workers – a difference of nearly 45 percent (U.S. Bureau of Labor Statistics 2010). This compensation includes 35 percent higher wages and nearly 69 percent greater benefits.

At the federal level, civilian government workers in 2009 had an average wage and benefits package of $123,049, or double the private-sector average of $61,051 (Bureau of Economic Analysis 2010).

(These figures were derived by dividing compensation by full-time equivalents to get average compensation. Data exclude the U.S. Postal Service.)

Government workers also enjoy greater job security than private-sector workers. Since the recession began in late 2007, the private sector through mid-July 2010 had shed 6.9 million jobs whereas state and local governments had added 110,000 jobs (Boyd and Dadayan 2010).

Finally, many government workers are retiring with six-figure pensions and some are even becoming on-the-job millionaires. In July 2010, for instance, the *Los Angeles Times* began reporting on the Los Angeles suburb of Bell, where the city manager had a pay and benefits package worth $1.5 million a year (Gottlieb, Becerra, and Vives 2010). The city manager, police chief, and assistant city manager resigned after outraged citizens called for their ouster because of their huge compensation packages.

Misuse of Union Dues

Members of public-sector labor unions are forced to pay dues, with much of the money going for political activity not supported by the rank and file. Although the U.S. Supreme Court in the *Beck* decision outlawed this practice, it continues (Almasi 1998; Denholm 2005).

State and local governments condone this practice when they collect union dues from public workers, including the portion used for political activities. Legally there is no reason why state and local governments should do this for unions, and ethically there is reason enough to believe they should be prohibited from doing so without the explicit written consent of individual employees.

As Thomas Jefferson wrote, "To compel a man to furnish contributions of money for the propagation of opinions which he disbelieves and abhors, is sinful and tyrannical."

A 2004 Zogby poll showed 63 percent of respondents support giving union members the right to object to their dues being used for political purposes. Nearly 61 percent of union members agreed (Zogby 2004).

David Denholm notes, "labor leaders face stiff opposition on key questions of union reform – not only from the general public but also from their own members. These questions include whether workers should be free to choose or decline union membership ('right to work'), who should control whether union dues are used for political purposes ('paycheck protection'), and whether there should be extensive financial disclosure of union expenditures" (Denholm 2004).

In each of these areas, elected officials can enact legislation protecting government workers from politics, thereby reducing pressure for bigger and more expensive government.

Recommended reading: David Y. Denholm, "Do Americans Support Labor Unions?" *Labor Watch,* Capital Research Center, June 2004, www.capitalresearch.org/pubs/pdf/06_04_LW.pdf; A. Summers, "California's Proposition 75: Paycheck Protection," *Commentary,* Reason Foundation, November 3, 2005, www.reason.org/commentaries/summers_ 20051103.shtml.

References

Almasi, D. 1998. Paycheck protection promotes union integrity. *National Policy Analysis* No. 197, The National Center for Public Policy Research, May. www.nationalcenter.org/NPA197.html.

Arnett, G.M, ed. 1999. *Empowering health care consumers through tax reform.* Ann Arbor, MI: University of Michigan Press.

Arnett, G.M. and J.S. Hoff. 1999. A vision for consumer-driven health care reform. The Health Policy Consensus Group. www.galen.org/fileuploads/vision.pdf.

Atkins, C. 2005. An analysis of misleading attacks on Colorado's taxpayer's bill of rights. *Fiscal Facts,* The Tax Foundation, March 25. www.taxfoundation.org/publications/show/316.html.

Bartlett, B. 1998. Taxing the poor. *Brief Analysis* No. 269. National Center for Policy Analysis.

Bast, J. and J. Beck. 1990. Taxes and economic growth. In *Coming out of the ice: a plan to make the 1990s Illinois' decade,* ed. Joseph Bast and Diane Bast, 15-32. Chicago, IL: The Heartland Institute.

Bast, J.L. and H.J. Walberg. 2004a. *Let's put parents back in charge!* Chicago, IL: The Heartland Institute.

Bast, J.L. and H.J. Walberg. 2004b. Can parents choose the best schools for their children? *Economics of Education Review* 23: 431-40. www.heartland.org/article/18622.

Boyd, Donald J. and Lucy Dadayan. 2010. State and local government employment is down in 31 states - and up in 18 - compared with a year ago. Data Alert. Nelson A. Rockefeller Institute of Government.

Buchanan, J.M. and G. Tullock. 1962. *The calculus of consent*. Ann Arbor, MI: The University of Michigan.

Bureau of Economic Analysis. 2010. National income and product accounts, tables 6.2D, 6.3D, and 6.5D. U.S. Bureau of Economic Analysis, www.bea.gov/national/nipaweb.

Cai, J. and J. Gokhale. 1997. The welfare loss from a capital income tax. *Economic Review* 33(1). www.clevelandfed.org/research/review97/q1caijag.pdf.

Denholm, D.Y. 2005. Government unions spend lavishly on politics. *Budget & Tax News*, September. www.heartland.org/article/17676.

Denholm, D.Y. 2004. Do Americans support labor unions? *Labor Watch*. Capital Research Center, June. www.capitalresearch.org/pubs/pdf/06_04_LW.pdf.

Denholm, D.Y. 2001. Hey teachers! Let's talk about decertification! Public Service Research Foundation. www.psrf.org/issues/hey_teachers.jsp.

Dubay, C. and S. Hodge. 2006. America celebrates tax freedom day. *Special Report* #140, April. www.taxfoundation.org/files/sr140.pdf.

Edwards, C., S. Moore, and P. Kerpen. 2003. States face fiscal crunch after 1990s spending surge. *Briefing Papers* No. 80. Cato Institute. www.cato-institute.com/pubs/briefs/bp80.pdf.

Entin, S.J. 2006. Exploring the effects of a flat federal income tax for the District of Columbia. *Advisory* No. 200, Institute for Research on the Economics of Taxation, March.

Evergreen Freedom Foundation. 2005. State expenditure and tax limit model language. www.effwa.org/ pdfs/tel.pdf.

Genetski, R.J. and J. Skorburg. 1991. The impact of state and local taxes on economic growth: 1975-1987. *Working Papers,* Chicago Association of Commerce and Industry. www.heartland.org/article/15788.

Gottlieb, Jeff, Hector Becerra, and Ruben Vives. 2010. Bell admits more hefty city salaries. Los Angeles Times, August 7.

Governor's Council on Information Technology. 1995. *Getting results*. Sacramento, CA. www.ca.gov.

Gulibon, G. 1999. Growing Pennsylvania's economy: tax cuts vs. economic development programs. Commonwealth Foundation, March. www.heartland.org/article/3071.

Guppy, P. 2005. Health savings accounts can help solve Olympia's budget mess. Washington Policy Center, February. www.washingtonpolicy.org/Misc/Op-Ed_HSAsA ndBudgetMess.html.

Hanushek, E. 1995. Making schools work: spending and student achievement. *Heartland Policy Study* No. 68. The Heartland Institute, September. www.heartland.org/article/9518.

Hartman, D.A. 2002. Does progressive taxation redistribute income? *The Road Map to Tax Reform Series*, Institute for Policy Innovation.

Herrick, D. 2005a. Fraud and waste infect New York medicaid. *Health Care News*, September.

Herrick, D. 2005b. Consumer driven health care: the changing role of the patient. *NCPA Policy Report*, No. 276, National Center for Policy Analysis, May. www.ncpa.org/pub/st/st276.

Hilke, J. 1993. *Cost savings from privatization: a compilation of study findings*. Los Angeles, CA: Reason Foundation.

Holland, R. 2005. Vouchers better than NCLB accountability. *School Reform News*, June.

Hoxby, C. 2001. How to improve school productivity. Interview by George Clowes, *School Reform News*, September. www.heartland.org.Article/10212.

John Locke Foundation. 2006. *Agenda 2006*. Raleigh, NC: John Locke Foundation.

Konig, S. 2005a. Florida, Pfizer team up to improve medicaid patients' use of health services. *Health Care News*, January.

Konig, S. 2005b. Medicaid reform: Florida, South Carolina lead the way. *Health Care News*, August.

Kotlikoff, L.J. 1993. The economic impact of replacing federal income taxes with a sales tax. *Cato Policy Analysis* No. 193, Cato Institute.

Matthews, M. 2005. State mandates drive up insurance costs. *Health Care News*, January.

McClaughry, J., G. Blankenship, and M. Van Winkle. 2004. A health care reform agenda for Illinois. Springfield, IL: Illinois Policy Institute, November.

McClaughry, J. 2001. A health care reform agenda. Richmond, CA: State Policy Network.

Meier, C. 1999. Extending affordable insurance to the uninsurable. *Heartland Policy Study* No. 91, The Heartland Institute. www.heartland.org/article/9500.

Miles, M.C *et al.* 2006. *2006 freedom index*. The Heritage Foundation and The Wall Street Journal.

Mitchell, D.J. 1996. The historical lessons of lower tax rates. *Heritage Foundation Backgrounder* No. 1086, The Heritage Foundation, July 19. www.heritage.org/Research/Taxes/BG1086.cfm.

Moore, A. 2002. Making privatization work for state government. *ALEC Policy Forum*, American Legislative Exchange Council.

Murphy Report. 1999. Summary of key recommendations. Arkansas Policy Foundation. www.reformarkansas.org.

Olson, M. 1971. *The logic of collective action*. Cambridge, MA: Harvard University Press.

Poulson, B. 2005. A taxpayer's bill of rights TABOR for Texas. *Policy Paper,* Americans for Prosperity Foundation, January.

Poulson, B. 2004a. Tax and spending limits: theory, analysis, and policy. *Issue Paper,* 2-2004, Independence Institute, January. www.i2i.org/article.aspx?ID=975.

Poulson, B. 2004b. The next generation of tax and expenditure limits. Americans for Prosperity Foundation.

Rabushka, A. 2002. The colonial roots of American taxation, 1607-1700. *Policy Review,* Hoover Institution, September. www.heartland.org/article/10285.

Savas, E.S. 2005. *Privatization in the city: successes, failures, lessons*. Washington, DC: CQ Press.

Segal, G. 2005. *Annual privatization report*. Los Angeles, CA: Reason Foundation. www.reason.org/apr2005/.

Sirico, R.A. 2004. Sin taxes: inferior revenue sources. *Budget & Tax News*, July. www.heartland.org/article/15293

Snell, R.K., C. Eckl, and G. Williams. 2003. State spending in the 1990s. National Conference of State Legislatures. www.ncsl.org/programs/ fiscal/stspend90s.htm.

Sobel, R.S., R.A. Lawson, and J.C. Hall. 2004. How California's steep income tax stifles economic growth. *Taxing Times*, April.

Stanek, S. 2005. Congress considers beer a luxury – but not mink coats, private jets, or yachts. *Budget & Tax News*, September.

Summers, A. 2005. California's proposition 75: paycheck protection. *Commentary,* Reason Foundation, November 3.

Uhler, L.K. and B. Poulson. 2003. How to limit taxes and spending. Oklahoma City, OK: Oklahoma Council of Public Affairs.

U.S. Bureau of Labor Statistics. 2010. May 2010 employer costs for employee compensation survey. May.

Vedder, R.K. 2005. Taxes fuel historic American migration. *Budget & Tax News,* December.

Vedder, R.K. 2003. State and local taxes and economic growth. *Virginia Viewpoint,* Virginia Institute. www.virginiainstitute.org/pdf/2003_14. pdf.

Vedder, R K. 2002. Crisis in state spending: a guide for state legislators. Washington, DC: American Legislative Exchange Council.

Vedder, R K. 2001. Taxes and economic growth. Taxpayers Network, Inc. www.heartland.org/article/8714.

Vedder, R.K. 1995. State and local taxation and economic growth: lessons for federal tax reform. Joint Economic Committee, Congress of the United States.

Vedder, R K, and L.E. Gallaway. 1999. Tax reduction and economic welfare. Joint Economic Committee, Congress of the United States, April.

Wagner, R. 2005. State excise taxation: horse-and-buggy taxes in an electronic age. *Background Paper* No. 48, Tax Foundation. www.taxfoundation.org.

Walberg, H.J. 2001. Achievement in American schools. In *American education: a primer*, ed. Terry M. Moe, 43-68. Stanford, CA: Hoover Institution Press.

Walberg, H.J. and J.L. Bast. 2003. *Education and Capitalism*. Stanford, CA: Hoover Institution Press. www.hoover.standford.educ/publications/books/edcap.html.

Walton, T. 2003. Adam Smith on taxes. *Budget & Tax News*, November.

Williams, B. and L. Harsh. 2003. The stewardship project. Olympia, WA: Evergreen Freedom Foundation. www.heartland.org/article/12614.

Wilson, J.Q. 1989. *Bureaucracy: what government agencies do and why they do it*. New York, NY: Basic Books Classics.

Wolf Jr., C. 1990. *Markets or governments: choosing between imperfect alternatives*. Cambridge, MA: The MIT Press.

Zogby, J. *et al.* 2004. Nationwide attitudes toward unions. Utica, NY: Zogby International, February 26.

Additional Resources

1. *Crisis in State Spending: A Guide for State Legislators*, by Richard Vedder *et al.* (Washington, DC: American Legislative Exchange Council, 2002), www.alec.org/meSWFiles/pdf/TaxCrisis.pdf.
2. *Tax and Spending Limits: Theory, Analysis, and Policy*, by Barry Poulson (Golden, CO: The Independence Institute, 2004), www.i2i.org/article.aspx?ID=975.

3. *PolicyBot*, The Heartland Institute's free online clearinghouse for the work of other free-market think tanks, contains thousands of documents on taxes, budgets, privatization, and other fiscal issues. It is on Heartland's Web site at www.heartland.org.

4. *www.budgetandtax-news.org*, a Web site devoted to the latest news and commentary about budget and tax issues. Read headlines, watch videos, or join the conversation by using Twitter or Facebook.

5. *Budget & Tax News*, a monthly publication from The Heartland Institute. Subscribe online at www.heartland.org.

Directory

The following national organizations support sound state fiscal policies. For a list of state organizations, go to www.heartland.org and click on "links."

American Legislative Exchange Council, www.alec.org
Americans for Fair Taxation, www.fairtax.org
Americans for Limited Government, www.getliberty.org
Americans for Prosperity, www.americansforprosperity.org
Americans for Tax Reform, www.atr.org
Cato Institute, www.cato.org
FreedomWorks, www.freedomworks.org
Heartland Institute, www.heartland.org
Heritage Foundation, www.heritage.org
Hoover Institution, www.hoover.stanford.edu
Manhattan Institute, www.manhattan-institute.org
National Center for Policy Analysis, www.ncpa.org
National Taxpayers Union, www.ntu.org
Reason Foundation, www.reason.org
Tax Foundation, www.taxfoundation.org

Chapter 8
Property and Casualty Insurance

Matthew Glans and Eli Lehrer

---

10 Principles of Property and Casualty Insurance

1. Price controls are unnecessary.
2. Emphasize solvency.
3. Minimize residual insurance markets.
4. Avoid tariff barriers to non-U.S. reinsurance.
5. Dismantle catastrophe funds.
6. Reform and phase out the National Flood Insurance Program.
7. Don't ban credit scoring.
8. Don't ban territorial rating.
9. Don't interfere in rate-setting.
10. Help only the truly needy.

Introduction

A chapter on property and casualty insurance belongs in any guide to public policy issues because insurance is an important economic activity; because it is regulated almost entirely at the state level and is thus of particular concern to state legislators; and because a look at the principles behind insurance regulation reveals the benefits of creating freer marketplaces for consumers and insurers.

Insurance Is Vital to a Growing Economy
Insurance is one of the key institutions that make economic prosperity

possible. Properly designed insurance makes the management of risk possible and, in so doing, makes long-term planning and investment more reliable. Insurance markets best accomplish their risk-management function when insurers are allowed to charge actuarially determined, risk-based rates that accurately reflect the risk their policyholders incur. When government regulation interferes with these price mechanisms, the result is either rate suppression or a redistribution of the cost burden, resulting in wealth redistribution from policyholders who behave prudently to those who take greater risks.

Political manipulation of insurance rates, regardless of its intentions, distorts the valuable competitive signals of the private market and reduces the range of products available for consumers. Price controls inevitably reduce the supply and lower the quality of insurance products.

Insurance Is Regulated at the State Level

Insurance is the largest and most important economic activity regulated almost entirely at the state level. In some cases, this regulation leads to inefficiency. Although federal and international entities oversee banking, trade, manufacturing, and many service industries, states alone have the power to oversee property and casualty insurance, under the federal McCarran-Ferguson Act of 1945. As a result, insurers and consumers must deal with a confusing and expensive maze of state regulations. International insurers have a difficult time entering the United States market because they must enter each state market separately.

State regulation makes insurance more expensive, on average, than it otherwise would be, because incumbent insurers often lobby political authorities for rules that limit competition and allow them to raise rates. Consumers use their political influence as voters to support rate caps and subsidies to socialize the cost of insuring against risks they face due to the choices they make, costs they should pay themselves. Both pressures lead to less consumer choice, as shown by the fact that major property and casualty insurers have not introduced a single major new product since modern homeowners insurance (the HO-3 and HO-8 policies, in industry parlance) became available in 1959.

Freedom Is Best

Government certainly has a role to play in regulating insurance. Enforcement of laws regarding reserve requirements to ensure solvency is needed in the insurance business, and that enforcement properly belongs in the hands of the state. Rules governing timely response to claims and the use of clear language in insurance contracts are also legitimate government functions that benefit consumers.

The current regulatory environment in many states, however, goes far beyond this limited role. It is characterized by heavy-handed regulation through processes that are generally unknown by the general public and dominated by special-interest groups and a small number of elected and unelected officials. These processes impose large, though undocumented, costs on businesses and individuals deprived of reliable and affordable insurance products, and they increasingly threaten to put U.S.-based financial services companies at a competitive disadvantage with those in Europe.

We believe most insurance decisions – especially the price charged for insurance products – should be determined by market forces and voluntary arrangements. The benefits of doing this are clear: States with more open and free regulatory environments provide more insurance choices to consumers and more insurance jobs. A free and open insurance environment makes sense. This chapter describes how to build one.

Recommended reading: Eli Lehrer and Michelle Minton, *Property and Casualty Insurance 2009 Report Card*, The Heartland Institute, 2009; Eli Lehrer, *2010 Property and Casualty Insurance Report Card*, The Heartland Institute, 2010.

1. Price controls are unnecessary.

Insurance should be priced based on supply, demand, and common-sense standards of fair play.

Despite claims to the contrary, insurance is not fundamentally different from many other consumer products. Considered properly, insurance is not an exotic product that needs different rules, but rather a conventional financial instrument for which government's primary role should be limited to policing against force and fraud. Government intervention in the insurance market in the form of price controls makes no sense.

How Underwriting Works

Underwriting is the process of evaluating the amount of risk a policy presents. Determining a proper premium for the predicted claims costs insurance companies millions of dollars per year. Using scientific models and actuarial science, insurers attempt to predict future losses, adjust their investments, and purchase reinsurance to absorb future claims.

Competitive underwriting benefits both consumers and insurers. "In jurisdictions where underwriting freedom prevails ... [c]ompetitive, risk-based underwriting facilitates fairness in pricing, prudent conduct, widespread availability of coverage, and risk sharing among insurers," argues Robert Detlefsen, director of public policy for the National Association of Mutual Insurance Companies.

Acquiring the data to build these models is costly and labor-intensive, so insurers are often protective of their loss-prediction models. Accuracy in predicting future losses in any given region provides a competitive advantage over other providers. With the introduction of computerized modeling, insurance underwriting has become increasingly sophisticated, and insurers have become more reliant on these types of models.

Restrictions Raise Prices

The injection of politics into the underwriting process (beyond ensuring that it is not fraudulent or discriminatory) unnecessarily complicates the matter further. Restrictions or bans on various underwriting practices limit the variety of products, raise prices, and do little to achieve their intended goals. Detlefson argues that because insurance rates determined by competition among insurers "assess risk with the greatest possible rigor, and group similarly situated insureds into precisely constructed risk classes," they "cannot, by definition, be unfairly discriminatory. Nor could rates established through competitive, risk-based underwriting be considered 'excessive,' because the same competitive forces that promote underwriting accuracy also conspire to drive down prices."

Efforts to ban certain underwriting practices can have negative effects on the insurance market; they do little to achieve their intended goals and, in many cases, prevent consumers from being able to choose from a larger variety of products. Accurate accounting for risk allows insurers greater freedom to provide new products tailored to the needs of consumers, and active competition leads to lower prices across the board.

Encouraging the creation of a competitive insurance market and avoiding excessive underwriting restrictions achieve the very goals regulators seek: the setting of rates that are adequate, not excessive, and not unfairly discriminatory.

Consumers Don't Need Price Controls

Even if one discards free-market thinking and turns to amorphous concepts of fairness and justice, there is no good case for price controls on insurance. The overwhelming majority of people who pay different rates than they would in a free insurance market do not need the "help" they get from the government. The truly poor cannot afford to own homes and often cannot afford automobiles. Nobody has ever perished for lack of property and casualty insurance.

Insofar as one considers automobile ownership and home ownership necessary for full participation in modern society, a case may exist for public or private efforts to help people of modest means pay insurance premiums, but it's difficult to see why the government ought to do this by controlling prices.

Food, after all, is clearly necessary for human existence, but instead of trying to keep prices down, government policies – such as the milk price-setting regime – often are designed to *increase* food prices. Public and private sources provide various forms of income assistance, such as food stamps, to help people buy food. This is a better model for improving access to insurance for people with low incomes.

Recommended reading: Steve Pociask, "Does Private Passenger Auto Insurance Price Regulation Benefit Consumers: Myths and Facts," Consumer Institute, 2009; National Association of Insurance Commissioners, "Personal Lines Regulatory Framework," *Speed to Market (EX) Task Force,* 2009; Insurance Information Institute, "Financial Responsibility Laws by State," *IIM Fact Book*, 2009.

2. Emphasize solvency.

> The government's primary role in regulating insurance should be making sure companies can pay their claims.

The government's leading role – by some standards its only legitimate role – in insurance regulation is to make sure insurance companies can pay their claims. This is a necessary function of government in preventing what is, for all intents and purposes, fraud. Insurance departments have a wide range of tools at their disposal to accomplish this.

Although pricing of insurance ought to follow the rules for pricing any other product, insurance is different from most other products in one way: It's useless if it's sold for too little. If a car manufacturer sells an automobile for less than it costs to produce or an airline sells a plane full of seats for less than its operating costs, consumers get a good deal even if the company goes bankrupt as a result. Insurance, however, must be sold at a price high enough that the insurer can have reasonable certainty of paying claims it can expect. This is called actuarial adequacy. An insurance company that doesn't remain solvent – that is, capable of paying its claims – commits fraud every time it sells a policy.

Preventing Fraud

There are three major reasons why the government should play a role in preventing this type of fraud before companies actually engage in fraud.

First, a dishonest insurance company that sells policies at inadequate rates could drive honest players from the market for a significant period of time. Because many insurers draw on reserves and reinsurance most heavily when catastrophes hit, an insurer that charged too little might be able to go years before being detected. In the meantime, it would likely drive truly solvent insurers out of the market.

Second, a thriving, trustworthy insurance system is necessary for a nation to have a healthy overall economy and significant levels of investment. The existence of insurance, on balance, leads to much more efficient allocation of capital throughout the economy.

Homeowners wanting to protect themselves against loss of their property, for example, rarely can afford to set aside all the capital necessary to protect it. Even if they did, a large portion of capital used to protect a single house would essentially have to sit dormant and would not be available for investment, consumption, or other purposes. In a country with a strong, trustworthy insurance system, the amount of resources an individual must use to insure a home is much smaller and, because it's pooled together in the hands of an insurer, it can be invested more efficiently. By providing assurance that insurance in general will be safe, government can encourage its use and thereby promote more efficient allocation of capital throughout the economy.

Third, all states provide a mandatory guarantee fund system. Under these systems, if an insurer is unable to pay its claims, a guarantee fund takes over its claims and pays policyholders some or all of what they would otherwise receive. In all states except New York, the payments come from mandatory taxes imposed on all insurers following a company's insolvency. Although most of these guarantee funds are theoretically "private" associations run by the insurance industry and are fire-walled from general state revenues, each of them creates a *de facto* taxpayer liability for insurance claims. If an insurance company becomes insolvent, in other words, all taxpayers end up paying.

Therefore, it's important for states to emphasize measures that provide for insurer solvency.

Recommended reading: Kevin McCarty, "Insurance Company Solvency Regulation: An Overview for the Financial Services Commission," Florida Department of Insurance Regulation, 2009; Robert Klein, "Hurricanes and Residual Market Mechanisms," Center for Risk Management and Insurance Research at the University of Georgia, 2009; National Association of Insurance Guarantee Funds, "Insolvencies ... an Overview," 2008.

3. Minimize residual insurance markets.

State-run markets of last resort should be small and for temporary use only.

Government policymakers and some insurance executives claim the insurance market simply cannot cover certain types of risks. In fact, this is hardly ever true: At some price, some insurance company will underwrite just about any home or automobile.

Nonetheless, all 50 states have laws establishing a residual automobile insurance market, and 31 states maintain residual homeowners insurance markets. These markets, which are usually state-mandated, industry-run "shared risk" consortiums, exist as markets of last resort for people supposedly unable to find insurance elsewhere. In a few states, they are state agencies.

Although almost all of these residual markets operate under statutes that specify they are markets of last resort and have no claim on general state revenues, state governments have never allowed them to collapse. In the wake of the particularly destructive 2005 hurricane season, Florida, Louisiana, and Mississippi all diverted taxpayer funds to stabilize government-mandated coastal insurance entities.

Some states maintain very large residual markets. Nearly one in five Florida homeowners, for example, buys property insurance from a state agency called the Florida Citizens Property Insurance Corporation. A similar percentage of North Carolina drivers get automobile insurance through a state-run reinsurance facility. Other states, such as Massachusetts, Michigan, New Jersey, and Rhode Island, also maintain outsized residual insurance markets.

Alternatives Are Available

For the most part, there's no reason such residual markets should exist at all. If market forces set rates, nearly everyone can find insurance. Through rate deregulation, states such as South Carolina and Texas have managed to reduce once-massive automobile insurance residual markets to near-nothingness. Hawaii, Illinois, and Wisconsin have managed to cut the size of their residual homeowners insurance markets significantly by letting market forces set rates. Most states have discovered this, and their residual markets are very small, containing fewer than 100 policies. In other states, the "markets" exist only on paper and don't operate or write coverage.

Of course, some risks do prove very difficult to insure. When a given risk seems extreme – a drunk driver with multiple convictions who wants to remain on the road, or a person who wants to have a home on top of a sand dune in a hurricane-prone area – many insurers will not take on the risk at any price. Even in cases such as these, however, people who really want insurance often can find it in the "excess and surplus" markets, a lightly regulated portion of the insurance market that allows for highly customized policies at high prices. E&S companies typically don't have to file rates with insurance departments and don't participate in guarantee funds. These policies often get very expensive, but the government best serves the public when it takes a light hand toward them, as society is better off with drunk drivers off the road and houses built in safe locations.

Keep it Small

If state officials still see a compelling need for a residual market even after exploring the possibilities of market-based rates and excess and surplus markets, they should do everything they can to minimize the risk to the taxpayers and keep the market small. If citizens buy policies in a residual market, they should be encouraged to exit the market as soon as possible.

States also should allow companies to "take out" policies from residual markets whenever they wish. (A "take out" happens when a private company assumes the full risk for a residual market policy at the same premium or a lower one than the government charged.)

Shrinking residual markets will minimize the risks imposed on taxpayers.

Recommended reading: Eli Lehrer, *Property and Casualty Insurance 2008 Report Card*, The Heartland Institute, 2008; Eli Lehrer, "Restoring Florida's Insurance Market," The James Madison Institute, 2009; Arin Greenwood, "Compounding Catastrophe," Competitive Enterprise Institute, 2008.

4. Avoid Barriers to Non-U.S. Reinsurance

Tariffs and similar barriers to offshore reinsurance would raise prices for consumers and could make private insurance unavailable to homeowners in high-risk areas.

Insurance in the United States – particularly insurance against catastrophes like hurricanes and earthquakes – depends heavily on international markets, where U.S.-based insurers buy "reinsurance" that allows them to turn over risk to a private third party that agrees to pay if losses exceed a predetermined amount.

According to the Coalition for Competitive Insurance Rates, non-U.S.-based reinsurers paid two-thirds of the claims for Hurricane Katrina and more than 70 percent of those associated with the private-sector losses from the terrorist attacks of September 11, 2001. Companies in Bermuda, the single largest source of offshore reinsurance capacity that affects U.S. consumers, cover about 60 percent of the hurricane risk in Florida and Texas, according to the Association of Bermuda Insurers and Reinsurers. Similarly, the California Earthquake Authority, a public-private hybrid that writes most earthquake coverage in California, purchases most of its coverage from offshore sources.

For more than a decade, a changing cast of politicians and several U.S.-based insurers have proposed placing substantial tariffs on many transactions involving offshore reinsurers. Rep. Richard Neal (D-MA) has championed these ideas in Congress, and the Obama administration has included them in its 2011 and 2012 budgets.

Tariffs and similar barriers to reinsurance are a bad idea for three reasons: They penalize an ordinary business practice; they will raise prices for American consumers; and they could lead to private insurance becoming entirely unavailable in some areas.

Penalizing a Common Business Practice

The proposed tariffs – technically called "deduction disallowance for excess non-taxed reinsurance premiums paid to affiliates" – penalize something ("affiliated reinsurance purchase") that all sizeable insurers do.

Almost all insurers buy insurance of their own, called reinsurance. When purchasing this insurance, all sizeable insurers (which invariably are part of larger "groups" of companies) mix unaffiliated reinsurance purchased from unrelated companies with "affiliated" reinsurance purchased from companies that share ownership and management ties.

Affiliated reinsurance is often worth purchasing because affiliated companies can be trusted with very sensitive information about their sibling company's liabilities, won't abandon them after a major loss, and can sometimes make investments that smaller affiliates couldn't make. Even when reinsurance is done within the same company, state insurance regulators and the IRS make sure these transactions are real transfers of risk, priced as they would be if the parties weren't related, and that they are taxed at rates functionally equivalent to the corporate income tax. Stiff penalties apply if these conditions aren't met.

The new taxes favored by Neal, the Obama administration, and some U.S.-based insurers would allow U.S. insurers to continue these transactions while making them financially unworkable for companies with official headquarters locations elsewhere.

Raising Rates for Consumers

A study from The Brattle Group, an economics research and consulting firm, found the Neal proposal would raise insurance rates for consumers by $110 billion to $130 billion over ten years. The rate increases would happen because the overall supply of reinsurance would drop by roughly 20 percent, Brattle's researchers found. With less competition, U.S.-based and offshore reinsurance companies could and would raise their prices.

The rate increases would not affect all consumers equally: Some lines of business and some states would see much higher premium increases than others. Earthquake insurance rates would rise more than 7 percent, Brattle found. And consumers in Florida would see their premiums soar almost $3.5 billion over a decade.

Making Private Insurance Unavailable

The proposed insurance tariffs could make private insurance completely unavailable for some types of perils.

The Brattle Group, and all other economic researchers who have looked at the question, assume insurers will pass increased reinsurance costs on to their consumers and that state regulators will let them do this. Experience, however, shows this does not always happen.

When reinsurance prices surged in the wake of Hurricane Katrina, for example, the State of Florida increased its own participation in the insurance and reinsurance businesses and refused to allow many insurers to raise rates. Most major national insurers decided to stop writing new business in the state. The maximum amount covered by the Florida Hurricane Catastrophe Fund was increased from $16 billion to $36 billion. Florida Citizens Property Insurance Corporation, previously a "market of last resort," was allowed to sell insurance to anyone receiving even one price quote more than 15 percent above its rates.

A similar price shock could easily encourage other governments to begin acting as Florida did, making insurance even less available in the private market.

The United States needs offshore reinsurance. Proposals to impose significant tariffs on it would hurt consumers and should be rejected.

Recommended readings: Michael Cragg et al., *The Impact on the U.S. Insurance Market of H.R. 3424 on Offshore Affiliate Reinsurance: An Updated Economic Analysis*, The Brattle Group, 2010; Coalition for Competitive Insurance Rates, "Taxing our Credulity: Refuting the Top Ten Myths about Overseas Reinsurers," 2001; Association of Bermuda Insurers and Reinsurers, "Bermuda Reinsurance Fact Sheet," 2010; Eli Lehrer. "The Worst Tax of All: An Attack on American Consumers," *Inside ALEC*, May 2010.

5. Dismantle catastrophe funds.

Government-run reinsurance entities, aka catastrophe funds, promote excessive risk-taking.

When a major disaster hits, private insurers currently fall back on insurance of their own. This product, called reinsurance, serves a vital function in making it possible for insurers to write large numbers of policies in disaster-prone areas. When an insurer's losses exceed a certain figure, reinsurance typically pays some or all of the losses.

Some politicians and some insurers want the government to establish government-run reinsurance entities, typically called "catastrophe funds," that supposedly would lower the cost for the "backstop" that companies now get privately. This is a bad idea.

International Risk Pooling Crucial

Government-run reinsurance can't work. Like insurance, reinsurance works by grouping significant numbers of similar risk exposures that are unlikely to result in claims at the same time. Through international reinsurance markets, risk gets spread all over the world. The risk of a hurricane hitting Florida, through international transactions, gets pooled with the risk of an Indonesian cyclone. Since the seasons are reversed, the two events won't happen at the same time. A reinsurer that pays out big claims on a Florida hurricane can be sure it will make large profits on insurance against an

Indonesian cyclone.

By focusing all risk within one state (as Florida has done with its Hurricane Catastrophe Fund), or even within the United States (as some in Congress want to do), a government-run catastrophe fund would lose the advantage of international risk pooling. To break even – as the proponents of the idea suggest it will do – a government catastrophe fund would have to charge higher rates than existing private coverage. If it did so, it seems unlikely anybody would participate in it. If, on the other hand, it were to do what Florida has done and underfund its liabilities, it will stick taxpayers with an enormous burden. Florida's fund has about $4 billion in assets and perhaps $12 billion in borrowing potential, to pay claims that could top $25 billion. Taxpayers will have to pay the difference.

Encouraging Risky Behavior

By charging lower-than-market prices for reinsurance and asking taxpayers to pick up the bill later, catastrophe funds also encourage development in areas where it would not otherwise happen. Quite often, additional development happens in coastal areas and along beaches. In many cases, catastrophe funds can fairly be called a "beach house bailout."

Environmental groups including the Sierra Club, American Rivers, and National Wildlife Federation oppose the idea of national and state catastrophe funds for this very reason. They should be joined by taxpayer advocates and enlightened elected officials, and together work to dismantle catastrophe funds.

Recommended reading: Eli Lehrer, "Catastrophe Funds and Reinsurance Frequently Asked Questions," Competitive Enterprise Institute, 2008; Eli Lehrer, "Restoring the Private Property-Insurance Market to Reduce Florida's Risk of Financial Insolvency," Competitive Enterprise Institute, 2008; Protecting America.org, "How a Catastrophe Fund Will Protect America," 2006; Robert E. Litan, "Preparing for Future 'Katrinas,'" *Brookings Institution Policy Brief #150*, March 2006.

6. Reform and phase out the National Flood Insurance Program.

The National Flood Insurance Program is deeply in debt and has not worked as intended.

Since Congress first passed legislation establishing it in 1968, the National Flood Insurance Program (NFIP) has provided flood coverage for homes and families around the country. Local governments with zoning authority must opt in to the program and implement zoning codes intended to prevent building in flood-prone zones. Since the late 1970s, almost all flood-prone communities have participated in the program. Private insurance companies administer the National Flood Insurance Program, but the federal government takes on all the risk.

Increasing Homeowners' Risks

NFIP does not work. Instead of discouraging construction in flood-prone places while encouraging construction in less flood-prone areas, the program has done just the opposite. Research by the National Wildlife Federation has shown that a small percentage of the insured buildings – including many built after the program began – has been responsible for a disproportionate percentage of the program's claims. Army Corps of Engineers spending on flood control – much of it done in concert with NFIP – also has done nothing to reduce the risk of flood damage.

NFIP currently owes the Treasury Department almost $20 billion, has no way to pay it back (and may even have trouble paying the interest), and uses dangerously outdated maps. Efforts to modernize the program's maps and thereby move its rates closer to adequacy have fallen behind schedule.

Move Toward Privatization

Since only a handful of private companies currently write private flood insurance, it would be impractical to do away with the program overnight. However, Congress should make efforts to limit its reach. Some policies likely can be sold to private companies immediately, while others might be "nudged" into the private market through steady rate increases, improved mapping, and even temporary subsidies to insurers willing to take them on.

For the handful of properties that may be impossible to insure at rates their current owners can afford, Congress should consider government-sponsored buyouts, long-term subsidies to incumbent property owners, and conversion of the property to open space, wildlife habitat, golf courses, or other such uses.

If Congress cannot find the will to privatize the program, it should work to improve it. It can do this by increasing rates on the most flood-prone properties, fully funding efforts to improve the program's maps, and denying future coverage to destroyed houses that already have been rebuilt in the same place.

Recommended reading: Eli Lehrer, "Reforming the National Flood Insurance Program after 35 Years of Failure," Competitive Enterprise Institute, 2008; David Conrad, "Higher Ground: A Report on Voluntary Property Buyouts in the Nation's Floodplains," National Wildlife Federation, 1998; Daniel Sutter, "Hurricane Damage and Global Warming," Competitive Enterprise Institute, 2009; Federal Emergency Management Agency, "The National Flood Insurance Program," 2009.

7. Don't ban credit scoring.

Credit scores are a valuable and accurate tool in determining risk.

Insurers have the difficult responsibility of crafting rate and premium structures that allow profitability for company owners while being attractive to consumers. To remain viable against competitors, an insurer must accurately measure risk and tailor rates accordingly. Maintaining accuracy in rate-making is important for consumers as well, as accurate rates ensure that one consumer does not end up subsidizing another's risky behavior.

Valuable Information

A consumer's credit score is one of dozens of factors that most insurers take into account when determining the risk involved in writing a new policy. Credit-based insurance scoring assigns a numerical ranking based on an individual's credit history. The insurance score is then used as one of many factors in determining the risk level of the applicant. Actuarial studies demonstrate a link between the number of claims filed by an individual and the level of credit reliability achieved by a consumer through careful management of personal finances.

In a 2005 study by the Texas Department of Insurance, researchers found drivers with poorer credit scores generated losses 65 percent higher than those with the highest scores when comparing credit scores to policy claims. It also found credit scoring is not discriminatory, because it is not based upon race or income. Credit scores work.

Prevents Cost-Shifting

The end result of credit scoring is better products for consumers. Most states, 46 as of May 2009, don't place significant restrictions on insurance companies' use of credit scores. However, self-styled "consumer advocates" such as the Consumer Federation of America argue credit scoring discriminates against minority and low-income applicants – despite the evidence to the contrary.

In recent years, state legislators across the country have proposed total or partial bans on using credit scoring in rate-making. According to the Insurance Information Institute, legislation aimed at limiting the use of credit scoring has been proposed in more than 19 states since the beginning of 2009, including Connecticut, Indiana, Maryland, Mississippi, Montana, and North Dakota, where attempts to ban it were rejected.

Report Card

In the 2010 edition of The Heartland Institute's *Property and Casualty Insurance Report Card*, Eli Lehrer considers credit scoring to be one of 11 key factors in evaluating a state's P&C insurance environment. He wrote, "States that allow the use of credit scores generally have lower overall rates than those that forbid their use. ... States that ban [the use of credit scoring] entirely or impose restrictions so severe it becomes useless, received a score of -5."

Five states – four of which fared poorly overall in the *Report Card* – achieved the lowest possible grade of -5 on the credit scoring measure.

Five Worst States for Credit Scoring Restrictions		
States	Overall Grade	Credit Scoring Grade
California	D+	-5
Hawaii	C-	-5
Maryland	D-	-5
Massachusetts	C-	-5
Washington	B-	-5

Recommended reading: Texas Department of Insurance, "TDI Credit Scoring Study Synopsis," 2006; Insurance Institute of Michigan, "What's Credit Got to do With It?" 2008; Federal Trade Commission, "Need Credit or Insurance? Your Credit Score Helps Determine What You'll Pay," *Facts for Consumers*, 2007.

8. Don't ban territorial rating.

Using geographical location in determining insurance rates results in better insurance prices that more accurately reflect risk.

The location of insured property, such as a residence or an automobile, can have a substantial effect on insurance rates. People who build houses on sand dunes should expect to pay higher homeowners insurance rates than those who live well inland, and those who live in neighborhoods plagued by auto theft and vandalism should expect to pay higher automobile insurance rates than those in more secure neighborhoods. Most states, sensibly, allow insurers to take such factors into account with only a few restrictions. Doing so results in fairer and often lower rates for average consumers.

Significant Limitations
This is especially true of auto insurance. According to the Insurance Information Institute, various studies have found that where a person garages his or her vehicle is the most accurate predictor of loss, while an

individual's driving history is among the least predictive, because the average driver has so few claims during his or her lifetime. A California Actuarial Advisory Committee study found geography explained 49.7 percent of the risk for bodily injury coverage.

Although no state makes it impossible for insurers to use geography in any way, many states place significant limitations on its use. Most states disallow the use of territorial rating as the "sole" factor in determining rates, and several – Colorado, Delaware, Florida, Hawaii, Maryland, Massachusetts, Missouri, New York, Pennsylvania, and Texas – place significant limitations on territorial rating in at least one major category of insurance. By contrast, Alabama, Alaska, Idaho, Mississippi, New Mexico, Tennessee, Utah, and Vermont place no limitations on the use of geography in rating insurance risks.

Distinct from Redlining

Using territorial data in setting rates results in lower rates for most customers while avoiding the problems of cross-subsidies and perverse incentives that arise when premiums are not based upon risk. But some advocacy groups contend territorial rating is a form of redlining, the illegal practice of arbitrarily denying or limiting financial services to specific neighborhoods.

Territorial rating is definitely not arbitrary, as the previously cited California Actuarial Advisory Committee report showed. It traditionally has been regarded by the insurance industry and legislators alike as an essential tool for insurers. The American Legislative Exchange Council passed a resolution in 1999 recommending the legal practice of territorial rating not be confused with redlining, and it endorsed territorial rating in the competitive insurance market as a means of ensuring that insurance prices are fair and reasonable and adequate coverage is provided.

Report Card

Territorial rating was another of the 11 key factors affecting property and casualty insurance examined by Lehrer in his *2010 Property and Casualty Insurance Report Card*, with states with outright or partial bans on territorial rating scoring -10. Many of the lowest-ranked states, and even some otherwise highly ranked states, scored low on this measure.

13 Worst States for Territorial Rating Restrictions		
States	Overall Grade	Territorial Rating Grade
California	D+	-10
Colorado	D	-5
Connecticut	B	-5
Florida	F	-10
Maryland	D-	-5
Missouri	B	-5
Nevada	A-	-5
New Hampshire	A-	-5
Oklahoma	C-	-5
Oregon	B-	-5
Pennsylvania	C	-5
Rhode Island	C	-5
Texas	D	-5

Recommended reading: Janet L. Kaminski, "Territorial Rating for Auto Insurance," Connecticut Office of Legislative Research, 2006; Howard Botts and Jeffery L. Kucera, "Time for Another Look at Personal Lines Territories," *Contingencies Magazine*, 2004; American Legislative Exchange Council, "Resolution Supporting Territorial Rating," *ALEC Model Legislation*, 1999; Insurance Information Institute, "Hurricane Katrina Fact File," *Rates and Regulation*, August 2006, p. 16.

9. Don't interfere in rate-setting.

Accurately accounting for risk allows insurers to provide new products tailored to the needs of consumers.

As was explained in Principle 1, insurance rates are best discovered by allowing insurers to compete and consumers to choose in competitive marketplaces. Underwriting is the sophisticated means used by insurers to predict future claims and set rates to cover their costs. Government's role is properly limited to ensuring that premiums are sufficient to cover expected claims.

In the real world, 48 states impose a significant degree of direct control over the rates insurance companies charge. Regulators typically set lower rates for politically favored groups and higher rates for disfavored groups. For example, in Florida a massive state-run insurance company – the largest homeowners insurer in the state – guarantees lower-than-market rates for people who live in coastal areas and, as a result, will tend to raise private homeowners insurance rates in inland areas.

Types of Regulation

One state, Florida, establishes rates through the political process. Florida operates a state agency, the Citizens Property Insurance Corporation (Citizens), which will sell insurance to anybody who receives a single insurance quote more than 15 percent above Citizens' rates.

More states require regulators to pre-approve all rates. Such "prior-approval" regulation, found in states like New Jersey and North Carolina, tends to lower rates for groups that take large risks and raise rates for those who avoid risks. Although prior approval generally tends to reduce the number of changes in rates, by making the approval process more difficult, insurers tend to request larger increases (and rate cuts) when they change the rates being charged.

A less-restrictive form of regulation is file-and-use, whereby companies are required to develop rates and file them with regulators, along with justifications explaining why the rates were set as they were. Upon acceptance of the paperwork by the regulators, the rates can be used by the insurance companies.

Other states use flex-rating systems, which often are paired with file-and-use systems. Flex-rating allows companies to charge rates within a certain range without any specific rate-filing.

Finally, two states, Illinois and Wyoming, operate under no-file or modified no-file systems. Insurance companies must maintain certain files and open them to inspection by the state. Insurance companies are required only to charge actuarially adequate rates (a *de facto* price floor) and may not charge unconscionable rates (a *de facto* ceiling). This system allows greater freedom than any other.

Report Card

According to Lehrer's *2010 Property and Casualty Insurance Report Card*, 47 states exert a significant degree of direct control over the rates insurance companies charge. Lehrer writes, "When regulators establish rates or require specific justification for the rates insurance companies establish, factors other than risk become more important to the rate-setting process than they should be. Regulators typically set lower rates for politically favored groups and higher rates for disfavored groups."

Regulatory environment was one of the more heavily weighted factors of the 11 examined in the *2010 Report Card*.

Six Worst States for Rate Regulation		
States	**Overall Grade**	**Rate Regulation Grade**
California	D+	-10
Florida	F	-20
Hawaii	C-	-10
New York	F	-10
Texas	D	-10
Washington	B-	-10

Recommended reading: Robert Detlefsen, "The Case for Underwriting Freedom: How Competitive Risk Analysis Promotes Fairness and Efficiency in Property/Casualty Insurance Markets," National Association of Mutual Insurance Companies, 2005; J. David Cummins, "Property-Liability Insurance Price Deregulation: The Last Bastion?" *Deregulating Property-Liability Insurance: Restoring Competition and Increasing Market Efficiency* (Washington, DC: AEI-Brookings Joint Center for Regulatory Studies, 2002), p. 12.

10. Help only the truly needy.

Instead of destroying the important information prices convey, government should provide direct help to the needy.

Prices can convey an incredible amount of information. If insurance for a certain type of construction becomes particularly expensive, it's a signal that type of construction is not safe. When insurers can take all risk factors into account, their prices can encourage better, safer construction.

In hurricane-prone areas, insurers invariably cut premiums for homes with roof tie-downs (which stop roofs from blowing off in high winds) and raise them for homeowners who don't make the necessary changes. The more freedom insurers have to set rates based on risk factors, the more they are able to reward consumers who invest in mitigation measures.

The government alone could never – and should never – take the responsibility for securing every private home against disaster. Homeowners are best equipped to take charge of that. Temporary, means-tested assistance to poorer homeowners may prove an adequate substitute for insurance price controls or permanent insurance subsidies.

Direct, Temporary Help Is Best

If homeowners living on low, fixed incomes cannot afford risk-based rates, it's certainly preferable to help them reinforce their homes and lower their insurance premiums than to use government regulation to control insurance premiums for everyone. Florida, Louisiana, and South Carolina have offered grants, tax credits, and other incentives to aid truly needy homeowners with mitigation efforts.

Many effective adaptations involve reasonably simple steps. Encouraging individuals to install storm shutters, providing advice on types of plantings that will survive storms, and even suggesting building standards that specify roof and garage door shapes can all make homes safer and lower insurance premiums. In many cases, these things can pay for themselves in a few years through lower insurance rates and decreased storm damage.

That said, some things that make communities and homes safer take longer or require larger-scale decision making. Governments, for example, shouldn't subsidize the destruction of coastal wetlands that can absorb storm surge from hurricanes, even when they're replaced by inland wildlife preserves, or encourage construction in box canyons that are particularly susceptible to wildfires. In many cases, eliminating these subsidies can do more to promote safety and decrease average insurance rates than any number of price controls.

Mitigation assistance programs are most valuable when offered as limited-duration aid for people of modest means and coupled with broad efforts to remove controls on insurance rates. In the end, however, homeowners who live in dangerous areas must step up to the plate and strengthen their own properties using their own resources.

When a compelling public policy reason exists to provide an insurance or risk mitigation subsidy to a group of people, government will achieve the best results if it uses a broad-based revenue source – rather than an insurance premium tax or other cross-subsidy – to fund the program. A cross-subsidy or additional premium tax distorts the price of insurance for everyone. A subsidy paid out of general revenue does not.

Recommended reading: Americans for Smart Natural Catastrophe Policy, "Why Mitigation?" 2009; Federal Alliance for Safe Homes, "If Disaster Strikes, Will You Be Covered," 2006.

References

Americans for Smart Natural Catastrophe Policy. 2009. Why mitigation? www.smartersafer.org/resources-and-tips/why-mitigation.

American Insurance Association. 2008. What every insurance agent needs to know about credit-based insurance scores. www.aiadc.org/AIAdotNet/landing.aspx?docid= 303972.

American Legislative Exchange Council. 1999. Resolution supporting territorial rating. ALEC Model Legislation. www.heartland.org/article/6421.

Association of Bermuda Insurers and Reinsurers. 2010. Bermuda reinsurance fact sheet.

Berrington, Craig. 2003. *Optional federal charter: A remedy for America's antiquated insurance regulatory system.* Wiley Rein, LLC, www.wileyrein.com/docs/publications/12433.pdf.

Botts, Howard and Jeffery L. Kucera. 2004. Time for another look at personal lines territories. *Contingencies,* American Academy of Actuaries. www.contingencies.org/septoct04/tradecraft.pdf.

Coalition for Competitive Insurance Rates. 2001. Taxing our credulity: refuting the top ten myths about overseas reinsurers.

Competitive Enterprise Institute. 2007. National regulatory modernization faq. www.nicpa.org.

Conrad, David. 1998. Higher ground: a report on voluntary property buyouts in the nation's floodplains. National Wildlife Federation. www.nwf.org/hurricanes/pdfs/NWFHigherGround.pdf.

Cragg, Michael et al. 2010. The impact on the U.S. insurance market of H.R. 3424 on offshore affiliate reinsurance: an updated economic analysis. The Brattle Group.

Cummins, J. David. 2002. Deregulating property-liability insurance: restoring competition and increasing market efficiency. Washington, DC: American Enterprise Institute Press.

Detlefsen, Robert. 2005. The case for underwriting freedom: how competitive risk analysis promotes fairness and efficiency in property/casualty insurance markets. National Association of Mutual Insurance Companies. www.heartland.org/ article/21071.

Epstein, R. 1999. Exit rights and insurance regulation: from federalism to takings. George Mason Law Review 7 (2): 293-311.

Federal Alliance for Safe Homes. 2006. If disaster strikes, will you be covered. www.flash.org/pdf/7-13-06FLASH_Insurance_Guide.pdf.

Federal Emergency Management Agency. 2009. The national flood insurance program. www.fema.gov/about/programs/nfip/index.shtm.

Federal Trade Commission. 2007. Need credit or insurance? Your credit score helps determine what you'll pay. Facts for Consumers. www.ftc.gov/bcp/edu/pubs/consumer/credit/cre24.shtm.

Greenwood, Arin. 2008. Compounding catastrophe. OnPoint, Competitive Enterprise Institute. cei.org/on-point/2008/12/02/compounding-catastrophe.

Grover, Nancy. 2008. NAMIC: Wisconsin senate's approval of credit-based insurance scoring legislation could jeopardize low rates. InsuranceNews.net. www.insurance newsnet.com/article.asp?a=top_pc&id=90774.

Insurance Information Institute. 2006. Hurricane Katrina fact file. Rates and Regulation, August.

Insurance Information Institute. 2009. Credit scoring. III Issue Updates, June. www.iii.org/media/hottopics/insurance/creditscoring/.

Insurance Information Institute. 2009. Optional federal charter. III Issue Updates, June. www.iii.org/media/hottopics/insurance/opt/.

Insurance Information Institute. 2009. Financial responsibility laws by state. IIM Fact Book. www.iii.org/individuals/auto/a/stateautolaws/.

Insurance Institute of Michigan. 2008. What's credit got to do with it?
www.iiminfo.org/consumers/InsuranceScoring/tabid/1723/Default.aspx.

Kaminski, Janet L. 2006. Territorial rating for auto insurance. Connecticut Office of
Legislative Research. www.cga.ct.gov/2006/rpt/2006-R-0542.htm.

Kaufman, George G. 2010. The financial turmoil of 2007-XX: sinners and their sins.
Heartland Policy Brief, April, http://www.heartland.org/custom/semod_policybot/pdf/
28098.pdf

Klein, Robert. 2000. *Regulating insurer solvency in a brave new world.* Center for Risk
Management and Insurance Research, University of Georgia. rmictr.gsu.edu/Papers/
Insurance_Solvency_Regulation.pdf.

Klein, Robert. 2009. *Hurricanes and residual market mechanisms.* Center for Risk
Management and Insurance Research, University of Georgia. opim.wharton.upenn.edu/
risk/library/2009-05-29Klein_ResidualMkt.pdf.

Lehrer, Eli. 2010. 2010 property and casualty insurance report card. *Heartland Policy
Study*, The Heartland Institute, May. www.heartland.org/article/27752.

Lehrer, Eli. 2010. The worst tax of all: an attack on American consumers. *Inside ALEC*,
May.

Lehrer, Eli. 2009. *Restoring Florida's insurance market.* The James Madison Institute.
cei.org/gencon/030,06398.cfm.

Lehrer, Eli. 2009. Restoring the private property-insurance market to reduce Florida's
risk of financial insolvency. Competitive Enterprise Institute. cei.org/study/2009/
03/22/restoring-private-property-insurance-market-reduce-florida%E2%80%99s-risk-fina
ncial-insolve.

Lehrer, Eli. 2008. Catastrophe funds and reinsurance frequently asked questions.
Competitive Enterprise Institute. www.smartersafer.org/uploads/
Digital%20Library/Eli_faq.pdf.

Lehrer, Eli. 2008. Reforming the national flood insurance program after 35 years of
failure. Competitive Enterprise Institute. cei.org/cei_files/fm/active/0/Eli%20
Lehrer%20-%20Reforming%20the%20National%20Flood%20Insurance%20Program.
pdf.

Lehrer, Eli. 2008. Property and casualty insurance: a state-by-state analysis of regulatory
burden. *Heartland Policy Study*, The Heartland Institute, March.
www.heartland.org/article/22907.

Lehrer, Eli. 2007. Uncle Sam, regulate me! *National Review* Online.
www.cei.org/gencon/019,05862.cfm.

Lehrer, Eli and Michelle Minton. 2009. Property and casualty insurance 2009 report card.
Heartland Policy Study, The Heartland Institute, May.
www.heartland.org/articles/25091.

Litan, Robert E. 2006. Preparing for future 'Katrinas.' *Policy Brief #150*, Brookings Institution, March 2006. www.brookings.edu/comm/policybriefs/pb150.pdf.

McCarty, Kevin. 2009. Insurance company solvency regulation: an overview for the financial services commission. Florida Department of Insurance Regulation. www.floir.com/pdf/CabinetPresentation01132009.pdf.

National Association of Insurance Commissioners. 2009. Personal lines regulatory framework. Speed to Market (EX) Task Force. www.naic.org/documents/committees _ex_speed_personal_lines_whitepaper.pdf.

National Association of Insurance Guarantee Funds. 2008. Insolvencies ... an overview. www.ncigf.org/media/files/primer_122607.pdf.

National Association of Mutual Insurance Companies. 2002. Regulation of property/ casualty insurance: the road to reform.

ProtectingAmerica.org. 2006. How a catastrophe fund will protect America. www.protectingamerica.org/how-a-catastrophe-fund-will-protect-America.

Sutter, Daniel. 2009. Hurricane damage and global warming. Competitive Enterprise Institute. cei.org/issue-analysis/2009/06/03/hurricane-damage-and-global-warming.

Texas Department of Insurance. 2006. TDI credit scoring study synopsis. www.tdi.state.tx.us/reports/credit3.html.

Additional Resources

- *PolicyBot*, The Heartland Institute's free online clearinghouse for the work of other free-market think tanks, contains thousands of documents on property and casualty insurance issues. It is on Heartland's Web site at www.heartland.org.

- *www.firepolicy-news.org* and *www.outofthestormnews.com*, are Web sites devoted to the latest news and commentary about property and casualty insurance and other finance and real estate issues. Read headlines, watch videos, or browse the thousands of documents available from *PolicyBot*.

- *FIRE Policy News*, a monthly publication from The Heartland Institute. Subscribe online at www.heartland.org.

Directory

The following national organizations support risk-based insurance rates, mitigation, and insurance reforms. For a longer list, go to www.heartland.org, click "FIRE," and see the links on that page.

American Enterprise Institute, www.aei.org
Cato Institute, www.cato.org
Competitive Enterprise Institute, www.cei.org
Federal Alliance for Safe Homes, www.flash.org
Heartland Institute, www.heartland.org
Insurance Information Institute, www.iii.org
Insurance Institute for Building and Home Safety, www.ibhs.org
James Madison Institute, www.jamesmadison.org
John Locke Foundation, www.johnlocke.org
Mercatus Center, www.mercatus.org
National Conference of Insurance Legislators, www.ncoil.org
National Wildlife Federation, www.nwf.org
Pelican Institute, www.pelicaninstitute.org
Sierra Club, www.sierraclub.org
Texas Public Policy Foundation, www.tppf.org

Chapter 9
Federal Tax Policy

Daniel J. Pilla

---

10 Principles of Federal Tax Policy

1. Simplicity
2. Noninvasiveness
3. Efficiency
4. Stability
5. Visibility

6. Neutrality
7. Economic Growth
8. Broad-based
9. Equality
10. Constitutionality

Introduction

"Of all the powers conferred upon government that of taxation is
most liable to abuse."

> Supreme Court of the United States
> *Citizens' Savings & Loan Ass'n v. City of Topeka*
> 87 U.S. 655 (1874)

The power to tax is the most ubiquitous of all government powers. It
reaches directly or indirectly to all classes of people, all industries, all
elements of society. Taxes always place at least some burdens on business,
individuals, and the economy. They are a necessary evil. However, citizens
should tolerate only those taxes that are lawful and used to support
legitimate functions of government.

For these reasons, policymakers and legislators have a responsibility to adhere to sound constitutional and economic principles when levying taxes, and citizens have a moral and legal duty to hold legislators accountable for violations of these principles. This trust is vital since abdication of these principles threatens liberty. The Supreme Court stated as much in *Citizens' Savings & Loan*, saying:

> It must be conceded that there are such [private] rights in every free government beyond the control of the State. A government which recognized no such rights, which held the lives, the liberty, and the property of its citizens subject at all times to the absolute disposition and unlimited control of even the most democratic depository of power, is after all but a despotism.

Thankfully, there is a body of constitutional law and economic evidence to guide the design of a tax system consistent with constitutional limitations and economic principles. As the nation clamors for solutions to the challenges of ongoing annual deficits, local, state, and national debt, and stagnant or sluggish economic growth, a renewal of these fundamental principles is timely.

This chapter focuses on the federal income tax, since this tax collects by far the most revenue and affects the most people in the United States. However, the ten principles presented here apply to any tax system, whether national, state, county, or local. Because income taxes are more likely to violate these ten principles than taxes on other things, elected officials at every rung of the federalism ladder should consider replacing income taxes with other types of taxes.

1. Simplicity

Citizens have a fundamental right to know what tax laws require, and compliance should be easy and inexpensive.

The Supreme Court, in its 1926 decision *Connally v. General Construction Co.*, recognized a fundamental right to know what legislation means, especially legislation that creates an affirmative duty to act. The majority wrote, "[A] statute which either forbids or requires the doing of an act in terms so vague that men of common intelligence must necessarily guess at its meaning and differ as to its application, violates the first essential of due process of law" (269 U.S. 385 (1926)).

The current tax code represents precisely the opposite of the constitutional standard for understandable legislation. The federal tax code is so complex that it is challenging just to count the words. The closest we are able to get is an estimate, produced by the National Taxpayer Advocate in her 2008 Annual Report to Congress, of 3.7 million words (NTA 2008, p. 4). The tax code has grown substantially since then.

A law this complicated is difficult to administer and impossible to obey. In every annual report presented to Congress since those reports were first required in 1999, the National Taxpayer Advocate identified "tax law complexity" as the biggest problem taxpayers face in dealing with the IRS. Former IRS Commissioner Shirley Peterson testified to Congress nearly 20 years ago:

> A good part of what we call non-compliance with the tax laws is caused by taxpayers' lack of understanding of what is required in the first place. ... Many taxpayers fail to comply because they are unaware of the requirements of the law or because they cannot easily understand what they are supposed to do (Peterson 1992).

When people do not know how to comply, they cannot be expected to comply. In 2001, the Treasury Inspector General for Tax Administration reported that IRS personnel in its taxpayer assistance centers answered taxpayers' questions "inaccurately or incompletely" up to 73 percent of the time (Treasury Inspector General 2001). A year earlier, former IRS Commissioner Charles Rossotti remarked, "Fundamentally, we are attempting the impossible. We are expecting employees and our managers to be trained in areas that are far too broad to ever succeed, and our manuals and training courses are, therefore, unmanageable in scope and complexity" (Rossotti 2000).

Very simply, these commissioners are conceding that the job of providing accurate information cannot be done given the scope, breadth, and complexity of the current tax code. This complexity in turn undermines people's willingness to comply with the law. Taxpayers are less willing to comply with a tax code they know to be rife with loopholes, exceptions, and ambiguities. Such complication breeds the not-unfounded idea that other taxpayers are paying less on the same or greater income. The President's

Advisory Panel on Federal Tax Reform reported in 2005:

> [T]axpayers think that with the myriad of targeted exclusions, deductions, and credits, others may not be paying their fair share – so why should they? Some call this "the cheat or chump syndrome." In addition, clever tax advisors mine the complexity of the tax code to develop and market tax shelters and other schemes clearly designed to manipulate the tax code's hidden loopholes for their clients' exclusive benefit. The perception that the tax code is unfair and easily manipulated undermines voluntary compliance – the foundation of our tax system (President's Advisory Panel 2005, p. 4).

The IRS Oversight Board's 2004 Taxpayer Attitude Survey showed that about one in five citizens believed that some amount of tax cheating is acceptable (IRS Oversight Board 2004). The board did not delve into why citizens feel this way. Certainly the perception that tax laws are unfair is a key factor driving this belief.

Lawmakers owe citizens and businesses a simple and understandable tax code. More than any other area of law, tax law touches and affects Americans with a growing list of affirmative duties. Given this, the constitutional guarantee of due process mandates a simple tax code that people can understand.

Recommended reading: President's Advisory Panel on Federal Tax Reform, *Simple, Fair and Pro-Growth: Proposals to Fix America's Tax System*, 2005, http://govinfo.library.unt.edu/taxreformpanel/ final-report/index.html.

2. Noninvasiveness

A minimally invasive tax code encourages voluntary compliance and reduces the need for enforcement.

It is widely agreed that citizens have a duty to pay the taxes they owe in full and on time. However, government has a duty to collect the revenue in the least invasive manner. The current income tax system is the most invasive part of the entire body of federal law.

A 1999 report of the General Accounting Office (GAO) to the Senate Small Business Committee found "by our count, there are more than 200 requirements – which we grouped into four layers – that may apply to small businesses as well as large businesses and other taxpayers" (Wrightson 1999, p. 4). The list of requirements grows annually. The National Taxpayer Advocate reported in 2008 that businesses are burdened with "a bewildering array of laws" (NTA 2008, p. 10).

Businesses are required to file information returns with the IRS reporting payments made to third parties in the course of business. Any payment of $600 or more to a "person"in a calendar year must be reported. In 2008 alone, businesses filed approximately 1.658 billion information returns with the IRS. That does not include income and employment tax returns (*Ibid.*). The 2010 Patient Protection and Affordable Care Act added a provision to the code that requires any person or corporation that pays another corporation more than $600 in a year to file a report with the IRS. The law is effective for payments beginning January 2012.

The new rule will require billions more information returns to be filed annually, putting a substantial additional burden on businesses to comply with a tax code that is already choking them. Since the passage of this law, the IRS has been overwhelmed with questions about its implementation and complaints about the burdens it creates.

According to the National Taxpayer Advocate, businesses and individuals spent approximately 7.6 billion hours meeting just the tax code's filing requirements in 2006. That is equivalent to 3.8 million full-time workers (NTA 2008). These numbers do not include the time and effort taxpayers spend each year dealing with IRS enforcement, which is no less staggering. In 2009 alone, more than 40 million citizens faced IRS collection actions, as shown in the table below (IRS 2009, pp. 41, 42).

Type of Action	Number of Taxpayers Affected
Penalty assessments	36,228,339
Wage and bank levies	3,478,181
Tax liens	965,618
Property seizures	581

Even these figures do not include time spent responding to millions of tax audits and tens of millions computer notices the IRS mails annually. Nor does it address the IRS's so-called "soft contacts." A soft contact is a letter the IRS mails to explain that you "might" have done something wrong and that you "should" examine your own tax return and records to make the correction before the IRS does.

All of this adds up to an incredibly invasive system that undermines the willingness of millions of Americans to comply voluntarily with tax laws.

A less invasive system also would benefit tax administrators. Administrators need fewer resources to manage a system that does not attempt to spy on every aspect of the financial lives of all taxpayers. Fewer reports mean less processing time and require fewer man-hours. Less enforcement action means fewer collectors spending fewer hours tracking down bank accounts, paychecks, and other assets to levy and seize.

The challenge for lawmakers is not to find new ways to squeeze more citizens, but to find a tax system that raises the revenue needed for legitimate government functions without placing a revenue officer in the home and office of every American.

Recommended reading: National Taxpayer Advocate, *Annual Report to Congress 2008*, Internal Revenue Service, www.irs.gov/advocate/article/0,,id=97404,00.html; Daniel J. Pilla, *How to Fire the IRS: A Plan to Eliminate the Income Tax and the IRS* (Stillwater, MN: Winning Publications, 1993).

3. Efficiency

> The total cost of collecting taxes can be reduced by lowering the number of collection points.

The IRS regularly asserts that it is extremely efficient in collecting taxes. In 2009, the agency reported collecting gross tax revenue of more than $2.3 trillion with a work force of 105,814 employees. Given the agency's budget of approximately $11.7 billion, the average cost of collecting $100 of tax was just 50 cents (IRS 2009, p. 63). However, these numbers are misleading.

The IRS's estimate does not take into account the cost *to the public* of complying with income tax laws. Only when we examine the compliance burden borne by the public do we see the true inefficiency of the system. Under the federal income tax withholding system, it is America's employers, not the government, who collect much of the tax.

Of the $2.3 trillion in gross revenue collected by the IRS in 2009, approximately $1.28 trillion, or about 56 percent, was collected by employers through taxes withheld from the paychecks of their workers (*Ibid.*, p. 3). Employers are responsible for paying the money to the IRS and reporting the withholding using various tax forms. The cost is borne by employers, not the government.

The cost to individuals and businesses to comply with the tax code is substantial. The National Taxpayer Advocate recently estimated that the out-of-pocket cost associated with tax return filing alone is approximately $193 billion annually. As the Taxpayer Advocate stated, "this is a staggering 14 percent of aggregate income tax receipts" (NTA 2008, p. 4). Even the NTA did not address the whole picture. We also must consider the cost of responding to the tens of millions of annual notices and letters, challenging penalty assessments, millions of annual audits and appeals, tax litigation and enforced collection, economic disincentive costs, and the cost of tax evasion and avoidance (Pilla 1993, p. 204).

When all these factors are accounted for, the cost of compliance is close to 65 percent of the amount collected (*Ibid.*; Payne 1993). That is to say, for every dollar of tax paid to the Treasury, it costs citizens and businesses 65 cents to get it there. Given that $2.3 trillion was paid to the IRS in 2009, society incurred a collection cost of nearly $1.5 trillion.

Paying taxes to government is a necessary evil, but incurring expenses of up to 65 percent of the tax in the process of paying is an intolerable evil. Lawmakers have a duty to design a system that is mindful of the costs businesses and individuals must bear to comply. Lawmakers have a duty to keep these costs as low as possible.

How can taxes be made more efficient? One way is to reduce the number of collection points. The number of tax returns filed represents the collection points of a tax system. The more the collection points, the less efficient the system. Back in 1999, I calculated the savings to a single state – Minnesota – of moving from an income tax to a broad-based sales tax as the principal means of collecting the state's revenue. The state could have expected to achieve:

- An 82 percent reduction in the number of collection points;

- Annual savings of at least $4.96 million in return processing costs;

- An 88 percent reduction in the number of taxpayer questions;

- A reduction of 63 percent in the state tax return filing obligation of the average Minnesota business; and

- An overall reduction in the state's administrative costs of about $38 million (Pilla 2000).

Of course, there are other issues to consider when proposing a major change in the way taxes are collected. But at a time when both taxpayers and governments are straining to find ways to save money, ways to improve the efficiency of tax collection need to be on the table.

Recommended reading: James L. Payne, *Costly Returns: The Burdens of the U.S. Tax System* (Richmond, CA: Institute for Contemporary Studies, 1993); Daniel J. Pilla, "Freedom to Prosper: Analyzing the Merits of Replacing Minnesota's Income Tax System with a Board-based Sales Tax," Tax Freedom Institute, Inc., January 2000, www.taxhelponline.com/resources-and-publications/research-reports/freedom-to-prosper.html.

4. Stability

> The tax code should be stable and reliable from year to year and generation to generation.

Tax laws directly affect what we do and how we do it. For example, the federal tax code contains provisions dealing with marriage, children, home ownership, personal investing, charitable giving, obtaining personal and professional education, changing employment, finding new employment, paying for medical care, purchasing and operating automobiles, making gifts to children and others, leaving an inheritance, and even death itself. These decisions comprise the most important and often the most personal elements of our lives.

No reasonable person would suggest that a person should make any of these decisions without some level of planning. And while we cannot plan the time or manner of our deaths, we certainly can plan what should happen before death and what happens to our assets after death. More than any other single factor, the tax code dictates the parameters of that planning. In order for any plan – whether business or personal – to be effective, the planning requirements must be stable. Yet the tax code requirements are constantly and unpredictably changing, making planning difficult.

Tax laws change frequently and the rate of change is rising. During the decade of the 1980s, Congress changed the tax code more than one hundred times. Those changes came through just a few major tax acts, such as the Tax Equity and Fiscal Responsibility Act of 1982 and the Tax Reform Act of 1986 (Pilla 1997, p. 25). The 1986 act changed more than 2,000 code sections and was responsible for the creation of more than one hundred new tax forms (Pilla 1995, p. 3).

During the decade of the 1990s, Congress was even busier. Four major tax laws were passed between 1996 and 1998, culminating in the Internal Revenue Service Restructuring and Reform Act, which took effect in July 1998. During the 1990s, more than 750 tax law changes were made.

According to the National Taxpayer Advocate's 2008 *Annual Report to Congress*, "Since the beginning of 2001, there have been more than 3,250 changes to the tax code, an average of more than one a day, including 500 changes in 2008 alone" (NTA 2008, p. 4). Some of these changes resulted in retroactive tax increases. For example, the 1994 Supreme Court ruling in *United States v. Carlton* (512 U.S. 26) approved a decision by

Congress to repeal a tax deduction retroactively, increasing an estate's tax liability by more than $600,000. In 2009 and 2010, 24 tax laws expired, and six more will expire by 2012 (Joint Committee on Taxation 2008).

This vicissitude in the tax code clearly interferes with people's right to plan their personal and business affairs. Between 1986 and 2000, Congress changed the requirements for making estimated tax payments seven different times (IRS 2000, p. 34). Changing the law on estimated taxes every other year is one reason IRS assesses the penalty for failure to pay estimated taxes so often. In 2009, the IRS assessed that penalty against 7.565 million individuals and more than 243,000 businesses (IRS 2009, p. 42).

The 2005 President's Advisory Panel on Tax Reform observed that the expiring provisions and phase-ins and phase-outs of various provisions "are a nuisance at best, and a negative force at worst, in the daily economic lives of American families and businesses" (President's Advisory Panel 2005, p. 5). The panel concluded:

> The tax system is both unstable and unpredictable. Frequent changes in the tax code, which often add to or undo previous policies, as well as the enactment of temporary provisions, result in uncertainty for businesses and families. This volatility is harmful to the economy and creates additional compliance costs (*Ibid.*, p. xiii).

A tax system that is sound fundamentally does not have to be changed often. A tax system that is firmly grounded in the principles discussed here will stand the test of time. Lawmakers must avoid frequent changes to tax laws and work instead to incorporate stability into the system. This would have a major positive impact on taxpayers' ability and willingness to comply.

Recommended reading: Daniel J. Pilla, "How the IRS Tries to Make You Die Poor," *Pilla Talks Taxes* (Stillwater, MN: Winning Publications, May 1997), www.taxhelponline.com/resources-and-publications/research-reports/die-poor.html; Daniel J. Pilla, "Why You Can't Trust the IRS," *Policy Analysis* No. 222, 1995, Cato Institute, www.cato.org.

5. Visibility

The cost of government should be readily apparent to taxpayers.

When asked how much money they paid in federal income taxes in the prior year, most people reply, "I didn't pay anything. I got a refund." They never saw, and therefore do not remember, the many thousands of dollars withheld from their paychecks by their employers.

About 85 percent of the income earners in America do not write a check to the government for their taxes. Since the tax is taken out of their paychecks by their employers, they do not even see the money. As a result, they generally have no idea how much they pay in taxes. The 1996 report of the National Commission on Economic Growth and Tax Reform called attention to the danger of this arrangement:

> The history of hidden taxes, rapidly rising rates, and perpetual budget deficits proves that what you don't know can hurt you. The current system hides the cost of government behind a chronic deficit and a maddening multiplicity of taxes – many of which are virtually invisible to the taxpayer who pays them. How much did we pay in payroll taxes last year? What excise taxes were hidden in the prices of the products we bought? What [is] the tax cost of exclusions, deductions, and corporate income taxes? Few of us know the answers (National Commission 1996, p. 21).

Social Security taxes are particularly invisible to taxpayers. The employee's share of Social Security and hospital taxes is figured at a flat rate of 7.65 percent of gross income. The tax is deducted from workers' paychecks as the income is earned. It then becomes the responsibility of the employers to pay the money to the IRS. Employees never file a Social Security tax return, never write a check to the IRS for the tax, and never do any recordkeeping to correctly figure the tax. They are never subject to an audit with regard to correctly reporting the tax. They are never subject to enforced collection if the tax is not paid by their employers. The money simply disappears from their paychecks.

(This is not true of self-employed persons. They must calculate their Social Security taxes on Schedule SE and include the tax on Form 1040.

Since the tax is figured as a flat percentage of business profit, they are subject to audit as to the amount of tax and collection if the tax is not paid.)

As "easy" as all this sounds, it means most taxpayers never know the true cost of Social Security – or, for that matter, government in general. This allows politicians to increase taxes without people knowing what is happening. That in turn allows politicians to blame the rising cost of living on outside devils such as Big Oil, Big Tobacco, or Big Whatever.

Taxes that are highly visible are much more stable, tend to stay low, and are not generally subject to tinkering. The best example of this is retail sales taxes imposed by state governments. Just compare the number of changes to your state's sales tax laws with the changes made in the Internal Revenue Code in the past ten years. The contrast is staggering. In Minnesota, one can practically count on one hand the number of sales tax law changes and increases that have occurred since the sales tax came into existence in 1963.

The National Commission on Economic Growth and Tax Reform concluded its discussion of the importance of tax visibility by noting, "A visible system gives taxpayers an honest accounting of government's expense and will make it far more difficult for politicians to tinker with the tax code without the democratic consent of those taxed" (*Ibid.*)

Recommended reading: National Commission on Economic Growth and Tax Reform, "Unleashing America's Potential: A Pro-growth, Pro-family Tax System for the 21st Century," Final Report, January 1996, www.galen.org/component,8/action, how_content/id,7/news_id,3074/type,33/?_highlight=kemp.

6. Neutrality

Taxes should not fall more heavily on one industry or class of individuals than on others.

Chief Justice John Marshall, in the 1819 case *McCulloch v. The State of Maryland,* wrote that the power to tax is "the power to destroy" (17 U.S. 316 (1819)). The case dealt with the 10 percent excise tax Congress imposed on the circulation of all bank notes other than those issued by the national bank. Within two years of its passage, the tax drove out of existence every state bank note.

A contemporary example of the destructive power of taxes is the Revenue Reconciliation Act of 1990. This law imposed the 10 percent "luxury tax" on high-priced boats and aircraft (priced at more than $100,000), autos (more than $30,000), and jewelry and furs (more than $10,000). The idea was to "tax the rich."

The politicians did not anticipate that the rich would simply stop buying the items subject to the tax. During the period the tax was in effect, sales of those products fell precipitously. In 1993, Congress repealed the luxury tax. In support of the vote to repeal, the House Ways and Means Committee stated:

> During the recent recession, the boat, aircraft, jewelry and fur industries have suffered job losses and increased unemployment. The committee believes that it is appropriate to eliminate the burden these taxes impose in the interests of fostering economic recovery in those and related industries (House Ways and Means Committee 1993, p. 188).

The Senate Finance Committee also acknowledged the negative effects of the taxes on the affected industries as the reason for repealing the tax hikes (Senate Finance Committee 1993, p. 213).

Selectively targeting industries for heavier tax burdens is an illegitimate use of the taxing power of government. The Supreme Court condemned the practice in *Citizens' Savings & Loan Ass'n v. Topeka,* an 1874 case involving the use of government bonds to finance railroads and the taxes imposed to pay for the bonds. Referring to government's power to impose selective taxes, the Court stated, "This power can as readily be employed against one class of individuals and in favor of another, so as to ruin the one class and give unlimited wealth and prosperity to the other, if there is no implied limitation of the uses for which the power may be exercised" (87 U.S. 655 (1874)). The Court went on to say:

> To lay with one hand the power of the government on the property of the citizen, and with the other to bestow it upon favored individuals to aid private enterprises and build up private fortunes, is none the less a robbery because it is done under the forms of law and is called taxation (p. 664).

There also is a pragmatic reason to keep government from interfering with the ability of legitimate businesses to compete in the marketplace on equal footing with one another. Otherwise, the only businesses with a chance to succeed are those that can afford and are willing to pay the lobbyists and influence peddlers who infest Congress and state houses. When government gets into the business of picking winners and losers in the marketplace, tax benefits and penalties become auction items, bought and sold at the expense of, and to the detriment of, those who cannot or will not play the game.

The idea that tax law ought to be neutral is widely recognized as an essential element of sound tax policy. The National Commission on Economic Growth and Tax Reform described it this way:

> The tax code should be used to raise revenue to run the government while doing the least possible damage to the economy. This means leaving individuals free to make decisions and to set priorities based on economic reality – not on the bureaucratic whims of Washington, D.C. … The result of the biases and distortions in the current system is to make the market less free, the system less fair, and families less financially secure (National Commission 1996, p. 20).

Recommended reading: Robert Carroll, John E. Chapoton, Maya MacGuineas, and Diane Lim Rogers, "Moving Forward with Bipartisan Tax Policy," *Working Paper* No. 5, Tax Foundation, February 2009.

7. Economic Growth

Taxes should not impede the investment and consumption decisions that make economic growth possible.

Three presidential commissions on taxes in the past 15 years each insisted that a sound tax system must be mindful of the profoundly negative consequences taxes can have on the economy: the Bipartisan Commission on Entitlement and Tax Reform, 1995; National Commission on Economic Growth and Tax Reform, 1996; and the President's Advisory Panel on Federal Tax Reform, 2005.

The National Commission on Economic Growth and Tax Reform declared in 1996 that promoting economic growth was the number one principle that must drive tax policy. The commission's report states, "economic growth, the engine of opportunity and prosperity, can only be unleashed by a tax code that encourages initiative, hard work, and saving" (National Commission 1996, p. 17).

What you tax you get less of; what you subsidize you get more of. These economic facts of life should be kept at the forefront of all discussions regarding taxation.

Americans want an economy that is diverse, dynamic, and growing. Such an economy requires rising employment, savings, investment, and productivity. Today's tax system imposes heavy and unnecessary burdens on the economy. How can the economy grow and create diverse opportunities if the very engines of that growth are heavily taxed? The bottom line is this: Taxes make you poorer. For this reason, taxes must be kept low and directed away from the engines of economic growth.

For every dollar paid in taxes, businesses have at least one less dollar available for capital improvements, wages, research and development, or inventory. For every dollar paid in taxes, individuals have at least one less dollar available to purchase a home, pay tuition or medical expenses, or build retirement savings.

The cost of collecting taxes and the negative and distorting impacts taxes have on incentives make their economic damage far greater than the dollars actually collected. Economists Ernest S. Christian and Gary A. Robbins of the Center for Strategic Tax Reform used econometric analysis to find that "the cost to the private sector of providing the government an additional $1 in tax revenue is about $2.50 and in some circumstances much more" (Christian and Robbins 2006). They say, "If taxes were both reduced and reformed (so that the drag on economic performance per $1 of tax would be less), the economy would be larger, government would be smaller, and everyone would be better off."

Economist Richard Vedder at Ohio University examined several dozen measures of taxes and spending in the years 1957, 1977, and 1997. In 2001 he reported, "In every single case, without exception, the results are consistent: High or rising taxes are associated with lower amounts of economic growth. The use of more sophisticated statistical models produces the same sort of result: higher taxes, lower growth" (Vedder 2001, p. 9).

Other researchers, including J. Scott Moody at the Maine Heritage Policy Center (Moody 2006) and Scott A. Hodge at the Tax Foundation (Stanek 2006) have found the same thing: High taxes lead to slower economic growth. According to Hodge, "Taxes are an important cost to business, as important as the cost of labor and raw materials. Nearly all of the best states raise sufficient revenue without imposing at least one of the three major state taxes: sales taxes, personal income taxes, and corporate income taxes" (*Ibid.*)

To minimize the negative effect of taxes on job creation, taxes on employment should be reduced. Our Founding Fathers had the wisdom and foresight to know that imposing direct taxes on the engines of economic growth would only inhibit growth. That is why the Founders expressly rejected the idea of imposing direct taxes on income, saving, and investment. Instead, they favored indirect (excise) taxes on consumption. The nation's first Treasury Secretary, Alexander Hamilton, observed that taxing the "articles of our own growth and manufacture are more prejudicial" to economic growth than excise taxes (Morris 1957, p. 258).

Recommended reading: Chris Edwards, "Options for Tax Reform," *Policy Analysis* No. 536, Cato Institute, 2005; Bipartisan Commission on Entitlement and Tax Reform, "Final Report to the President," January 1995, www.ssa.gov/history/reports/ KerreyDanforth/KerreyDanforth.htm.

8. Broad-based

Broad tax bases allow rates to be kept low, which in turn encourages voluntary compliance.

The tax base is the pool of economic activity from which tax revenue is generated. If the government operates on an income tax system, all items constituting accessions to wealth constitute the base. All other factors being equal, the broader the tax base, the more revenue a tax system will generate at a given tax rate.

Low tax rates are beneficial because they do not distort incentives as much as do high tax rates. A high tax rate on income, for example, discourages work and encourages tax evasion. High excise taxes lead to product substitutions and black markets.

Unfortunately, elected officials are shrinking the bases of existing federal and state income taxes. As state and federal lawmakers add more tax breaks for lower-income citizens and limit those for higher-income citizens, the tax burden is being disproportionately loaded onto an increasingly smaller segment of income earners. For example, drawing from Treasury data, the President's Advisory Panel reported in 2005:

> Taxpayers in the top 20 percent of the [income] distribution pay 70.6 percent of all federal taxes, while taxpayers in the bottom 20 percent pay 0.4 percent. More than half of federal taxes are paid by taxpayers in the top 10 percent of the [income] distribution. ...

> Taxpayers in the lowest two quintiles actually receive more in refunds from the federal government than they pay in income taxes and, as a result, have negative income tax burdens. Those taxpayers in the third and fourth quintile pay a relatively small share of the income taxes, 3.8 percent and 13.4 percent, respectively, while those in the top quintile pay over 84 percent of federal income taxes (President's Advisory Panel 2005, p. 31).

As more people are removed from the tax rolls through credits, deductions, exemptions, and the like, the burden on the remaining taxpayers must necessarily grow heavier. Tax rates have to increase to potentially confiscatory levels to continue raising the money to support government spending, which itself is growing.

Such a disproportionate distribution of the burden creates a host of problems, not the least of these being a growing share of the population who pay little or no taxes yet have the electoral power to dictate spending policy at the ballot box. The power of this electorate has led to the imposition of a growing list of entitlement programs for their benefit for which they do not have to pay. These entitlement programs now threaten the solvency of our federal, state, and local governments.

Before the passage of the massive new health care entitlement program, prior to the Medicare supplement program, and before any of the recent stimulus packages, student loan programs, and bailouts, our entitlement programs already were on a path to bankrupt America. In 1995, the Bipartisan Commission on Entitlement and Tax Reform stated in its final report,

> The Commission's Interim Report graphically displays the need to address our future fiscal imbalance. The conclusion of the Report is clear and inescapable: If we do not plan for the future, entitlement spending promises will exceed financial resources in the next century. The current spending trend is unsustainable (Bipartisan Commission 1995, p. 8).

Rather than make the systemic changes needed to control the problem, Congress and every president since 1995 have allowed entitlement programs and spending to grow. Even worse, the number of taxpayers asked to pay for them is shrinking. For there to be any real hope of avoiding a crippling national debt crisis, those who benefit from the system must pay something for those benefits.

Most states attempt to raise taxes simultaneously from several bases. For example, the State of Minnesota raises revenue from taxes on personal income, retail sales, corporate income, and excise taxes on some specific products (e.g., gasoline and cigarettes). This requires administrative infrastructure to handle all four tax systems. This diversified tax base is often defended in the tax literature as being necessary to ensure stable revenues and compete with other states.

If states opted for one form of taxation, say a retail sales tax, then instituted a broad base so that all consumption goods and services were subject to the tax while repealing other taxes, the state could raise the revenue necessary to fund legitimate government functions simply and efficiently, with the least cost of collection and lowest burden on taxpayers. More importantly, every resident of the state would have a vested interest in keeping taxes low because they all would be taxpayers.

Recommended reading: National Taxpayer Advocate, "A Taxpayer-Centric Approach to Tax Reform," in *2005 Annual Report to Congress*, Internal Revenue Service, 2005; National Commission on Restructuring the Internal Revenue Service, "A Vision for a New IRS," June 25, 1997, www.house.gov/ natcommirs/report1.pdf.

9. Equality

The tax system should treat people equally and fairly.

One of the biggest problems affecting the public's willingness to comply with the tax law is that it is widely perceived as being unfair. We have known this for decades. It was reported as early as 1977 that as many as 60 percent of the public felt the federal tax system was either "somewhat unfair or quite unfair" (Pilla 2001, p. 12). Thirty years later, in a report titled "Reducing the Federal Tax Gap," the Treasury Department stated, "Special rules, subtle distinctions in the tax law and complicated computations add to this complexity and foster a sense of unfairness in our tax system, which ultimately discourages compliance" (U.S. Treasury 2007, p. 50).

The public widely perceives the tax law as unfair because the tax law *is* unfair. The report of the President's Advisory Panel on Tax Reform states:

Taxpayers with the same income, family situation, and other key characteristics often face different tax burdens. Such differing treatment creates a perception of unfairness in our tax code. For example, taxpayers in states with high state and local income and property taxes receive higher deductions than taxpayers who live in lower-tax states with fewer state-provided services. Taxpayers with substantial employer-provided health insurance benefits receive in-kind compensation that is not taxed, while taxpayers who buy the same health insurance on their own usually pay tax on the income used to purchase the insurance. And Social Security benefits are taxed at a higher rate for married seniors than for those not married. How much or little taxpayers pay in tax is sometimes dependent on where they happen to live, the choices made by their employers, and whether they are married (President's Advisory Panel 2005).

The touchstone of American liberty is found in this clause in the Declaration of Independence: "all men are created equal." Our chief guiding principle of jurisprudence is that everyone stands equal before the law. This most fundamental precept of American liberty is undermined by the tax code with its quagmire of arbitrary rules.

The problem begins with graduated income tax rates, the foundation of the current system. Tax rates and brackets have been in a nearly constant state of flux since the income tax was imposed in 1913. At that time, the bottom tax bracket was 1 percent on incomes more than $20,000 and the top bracket was just 6 percent on incomes more than $500,000. While the first tax bill was debated in Congress, North Dakota Senator Porter J. McCumber declared:

> Mr. President, it is quite evident that no two Senators will agree upon the number of steps [brackets] in the sliding scale of this bill, and it is equally clear that no two of them will agree upon the ratio of rate for each particular step (McCumber 1913, p. 3834).

The rates and brackets were then and are now arbitrary. They are not based upon economic principles or constitutional standards. The rates and brackets in today's tax code – indeed all of the phase-ins, phase-outs, exceptions, exclusions, and temporary provisions – are "invidiously discriminatory": it is "unfair" that some earn more than others and that the masses can "get even" with those better off by raising their taxes.

Such invidious discrimination is unacceptable in other areas of law. Who would suggest that groups of people – rich or poor – should be more or less liable under, say, the fraud statutes, merely because of their social standing? In tax law, not only is this tolerated, it is embraced. Politicians and policymakers present it as though it were a noble, high-minded pursuit. Think about this: We embrace the idea that the power of law can and should be used as a sword to attack the lawful and peaceful pursuits of entire segments of our population. No free nation can long countenance such thinking.

But such discrimination does not stop with tax brackets. The tax code is rife with examples of how similarly situated people are treated differently merely because of their social or economic standing. For example, the code:

- has five different filing status classifications based upon a person's marriage and family circumstances;

- contains eight different provisions where the definition of the term "child" depends upon a person's social status;

- expressly phases out otherwise legal and proper itemized deductions and dependent exemptions solely upon a person's economic standing; and

- through the Alternative Minimum Tax, deprives certain people based solely on their economic standing of their otherwise perfectly legal and valid dependent exemptions, itemized deductions, and tax credits, raising their taxes beyond what other similarly situated citizens pay.

These provisions are arbitrary acts of discrimination by a government founded on the idea that "all men are created equal." Americans know these things are fundamentally unfair.

The profound unfairness of income taxes is why the Founders generally rejected such tax schemes in favor of excise taxes on consumption. Hamilton stated that consumption taxes "have, upon the whole, better pretensions to equality than any other" (Morris 1957, pp. 259-260).

Recommended reading: Daniel J. Pilla, "A Monument of Deficient Wisdom: The Constitutional Conflict in the Federal Income Tax Law Enforcement," part of *Road Map to Tax Reform Project* (Lewisville, TX: Institute for Policy Innovation, December 2001), www.taxhelponline.com/resources-and-publications/research-reports/con stitutional-conflict-fed-tax-law.html.

10. Constitutionality

Taxes must be imposed solely to fund clearly defined constitutional functions.

Since the 1930s, Congress has used the federal tax laws for purposes other than raising revenue. Specifically, taxes are used to implement social programs and spending. One way this is done is through tax credits. Some of the more prominent federal tax credits are the Earned Income Tax Credit, Child Tax Credit, and First-time Homebuyers Credit. These are just a few of the dozens of personal and business credits in the code, but they are especially important because they are *refundable* credits. This means even citizens who owe no taxes can get cash from the government.

Refundable credits are welfare programs. The Congressional Budget Office estimates that payment of refundable credits will increase by approximately $500 billion by 2019 (Elmendorf 2009). Through these credits, the tax laws are not used to raise revenue, but to achieve social planning goals by enforcing transfer payments: Taking money from some citizens and giving it to others.

Such use of the government's taxing power is unconstitutional. Article I, Section 8 of the Constitution authorizes the federal government to collect taxes for just three narrow purposes: to pay the debts of the nation, to provide a national defense, and to ensure the "general welfare" of the nation. The Founders were adamant that the taxing authority granted in the Constitution be used only to benefit the nation as a whole, not its individual inhabitants or locales, and certainly not individual classes of citizens at the expense of others (Pilla 2001, pp. 8-12). And yet, a great portion of the budgets of government at all levels finances transfer payments imposed to achieve social planning goals.

The Bipartisan Commission on Entitlement and Tax Reform hit the issue head-on when it said, "Government does not create wealth by distributing entitlement benefits; rather, it is engaging in a willful choice to take dollars from one segment of the population and to distribute that money in the form of benefits for others" (Bipartisan Commission 1995, p. 37).

In the 1933 case *United States v. Butler,* the Supreme Court was called on to address the government's claim that redistribution is justifiable under the "general welfare" clause of the Constitution. This decision struck at the core of what today has become a habitual legislative practice: using the power to tax as a means of imparting social benefits to certain classes of society at the expense of others. The Court ruled that "A tax, in the general understanding of the term, and as used in the Constitution, signifies an exaction for the support of the government. The word has never been thought to connote the expropriation of money from one group for the benefit of another" (297 U.S. 1, 61 (1933)).

In *Citizens' Savings & Loan Ass'n v. Topeka,* discussed earlier under the principle of neutrality, the Supreme Court ruled that using taxes to transfer wealth is a wholly illegitimate use of governments' taxing authority. The Court correctly labeled the practice "robbery." And Thomas Jefferson – lead author of the Declaration of Independence and third President of the United States – condemned the practice as an attack upon the ideal of liberty. He stated:

> To take from one, because it is thought his own industry and that of his father has acquired too much, in order to spare to others who (or whose fathers) have not exercised equal industry and skill, is to violate arbitrarily the first principle of association, "the *guarantee* to everyone a free exercise of his industry and the fruits acquired by it" (Ellis 1973, p. 94, emphasis in original).

There is simply no legal or moral authority in a free society that justifies using the power of government to take from some what they have legally and peacefully acquired and give it to others who have not earned it.

Frederick Bastiat (1801-1850), a French economist, statesman, and author, addressed the practice of using the power of taxation to take from producers and give to non-producers. He called this practice "legal plunder." In the strongest terms, he called for the elimination of any such law because "it is not only an evil itself, but it is a fertile source for further evils because it invites reprisals. If such a law – which may be an isolated case – is not abolished immediately, it will spread, multiply, and develop into a system" (Bastiat 1850 (1977), p. 21).

So long as such laws permeate the tax culture in America, there will never be enough money to satisfy government. No tax system can ever produce sufficient revenue to provide for the social programs formulated by those seeking more ways to spend money they have not earned. Tax burdens for the producers grow to confiscatory levels while the non-producers have further incentive to remain non-producers. The only hope of controlling the burden is to hold government strictly accountable to the constitutional limitations on its taxing authority.

Recommended reading: Frederick Bastiat, *The Law* (Irvington-on-Hudson, NY: Foundation for Economic Education, 1850 (reprint 1977)).

References

Bastiat, Frederick. 1850. *The Law.* Foundation for Economic Education edition, 1977.

Bipartisan Commission. 1995. *Final Report to the President.* Bipartisan Commission on Entitlement and Tax Reform, January.

Carroll, Robert, John E. Chapoton, Maya MacGuineas, and Diane Lim Rogers. 2009. Moving Forward with Bipartisan Tax Policy. *Working Paper* No. 5, Tax Foundation, February.

Christian, Earnest and Gary A. Robbins. 2006. *The Private Sector Cost of $1 in Government Tax Revenue.* Center for Strategic Tax Reform, July 26, www.cstr.org/commentaries/taxreform/taxnotes-july2606.html.

Ellis, Richard E. 1973. The Political Economy of Thomas Jefferson. In *Thomas Jefferson, The Man, His World, His Influence,* ed. Lally Meymouth. New York, NY: G.P. Putnam's Sons.

Elmendorf, Doug. 2009. *Federal Budget Challenges.* Congressional Budget Office, April 20.

House Ways and Means Committee. 1993. *Fiscal Year 1994 Budget Reconciliation Recommendations.*" May 18.

IRS 2000. *Annual Report from the Commissioner of IRS on Tax Law Complexity.* Internal Revenue Service, June 5.

IRS. 2009. *Internal Revenue Data Book.* Internal Revenue Service, www.irs.gov/taxstats/article/0,,id=102174,00.html.

IRS Oversight Board. 2004. *2004 Report.* Internal Revenue Service, www.treas.gov/irsob/reports/2009/.

Joint Committee on Taxation. 2008. *List of Expiring Federal Tax Provisions, 2007-2020* (JCX-1-08). January 11, www.jct.gov/x-1-08.pdf.

McCumber, Porter J. 1913. *Congressional Record.* United States Senate, August 28.

Moody, J. Scott. 2006. Higher Taxes Lower Economic Performance. *Maine Issue Brief,* Maine Heritage Policy Center, September 19.

Morris, Richard B. 1957. *The Basic Ideas of Alexander Hamilton.* New York, NY: The Pocket Library, Pocket Books.

National Commission on Economic Growth and Tax Reform. 1996. *Unleashing America's Potential: A Pro-growth, Pro-family Tax System for the 21st Century.* January, w₋w w w . g a l e n . o r g / c o m p o n e n t , 8 / a c t i o n , show_content/id,7/news_id,3074/type,33/?_highlight=kemp.

National Commission on Restructuring the Internal Revenue Service. 1997. A Vision for a New IRS. June 25. www.house.gov/natcommirs/report1.pdf.

NTA. 2005. National Taxpayer Advocate. *Annual Report to Congress.*

NTA. 2008. National Taxpayer Advocate. *Annual Report to Congress.* Vol. 1, www.irs.gov/advocate/article/0,,id=97404,00.html.

Payne, James L. 1993. *Costly Returns: The Burdens of the U.S. Tax System.* Richmond, CA: Institute for Contemporary Studies.

Peterson, Shirley. 1992. Testimony to House Government Operations Committee. June 3.

Pilla, Daniel J. 1993. *How to Fire the IRS.* Stillwater, MN: Winning Publications.

Pilla, Daniel J. 1995. Why You Can't Trust the IRS. *Policy Analysis* No. 222, Cato Institute, April 15.

Pilla, Daniel J. 1997. How the IRS Tries to Make You Die Poor. *Pilla Talks Taxes.* S t i l l w a t e r ,   M N :   W i n n i n g   P u b l i c a t i o n s ,   M a y , www.taxhelponline.com/resources-and-publications/research-reports/die-poor.html.

Pilla, Daniel J. 2000. *Freedom to Prosper: Analyzing the Merits of Replacing Minnesota's Income Tax System with a Board-based Sales Tax.* Tax Freedom Institute, Inc., January, www.taxhelponline.com/resources-and-publications/research-reports/ freedom-to-prosper.html.

Pilla, Daniel J. 2001. A Monument of Deficient Wisdom: The Constitutional Conflict in the Federal Income Tax Law Enforcement. In *Road Map to Tax Reform Project.* Lewisville, TX: Institute for Policy Innovation, December, www.taxhelponline.com/ resources-and-publications/research-reports/constitutional-conflict-fed-tax-law.html.

President's Advisory Panel. 2005. *Simple, Fair and Pro-Growth: Proposals to Fix America's Tax System.* President's Advisory Panel on Federal Tax Reform, http://govinfo.library.unt.edu/taxreformpanel/final-report/index.html.

Rossotti, Charles O. 2000. Comments on Customer Service Employee Feedback Report. Internal Revenue Service, May 25.

Senate Finance Committee. 1993. Reconciliation Submissions of the Instructed Committees Pursuant to the Concurrent Resolution on the Budget. June 23.

Stanek, Steven. 2006. Lowest Business Tax States Have Best Economies: Study. *Budget & Tax News,* December, www.budgetandtax-news.org/article/20233.

Treasury Inspector General. 2001. Letter Report, 2001-40-077. May, www.treas.gov/tigta/index.shtml.

U.S. Treasury. 2007. *Reducing the Federal Tax Gap: A Report on Improving Voluntary Compliance.* August.

Vedder, Richard. 2001. *Taxes and Economic Growth.* Taxpayers Network Inc., September.

Wrightson, Margaret T. 1999. Small Business: Taxpayers Face Many Requirements. General Government Division, GAO/T-GGD-99-76, April 12.

Additional Resources

Additional information about tax policy is available from The Heartland Institute.

- *PolicyBot,* The Heartland Institute's free online clearinghouse for the work of other free-market think tanks, contains thousands of documents on tax policy issues. It is on Heartland's Web site at www.heartland.org.

- www.budgetandtax-news.org, a Web site devoted to the latest news and commentary about budget and tax issues, often addresses local, state, and federal tax policy issues. Read headlines, watch videos, or browse the thousands of documents on tax policy available from PolicyBot.

- *Budget & Tax News,* a monthly publication from The Heartland Institute. Available for free online at the Web sites described above, or subscribe to the print edition for $36 a year (ten issues).

Bruce Bartlett, a columnist for Forbes.com, the online side of *Forbes* magazine, blogs on a site called capitalgainsandgames.com. Under the title "Tax Reform Resources," he has assembled a list of links to studies, reports, and papers on all matters relating to tax reform. Material is organized by date and title, allowing one to read reports and studies dating back several years, at www.capitalgainsandgames.com/blog/bruce-bartlett/1273/tax-reform-resources

Another excellent source is the Center for Strategic Tax Reform, an organization whose purpose is to study, evaluate, and develop options for fundamentally restructuring the American tax system. Visit its Web site at www.cstr.org.

Directory

The following national organizations support sound tax policies. For a longer list, go to www.heartland.org, click on "Taxes" to go to the Budget & Tax News Web site, and see the Links list on that page.

Americans for Tax Reform Foundation, www.atr.org
American Legislative Exchange Council (ALEC), www.alec.org
Beacon Hill Institute, www.beaconhill.org
Cato Institute, www.cato.org
Center for Strategic Tax Reform, www.cstr.org
Council on State Taxation (COST), www.cost.org
Heartland Institute, www.heartland.org
Heritage Foundation, www.heritage.org
John Locke Foundation, www.johnlocke.org
Pacific Research Institute, www.pacificresearch.org
Small Business & Entrepreneurship Council (SBEC), www.sbecouncil.org/
Tax Foundation, www.taxfoundation.org
Tax Freedom Institute, www.taxfreedominstitute.com
Winning Publications, Inc., www.taxhelponline.com

Chapter 10
Higher Education Reform

Richard Vedder and Matthew Denhart

10 Principles of Higher Education Reform
1. Reduce third-party payments.
2. Fund students, not institutions.
3. Increase transparency.
4. Don't push college on everyone.
5. Promote lower-cost alternatives.
6. Emphasize instruction.
7. Restructure university ownership and governance.
8. Raise academic standards.
9. Measure institutional success by student performance.
10. Reduce barriers to entry and encourage accreditation reform.

Introduction

The dissemination and expansion of knowledge is important to the advancement of our civilization and our nation's economic productivity, yet the cost of that effort is considerable and rising dramatically. Better efficiency in delivering higher education would increase the nation's economic growth and living standards.

The United States spends more than $430 billion annually on various forms of post-secondary education – the equivalent of 3 percent of the nation's total economic output – triple the proportion of a half-century ago (Digest 2009a). This chapter offers innovative ways that higher education, also known as postsecondary education, could be reformed to improve outcomes and lower costs. "Postsecondary education" is defined rather broadly, referring to American degree-granting colleges and universities.

There is a widespread feeling that university training is important for economic success at the individual level as well as to the nation, yet increasing evidence suggests U.S. institutions of higher education are less efficient and decreasingly effective at creating the foundations for such success:

- The cost of obtaining a four-year degree has more than doubled since 1975 in inflation-adjusted dollars (Digest 2009c).

- Statistics from the 2003 National Assessment of Adult Literacy suggest college graduates have a lower level of reading comprehension than their counterparts of a decade ago (NAAL 2003).

- Although difficult to quantify, by any reasonable measure productivity in higher education is at best stagnant, and probably falling (Vedder 2004).

- The typical college student of today spends about 30 percent less time on academic pursuits than his or her counterpart of a half-century ago, as grade inflation makes it easier to seem to perform well with less work (Babcock and Marks 2010).

- Some 42 percent of all students enrolling in bachelor's degree programs full-time fail to earn a degree within six years (Digest 2009b).

- Falling teaching loads have led to a proliferation of articles published in obscure academic journals that few persons read (Bauerlein *et al.* 2010).

- Universities devote more of their budgets to non-instructional pursuits than previously, including swollen (and very well paid) bureaucracies, luxurious country club-like recreational facilities, and research that has low value outside the academic community.

- The effort to have everyone obtain a college degree has led to many workers becoming over-trained for the low-skill jobs they take after graduation.

- Students are burdened with excessive debt from college training, sometimes larger than can be sustained on their modest post-college incomes.

Can something be done to reverse these trends? Adherence to sound principles can lead to reforms of higher education that make it more affordable, more productive, more efficient, and more useful to society. Alternatives to existing modes of educational delivery can and are being developed, including training more appropriate for the aptitudes and interests of students. The ten principles that follow show how our higher education system can be restructured to provide a better education to Americans at a lower cost.

Recommended reading: Richard Vedder, *Going Broke by Degree: Why College Costs Too Much* (Washington, DC: AEI Press, 2004); Richard Vedder, "Over Invested and Over Priced," Center for College Affordability and Productivity, 2007.

1. Reduce third-party payments.

> Ending government subsidies to higher education and removing tax breaks for third-party subsidization would more directly align the costs of higher education to the benefits of those who attend.

When someone other than the customer is paying the bills, a producer has little incentive to cut costs or even make the customer happy. Consumers in such circumstances have little power over producers. This happens in both health care and in higher education. Customers pay some of the costs of education, but much is paid through government subsidies, loan programs, private gifts, and the like. Because of this reliance on third-party payments, spending on higher education has soared, just as it has on medical care.

Government and private subsidies to colleges are often justified on two grounds. First, it is argued that higher education is a "public good" that confers benefits not just on the individual educated but on the broader society as well. However, the empirical evidence relating to these positive spillover effects is murky at best, with some of it even suggesting government subsidies have an important negative spillover effect: lower rates of economic growth (Vedder 2004). Second, subsidy proponents contend higher education is a means to achieve the American Dream, to ensure that anyone, no matter their economic or family circumstances, can succeed in the United States. Yet here too the evidence that third-party payments have brought about educational equality is scant. Among all college students earning bachelor's degrees, the proportion of those from families in the bottom quartile of income has increased negligibly compared with 40 years ago, despite large increases in federal student aid in the form of Pell Grants and college loans (Mortenson 2009).

There is little doubt that, on average, college graduates benefit from having their degrees, with the earnings differential between college graduates and high school graduates averaging well over 60 percent since 1980 (O'Keefe and Vedder 2008). Given that higher education is a good investment for many, why not let students pay the costs, just as we do with other personal investments?

As state government budgets get squeezed by rising Medicaid, corrections, and other costs, many states are starting to resist new higher education spending. In fact, perhaps the time has come to begin to privatize some public universities. Institutions such as the universities of Colorado, Michigan, and Virginia now get 10 percent or less of their budgets from state appropriations (IPEDS 2008). Why not phase out the state subsidies altogether?

Another big subsidy is the tax breaks for those who give money to a college or university, even if the money goes to fund non-educational facilities such as stadium renovations or luxury dormitories. Removing this tax break and lowering tax rates for everyone is a more direct way to facilitate economic growth. Tax-incentivized private giving also has increased the resource gap between elite private and public colleges and contributes to rising costs through the "academic arms race" of schools spending ever-larger amounts of money to entice good students to attend.

As paradoxical as it may seem, the best thing taxpayers can do for higher education could be to stop funding it. A system that relied more on tuition and profits, and less on government subsidies and tax-advantaged charity, would be more efficient and more responsive to the needs of its customers.

Recommended reading: Richard Vedder, "Over Invested and Over Priced," Center for College Affordability and Productivity, 2007; Armen Alchian, "The Economic and Social Impact of Free Tuition," *New Individualist Review,* 1961.

2. Fund students, not institutions.

Giving subsidies directly to students would create much-needed competition among institutions, forcing them to be more conscious of student needs and budgets.

Government subsidies given directly to schools do not target assistance to those students needing support the most. Most third-party support for higher education, other than that explicitly targeted for research, assumes funds will be used to enhance the quality or reduce the cost of the undergraduate experience. Yet that assumption is often wrong. Undergraduate students are neglected at many institutions, particularly research universities, where the emphasis is on graduate and professional education and research (NSSE 2010). The proportion of resources going for undergraduate instruction has been on the decline (Delta 2009).

If subsidies were given directly to students, not schools, the balance of power would change. Students would gain the power to direct the subsidies to the schools that best serve their needs. Instead of going begging to state legislators, university presidents would have to pay more attention to the students themselves. Vouchers given to students can be limited to four years, creating incentives for students to graduate in a timely manner. They can be made progressive, allowing larger sums for poorer students and eliminating subsidies for students who would go to college without a grant. Bonuses can be given for excellent academic performance, and penalties assessed for poor performance.

The Pell Grant has some aspects of a voucher, but it suffers from major limitations. It rewards low-achieving students as much as good ones, instead of targeting funds to those most likely to succeed. It probably contributes to the rising completion time for those who graduate, and even to higher dropout rates by enticing students with little prospect for academic success to attend college (CCAP 2010). In addition, the funds are sent to schools for administration. It would empower students more if vouchers, usable only for higher education expenses, were made available directly to the students themselves – which would be easy to do in this era of modern computer technology (CCAP 2010).

A good voucher approach would allow students to attend institutions other than state-supported ones – traditional private schools, for-profit institutions, and specialized career colleges that offer certificates for learning specific skills rather than diplomas. Such vouchers thereby would enhance competition for students and make universities more dependent on revenues generated from consumers than from the political process.

Recommended reading: Milton Friedman, "The Role of Government in Education," Chapter 6 of *Capitalism and Freedom* (Chicago, IL: University of Chicago Press, 1962); Andrew Gillen, "Financial Aid in Theory and Practice," Center for College Affordability and Productivity, 2009.

3. Increase transparency.

Competition among providers requires transparency in gathering and reporting data on student performance, research output, and institutional finances.

It is impossible to make judgments about the value of a particular institution of higher education or college degree without good information on costs and performance. Did Harvard have a good year in 2010? Who knows? Do its senior students know more than its freshmen? Is the research of its humanities faculty read by many people, and has it materially improved our understanding of the human condition?

Do students graduating from Harvard get good jobs, and does that vary greatly by major? Does it cost more to educate a historian than a sociologist? How much time do students spend studying, as opposed to partying or other nonacademic pursuits? How much of the university's resources are used for Ph.D. training relative to undergraduate learning? How do its performance measures compare with five years ago, or with competing institutions such as Yale and Princeton?

By and large, the answers to questions like these are unknown, and that is as true at Slippery Rock State University or Montgomery Community College as at Harvard. And where schools do have this information, they typically guard it like a state secret, fearing that revealing it might show weaknesses of performance relative to comparable, competing institutions.

With only a few exceptions, all postsecondary institutions receive significant amounts of government or private philanthropic aid. Yet those subsidies are provided blindly, with taxpayers getting little information about how efficiently their hard-earned money is being used. Colleges often have information from instruments such as the National Survey of Student Engagement (NSSE 2010) or the Collegiate Learning Assessment (Collegiate n.d.) that provide valuable information on how students use their time or how much critical thinking skills they have obtained. This information is rarely shared with the public, however. Similarly, information on the postsecondary occupational success of students by institution is available – the Internal Revenue Service and Social Security Administration have it, for example – but it is either not compiled or just not published.

Likewise, there is a lack of precise information on faculty teaching loads, the salary and fringe benefits of key employees, the allocation of resources among undergraduate and graduate teaching and nonteaching activities. Extremely costly nonacademic facilities receive little evaluation on cost-benefit grounds. Princeton, for example, recently constructed Whitman College, a residential housing facility for 500 undergraduates, for a cost of $136 million. Meg Whitman received federal income tax deductions for her family's gift of $30 million for naming rights (Marks 2002).

States could readily obtain and publicly report performance and cost data on their institutions. Some institutions have started making some of this information available themselves. The University of Pennsylvania, for example, has an excellent alumni survey that details factors such as graduates' average salaries, how they landed their first jobs, and average salaries while on student internships (Matgouranis and Denhart 2010). Cornell University has a similar survey (Cornell 2010). However, these voluntary efforts are very limited, leaving students and the public with little useful outcomes-based information about higher education.

Given that they support public universities and community colleges, state governments have a responsibility to collect and report the data needed to hold higher education's leaders accountable for results. Simply supplying students and their parents with accurate outcomes information would force the state's colleges and universities to be more responsive to students. Students and their families who were really in charge of their spending on higher education increasingly would demand this information. In addition, making institutions directly accountable to students would allow the state to reduce its oversight role – thus saving taxpayer dollars and reducing government intrusion.

Recommended reading: Derek Bok, *Our Underachieving Colleges* (Princeton, NJ: Princeton University Press, 2006).

4. Don't push college on everyone.

Traditional four-year degrees are not the best option for everyone. Alternative postsecondary training programs may be suitable for many Americans.

A major effort of politicians from President Barack Obama on down at both the federal and state levels has been to increase college enrollments, arguing that the percentage of young adults with college degrees is lower in the U.S. than in many other nations (Obama 2010). It is argued that increases in college attendance will increase worker skill levels, "human capital," and the rate of economic growth.

This attempt to increase postsecondary enrollment has at least three major drawbacks. First, there are wide variations in human cognitive skills and motivation. Many of those who choose not to pursue postsecondary education do so for a perfectly rational reason: They consider it unlikely that they will succeed. Even among those already going to college, nearly half drop out, and others take longer to get a degree than anticipated (Digest 2009b). Expanding the pool of those entering college also will increase the number of college dropouts.

Second, as greater numbers of less academically qualified persons enter college, remedial education costs will rise and the standards of rigor will decline in order to maintain respectable graduation rates. Data already show declining literacy skills among the nation's college students (NAAL 2003).

Third, Bureau of Labor Statistics job projections suggest most new jobs created over the next decade will *not* require skills acquired in traditional college or university programs (Occupations 2010). For example, some 461,000 new home health aides, 375,000 new retail salespersons, and 233,000 new truck drivers will be needed by 2018; those are skills best learned mostly on the job or in specialized postsecondary career schools, not through a college degree program (Occupations 2010).

The United States is beginning to accumulate large numbers of college-educated people who perform jobs for which they are overqualified. Currently, more than 13 percent of the nation's parking lot attendants and more than 14 percent of our hotel clerks have at least a bachelor's degree (Occupation Profiles 2010). "Credential inflation" has led many people to pursue degrees to try to stay ahead of other applicants, even though the jobs do not require such training (Vedder *et al.* 2010).

The use of post-secondary education vouchers would provide greater incentives for students to attend nontraditional schools such as for-profit schools, including those offering short (perhaps six months) training in skills such as truck driving or plumbing. For many, a six-month course in learning how to drive large semi-trailer trucks is likely to have a bigger payoff than a four-year course resulting in a bachelor's degree in, say, sociology. Less debt is incurred, the probability of successfully completing the program is greater, and the postgraduate earnings are likely to compare favorably with the four-year college alternative.

Recommended reading: Charles Murray, *Real Education: Four Simple Truths for Bringing America's Schools Back to Reality* (New York, NY: Crown Forum, 2008); Richard Vedder, "From Wall Street to Wal-Mart: Why College Graduates Are Not Getting Good Jobs," Center for College Affordability and Productivity, 2010.

5. Promote lower-cost alternatives.

Traditional four-year institutions are expensive. Students can obtain quality degrees at a lower cost by exploring alternatives.

Higher education costs per student are higher in the United States than in any other major country. Within the United States, some students are educated for less than $10,000 a year annually, whereas for others costs in excess of $100,000 are commonplace (IPEDS 2008). Public policy has actually provided more subsidies and recognition to the high-priced schools (elite private institutions and flagship public research universities) than to others (Digest 2009d).

In addition, accreditation proves a major barrier to entry to for-profit firms and other less-expensive alternatives (see Principle 10 below). On top of that, proposed federal regulations would require government regulators in each state to approve online instruction within the state. Yet there is evidence that online education very often is better than traditional classroom instruction (U.S. Dept. of Education 2009). Private online programs cost state governments nothing at all and would cost relatively little under a voucher plan.

Some of the proposals discussed above (reduction in third-party payments, the use of student vouchers) could help reduce the excessive public investment in exceedingly costly schools. States giving vouchers might make them usable only at relatively lower-cost community colleges and proprietary institutions for students whose academic profile suggests a high probability of academic failure in four-year schools. This would reduce the financial exposure of taxpayers in cases where students fail to take advantage of the academic resources provided them. Students completing courses with a satisfactory academic record at, say, community colleges could then receive vouchers for an additional two years at a four-year university.

States moving to student-centered funding of higher education might consider funding Higher Education Investment Accounts for eligible students. For example, each student who performs satisfactorily could withdraw up to $20,000 over a lifetime, at a rate not to exceed $5,000 a year, from his or her account. Those attending a community college that costs $3,500 in tuition for two years and then for two more years at a four-year school costing $6,000 annually would need a total of $19,000. The program could allow them to keep all or a portion of the amount below $20,000 after graduation, giving students an incentive to attend low-cost schools and finish their studies.

The greatest inefficiencies today arise from the various federal financial assistance programs. The negative unintended consequences of such programs cancel out any contributions they may be making toward their ostensible objective: more access to higher education among lower-income Americans (Gillen 2009). Pell Grant recipients who attend a low-cost community college may receive a grant of, say, $2,500, but would get $5,000 if they attended an expensive school, giving them a strong incentive to opt for higher-priced institutions. Student loans are even worse in this regard, with the size of the loan (and the implicit government subsidy) directly proportional to school costs.

A strong case can be made that the current federal program should be eliminated entirely. Despite their proponents' stated intentions of making college more affordable, existing federal financial aid programs have contributed significantly to the higher education cost explosion in recent decades (Vedder 2004).

If eliminating federal financial aid programs is politically infeasible, the Pell Grant at least should be converted into a fixed-sum voucher. The amount of this voucher should not vary depending on the tuition price of an institution, and therefore would give recipients an incentive to choose lower-cost alternatives instead of expensive four-year universities or liberal arts colleges.

Recommended reading: "25 Ways to Reduce the Cost of College," Center for College Affordability and Productivity, 2010; Richard Vedder, *Going Broke by Degree: Why College Costs Too Much* (Washington, DC: AEI Press, 2004).

6. Emphasize instruction.

Costs will continue to rise until frivolous activities subside in favor of a tighter focus on undergraduate instruction.

Most comprehensive universities, and even some liberal arts colleges, engage in many activities unrelated to the academic enterprise. They operate restaurant and lodging operations, conference centers, hospitals, entertainment enterprises (notably intercollegiate athletics), and recreational facilities such as golf courses and weight/conditioning operations, etc.

These ventures have very little to do with the twin goals of any university: the dissemination (teaching) and production (research) of knowledge. On average, universities are not as effective and efficient as private restaurant and lodging companies at food and housing services. To their credit, many schools have outsourced these activities. But they could, and usually should, outsource building maintenance, the teaching of remedial courses, the running of hospitals, and myriad other things they now do (CCAP 2010).

Also, much of the so-called "research" done by higher education institutions is of dubious value. A significant decline in teaching loads has occurred over time to allow time for more "research," and the number of academic journals has multiplied several-fold (Vedder 2004). As a consequence, diminishing returns to research have set in: More than 35,000 articles have been written about William Shakespeare since 1950; have the last 34,000 of those articles really added much to our understanding of either Shakespeare or the advance of Western civilization (Bauerlein 2010)? Weren't 1,000 articles enough?

Research should be subject to cost-benefit scrutiny, and that examination almost certainly would lead to some increase in teaching loads, allowing for a reduction in college costs (fewer faculty members would be needed to provide any given amount of instruction). Having aid money follow the student instead of being given directly to institutions would help ensure that such research would be concentrated on areas that enhance learning and increase the educational value to the students instead of merely being conducted for the professional advancement of college professors.

A special issue is intercollegiate athletics. Some would argue it has contributed to the downplaying of academics. One school recently cancelled classes for two days to be sure all students could attend the school's football bowl game (Low 2010). Other legitimate issues include the overpaying of coaches and the underpaying of student athletes (Vedder and Denhart 2009).

Those issues aside, intercollegiate athletics are increasingly a financial burden, particularly on schools with aspirations of being athletic powers but without much commercial appeal – there are many schools where athletic subsidies absorb 10 percent or more of state appropriations or, alternatively, of tuition and fees (Denhart and Vedder 2010). The athletic cartel (the National Collegiate Athletic Association, or NCAA) has worked to raise costs. Federal government policy treating gifts to intercollegiate athletics as a charitable, tax-deductible contribution has condoned and abetted the intercollegiate athletics "arms race."

It is time now for a new, collective effort to contain exploding athletic costs, perhaps by ending the tax-deductibility of gifts earmarked for athletic programs, divesting commercial sports from university operations, or by multiuniversity agreements to contain costs and redirect commercial sports revenues to core academic activities. In any case, government budget and tax policies should be changed to stop encouraging the waste of resources on intercollegiate athletics.

Recommended reading: Harry Lewis, "Excellence Without a Soul: How a Great University Forgot Education," *Public Affairs,* 2006; Richard Arum and Josipa Roksa, *Academically Adrift: Limited Learning on College Campuses* (Chicago, IL: University of Chicago Press, 2011); Andrew Hacker and Claudia Dreifus, *Higher Education?* (New York, NY: Times Books, 2010).

7. Restructure university ownership and governance.

> University management structures need to be simplified, which can be encouraged through student-centered aid and the consequent emphasis on delivering real educational value.

Most American universities are organized on a management model developed in the Middle Ages and essentially unchanged for more than a century. It is not clear at all who "owns" the university and who has the right to govern it. This vagueness leads to costly, often delayed, and timid decision-making (Vedder 2004). Bold innovations are stifled by the politics associated with operation by committees containing members of all interested groups.

At a typical university, the president raises funds to placate the needs of the faculty (high salaries, low teaching loads, good parking), students (decent housing, low work expectations, plenty of free time, and easy access to recreational facilities), alumni (good football and basketball teams, a nice alumni/conference center), senior administrators (high pay and perks such as international travel, a fancy office, and lots of assistants to do the heavy lifting), trustees (nice perks, luxurious facilities for meetings, appearances of institutional success), etc. The president is not an entrepreneur but instead a person who cajoles funds from third parties to pay what economists call the "economic rents" (payments beyond what is necessary to provide the service) to all those who could create trouble.

"Shared governance" is much revered by faculty, but it adds vastly to administrative costs and stifles innovation and change. Shared governance is a byproduct of academic tenure, where faculty members with lifetime appointments face little consequence from trying, often successfully, to obstruct changes that might reduce their power or influence or increase their teaching load. Most university decisions are made by committee, and implicitly various interest groups represented on the committees usually have some limited sort of veto power, forcing compromises that are often costly (adding faculty in department A as a condition of approving new programs for department B) and illogical on any rational cost-benefit ground.

One promising development, however, can reduce the governance problem: market-based higher education. For-profit colleges are growing rapidly, gaining market share to the point that in some cases they are forcing traditional universities to at least partially abandon the inefficiencies of the current management model (Bennett *et al.* 2010). Institutions such as Apollo Corp. (University of Phoenix), Kaplan Higher Education, Bridgepoint Education, and other companies have clearly defined ownership and management. Institutional priorities are concentrated on improving the bottom line (profits, perhaps stock price or market share), something traditional schools do not do as there is no clearly defined bottom line (Bennett *et al.* 2010). Removing barriers to the spread of market-based education and letting that sector absorb future enrollment increases would reduce the ownership/governance problem discussed above.

The for-profit higher education industry has recently been demonized by a federal investigation that has questioned the large debts accrued by students and their lackluster graduation and loan repayment rates. Such criticisms may be warranted, but the investigation has missed the larger point: *all* postsecondary institutions should be accountable on these issues, and in many cases traditional nonprofit institutions are worse offenders than the for-profits.

Recommended reading: Robert Zemsky, *Making Reform Work: The Case for Transforming American Higher Education* (Chapel Hill, NC: Rutgers University Press, 2009); Daniel L. Bennett *et al.*, "For-Profit Higher Education: Growth, Innovation, and Regulation," Center for College Affordability and Productivity, 2010.

8. Raise academic standards.

> Low standards and grade inflation are damaging the educational quality of U.S. higher education institutions and creating a culture of mediocrity.

Today's college students, on average, learn less than those of preceding generations. In part this is a consequence of a dysfunctional and costly system of government primary and secondary schools, but partly it is a result of the low academic standards of many colleges.

The U.S. Department of Education's Adult Literacy Survey shows declining literacy among college graduates (NAAL 2003). The Intercollegiate Studies Institute Survey of Civic Knowledge suggests seniors typically know little more than freshmen about basic facts and principles concerning our economy, government, and historical evolution (American Civic 2010). Data from time use surveys show students today typically study vastly less than their counterparts of a half-century ago (Babcock and Marks 2010).

An analysis of data about more than 2,300 undergraduates at 24 institutions found 36 percent experienced no significant improvement in learning over four years of schooling; more than 45 percent showed no significant improvement in a range of skills such as critical thinking, complex reasoning, and writing during their first two years of college (Arum and Roksa 2011). Scholarship from earlier decades also suggests there has been a sharp decline in both academic work effort and learning.

The Washington Post (Washington Post 2005) reported far fewer students "are leaving higher education with the skills needed to comprehend routine data, such as reading a table about the relationship between blood pressure and physical activity, according to the federal study conducted by the National Center for Education Statistics." In 2008 the National Survey of Student Engagement found 43 percent of U.S. higher education students spent ten hours or less per week "preparing for class (studying, reading, writing, doing homework or lab work, analyzing data, rehearsing, and other academic activities)." Seventeen percent spent *five* hours a week or less, and half of all college seniors have never written a paper 20 pages or longer while in college (NSSE 2008).

The "What Will They Learn?" project of the American Council of

Trustees and Alumni extensively documents the watering-down of general education requirements at U.S. colleges and universities. According to the project's Web site, "While most colleges today claim they are providing a strong core curriculum, in fact, they do so in name only. Instead of a limited number of courses, broad-based in focus, institutions now typically demand that students take courses in several wide subject areas – the so-called distribution requirements." (ACTA n.d.)

Better academic performance, as measured by grades, is associated with greater postgraduate earnings (Stinebrickner and Stinebrickner 2008). However, grade inflation has reduced college work effort and almost certainly learning (Babcock and Marks 2010). Accordingly, it would not be overly intrusive for governments to deny vouchers to students attending institutions where the aggregate undergraduate grade point average is greater than, say 3.00, and perhaps allow only a half-voucher for schools where the average GPA is between 2.80 and 2.99. Using the voucher amount to create incentives for the reintroduction of more rigorous curricula, grading standards, and core education requirements probably would help improve overall academic performance by U.S. higher education institutions.

Holding colleges accountable for maintaining high standards is difficult, largely because of the lack of transparency and failure to measure academic progress discussed earlier. For that reason, value-added measures of academic performance are needed, and third-party financial support should be dependent on demonstration that colleges are positively adding to the learning, critical thinking skills, or other desired qualities expected in a college graduate. The standards movement within K-12 education led to some improvement in learning outcomes, a lesson that could be learned profitably by universities.

Recommended reading: Philip Babcock and Mindy Marks, "Leisure College, USA: The Decline in Student Study Time," American Enterprise Institute, 2010; Richard Hersch and John Merrow, *Declining by Degrees: Higher Education at Risk* (New York, NY: Palgrave Macmillan, 2005); "Literacy of College Graduates Is on Decline," *Washington Post*, December 25, 2005; Philip Babcock, "Real costs of nominal grade inflation? New evidence from student course evaluations," *Economic Inquiry*, 48, 2010.

9. Measure institutional success by student performance.

Introducing market principles will provide incentives for faculty and administration to concentrate on making students' financial investments pay off.

The private business sector has achieved productivity growth averaging 2 percent per year ever since 1870. An important reason is that the private business sector is disciplined by market forces. Reducing costs and improving product quality enhances profits, and thereby stock prices, employee bonuses, the value of stock options, etc. Being efficient increases the income and wealth of managers and key employees, as does improving the quality of the product offered to consumers.

Those market incentives are muted or totally absent in higher education. A typical department chairman of a university wants to increase his budget. That typically increases the cost per unit of outcomes delivered. There are few or no incentives to cut costs. Classrooms are poorly utilized because there are no incentives to use them during less-desirable times (early mornings, late in the afternoon, evenings, Fridays, or in the summer). Professors continue to teach unpopular courses that they like, rather than what students want. Administrative staffs are decreasing at large corporations but increasing in universities, because the latter have few incentives to economize (Bennett 2009).

Market principles can be introduced more extensively into the academy, and government aid should encourage this. One method of introducing market forces is the outsourcing of services to competitive private companies. In addition, universities can introduce internal markets by, for example, renting space to departments, with rental prices set to encourage non-peak use. Tuition charges can be made to vary by the costs of instruction and the popularity of course offerings. Courses taken in the evening or on weekends can be priced lower than those taken in prime-time from Monday through Thursday.

More radically, colleges could adopt the professorial compensation model praised by Adam Smith in 1776, in which students directly pay professors (who in turn remit some of the funds to the university for administrative, academic support, and facility services), so that instructor compensation increases with the number of students taught and the popularity of the instruction. Alternatively, colleges could contract with groups of professors operating private firms to provide instructional services, instead of paying salaried professors individually.

Students who do well academically are already rewarded by merit scholarships, but the more aggressive tying of student financial assistance to student performance is a means of reducing dropouts and lengthy periods to degree completion. This is very easily done with a voucher program, which can use financial incentives to promote worthwhile goals such as timely graduation or good academic performance.

Recommended reading: "25 Ways to Reduce the Cost of College," Center for College Affordability and Productivity, 2010.

10. Reduce barriers to entry and encourage accreditation reform.

Reforming the accreditation system would allow more competitors to enter the higher education market by reducing barriers to entry.

Starting a college or university is not easy, especially given state and federal government obstacles to entry into the higher education business. Most important, students cannot get federal loans or grants to attend non-accredited schools.

The key problem is that accreditation tends to be based on inputs – spending money – instead of outputs – the demonstrated proof that students are actually receiving a beneficial education. The cost of meeting accreditation standards is often very high, measured in millions of dollars (Gillen *et al.* 2010). Small entrepreneurs are frozen out of competition, which reduces incentives for efficiency in the system. In addition to accreditation rules, many states require schools to get approval from state governments in order to be licensed to operate. For online companies operating in all 50 states, these costs can amount to millions of dollars.

What is the point of these regulatory barriers? "Accreditation" serves as an informational and quality control device: It endorses a school as being of decent quality and financially responsible, not a diploma mill offering nothing in return for tuition payments. Yet are accrediting agencies really needed for that? People buy all kinds of big-ticket items that are not "accredited," including houses, cars, and expensive electronic devices. Magazines or agencies such as *Consumers Report* or J.D. Powers and Associates help consumers assess the quality of products and services offered for sale. There is no huge problem with unscrupulous or unreliable auto manufacturers. Some currently available consumer protection devices, such as bonding requirements, probably could provide some of the safeguards expected of accreditation.

As stated earlier, a reliable, easy to use, and relatively uniform system of data on both the performance and financial conditions of undergraduate institutions could go a long way toward doing the job of accreditation. No large school, to our knowledge, ever lost accreditation on the basis of poor academic quality. The accreditation label thus says very little about the quality of an institution, yet accreditation often is costly to obtain because schools have to meet costly input-based criteria (for example, a certain percent of the faculty possessing Ph.D. or other terminal degrees) (Gillen *et al.* 2010). While reformers are calling for accrediting agencies to emphasize outcomes and not inputs, that goal has not been fully realized.

Continued third-party financial payments to institutions to cover instructional costs are of dubious value. But if such payments are going to occur, they should be related to aggregate student outcomes, such as the income and job prospects of graduates, or the proportion of graduating students scoring well on the Graduate Record Exam (GRE), Critical Learning Assessment, or some other instrument. Colleges and other institutions should compete to achieve these outputs and be rewarded if they succeed, without the formality of accreditation getting in the way.

Recommended reading: Andrew Gillen *et al.*, "The Inmates Running the Asylum? An Analysis of Higher Education Accreditation," Center for College Affordability and Productivity, 2010; Anne Neal, "Dis-Accreditation," *Academic Questions*, 2008; George Leef and Roxana Burris, "Can College Accreditation Live Up to Its Promise?" American Council of Trustees and Alumni, 2002.

Conclusion

Higher education has been notoriously resistant to reform. Tenured faculty bitterly resist major changes, and they often have the power to veto them. University presidents wanting a peaceful and successful career engage in large-scale spending to placate various constituencies. Decisions are made slowly and timidly, and innovation is discouraged. As a result of these impediments to change, calls for reform usually are just that: calls or pleas, nothing that results in tangible constructive action.

Yet there are reasons to believe that financial pressures could begin to force bold action. Those financial pressures are on governments as well as universities themselves. The political resistance to change, in the political arena generally and within universities, is more vulnerable than usual.

In the short run, the aftermath of the financial crisis of 2008 and accompanying recession have left both governments and universities weakened. Most state governments face huge potential budget deficits, making them eager to cut costs. For the longer term, the aging of the population and soaring health care costs are causing huge fiscal pressures at both the federal (the precarious financial shape of Social Security and Medicare) and the state (soaring Medicaid costs) levels. The current budget deficits are unsustainable, meaning federal fiscal constraint is likely to be reestablished to some degree in the near future. A reduction of government third-party payments to higher education seems more feasible than usually would be the case.

Cheerleaders for higher education who argue that expanding universities is vital to our nation's economic vitality are exaggerating and overstating their point. It is true that well-educated persons are important human resources in a sophisticated, advanced economy and that innovation based on research is needed for economic growth. However, the evidence shows the nation's higher education institutions are not turning out well-educated persons. We spend hundreds of billions of dollars on universities every year, so making more efficient use of those resources should be a significant national goal. Implementing the ten reforms discussed here is a necessary, if not sufficient, step toward achieving that goal.

References

Alchian, Armen. 1961. The economic and social impact of free tuition. *New Individualist Review.*

American Civic Literacy. 2010. *Civic Literacy Report – Major Findings.* Intercollegiate Studies Institute. www.americancivicliteracy.org/2010/major_findings_finding1.htm.

American Council of Trustees and Alumni. n.d. FAQ: My college says it has a good curriculum; why is its grade low? http://whatwilltheylearn.com/faq#My-college. Last visited February 22, 2011.

Arum, Richard and Josipa Roksa. 2011. *Academically Adrift: Limited Learning on College Campuses.* Chicago, IL: University of Chicago Press.

Babcock, Philip and Mindy Marks. 2010. *Leisure College, USA: The Decline in Student Study Time.* American Enterprise Institute. www.aei.org/outlook/100980.

Bauerlein, Mark, Mohamed Gad-el-Hak, Wayne Grody, Bill McKelvey, and Stanley W. Trimble. 2010. We must stop the avalanche of low-quality research. *The Chronicle of Higher Education.* chronicle.com/article/We-Must-Stop-the-Avalanche-of/65890/.

Bauerlein, Mark. 2010. Diminishing returns in humanities research. *The Chronicle of Higher Education.* chronicle.com/article/Diminishing-Returns-in/47107/.

Bennett, Daniel L., Adam R. Lucchesi, and Richard K. Vedder. 2010. *For-Profit Higher Education: Growth, Innovation and Regulation.* Center for College Affordability and Productivity. www.centerforcollegeaffordability.org/uploads/ForProfit_HigherEd.pdf.

Bennett, Daniel L., 2009. *Trends in the Higher Education Labor Force: Identifying Changes in Worker Composition and Productivity.* Center for College Affordability and Productivity. www.centerforcollegeaffordability.org/uploads/Trends_LaborForce.pdf.

Bok, Derek. 2006. *Our Underachieving Colleges.* Princeton, NJ: Princeton University Press.

Center for College Affordability and Productivity (CCAP). 2010. 25 ways to reduce the cost of college. centerforcollegeaffordability.org/uploads/25Ways_to_Reduce_the_Cost_of_College.pdf.

Cornell University. 2010. *Cornell Post Graduate Survey Results.* Cornell Career Services. www.career.cornell.edu/surveysAndSalary/postgrad.html.

Collegiate Learning Assessment. n.d. *CLA: Returning to Learning.* Council for Aid to Education. www.collegiatelearningassessment.org/.

Delta Cost Project. 2009. *Trends in College Spending.*
www.deltacostproject.org/resources/pdf/trends_in_spending-report.pdf.

Denhart, Matthew and Richard Vedder. 2010. *Intercollegiate Athletics Subsidies: A Regressive Tax.* Center for College Affordability and Productivity.
www.centerforcollegeaffordability.org/uploads/ICA_Subsidies_RegressiveTax.pdf.

Digest of Education Statistics. 2009a. Table 26. Expenditures of educational institutions related to the gross domestic product, by level of institution: Selected years, 1929-30 through 2008-09. National Center for Education Statistics.
nces.ed.gov/programs/digest/d09/tables/dt09_026.asp?referrer=list.

Digest of Education Statistics. 2009b. Table 331. Graduation rates of first-time postsecondary students who started as full-time degree-seeking students, by sex, race/ethnicity, time between starting and graduating, and level and control of institution where student started: Selected cohort entry years, 1996 through 2004. National Center for Education Statistics.
nces.ed.gov/programs/digest/d09/tables/dt09_331.asp?referrer=list.

Digest of Education Statistics. 2009c. Table 334. Average undergraduate tuition and fees and room and board rates charged for full-time students in degree-granting institutions, by type and control of institution: 1964-65 through 2008-09. National Center for Education Statistics. nces.ed.gov/programs/digest/d09/tables/dt09_334.asp?referrer=list.

Digest of Education Statistics. 2009d. Table 359. Revenue received from the federal government by the 120 degree-granting institutions receiving the largest amounts, by control and rank order: 2006-07. National Center for Education Statistics.
nces.ed.gov/programs/digest/d09/tables/dt09_359.asp?referrer=list.

Friedman, Milton. 1962. The role of government in education. *Capitalism and Freedom.* Chicago, IL: University of Chicago Press.

Gillen, Andrew. 2009. *Student Financial Aid in Theory and Practice: Why It Is Ineffective and What Can Be Done About It.* Center for College Affordability and Productivity. www.centerforcollegeaffordability.org/uploads/
Financial_Aid_in_Theory_and_Practice(1).pdf.

Gillen, Andrew, Daniel L Bennett, and Richard Vedder. 2010. *The Inmates Running the Asylum? An Analysis of Higher Education Accreditation.* Center for College Affordability and Productivity. www.centerforcollegeaffordability.org/uploads/
Accreditation.pdf.

Hacker, Andrew and Claudia Dreifus. 2010. *Higher Education?* New York, NY: Times Books.

Hersch, Richard and John Merrow. 2005. *Declining by Degrees: Higher Education at Risk.* New York, NY: Palgrave Macmillan.

Integrated Post Secondary Education Data System (IPEDS). 2008. National Center for Education Statistics. nces.ed.gov/ipeds/datacenter/.

Leef, George and Roxana Burris. 2002. *Can College Accreditation Live Up to Its Promise?* American Council of Trustees and Alumni.

Lewis, Harry. 2006. Excellence without a soul: How a great university forgot education. *Public Affairs*.

Low, Chris. 2010. Alabama cancels classes during title game. ESPN: The Worldwide Leader in Sports. espn.go.com/blog/sec/post/_/id/7075/alabama-cancels-classes-during-title-game.

Marks, Marilyn. 2002. Meg Whitman to support new residential college at Princeton. Princeton University. www.princeton.edu/pr/news/02/q1/0204-whitman.htm.

Matgouranis, Christopher and Matthew Denhart. 2010. Ignorance is not bliss. *Forbes*. www.forbes.com/2010/08/18/higher-education-rankings-college-opinions-contributors-denhart-matgouranis.html.

Mortenson, Tom. 2009. Higher education equity indices for students from bottom family income quartile, 1970 to 2007. *Postsecondary Education Opportunity*. www.postsecondary.org/topicslist.asp?page=1&od=&search=Demographics.

Murray, Charles. 2008. *Real Education: Four Simple Truths for Bringing America's Schools Back to Reality.* New York, NY: Crown Forum.

National Assessment of Adult Literacy (NAAL). 2003. National Center for Education Statistics. nces.ed.gov/naal/kf_dem_edu.asp.

National Survey of Student Engagement (NSSE). 2010. nsse.iub.edu/.

Neal, Anne. 2008. Dis-accreditation. *Academic Questions*.

Obama, Barack. 2010. Making college more affordable. The White House. www.whitehouse.gov/issues/education/higher-education.

Occupation Profiles – Descriptions, Earnings, Outlook. 2010. Careers.org. occupations.careers.org/.

Occupations with the Largest Job Growth. 2010. U.S. Bureau of Labor Statistics, U.S. Department of Labor. www.bls.gov/emp/ep_table_104.htm.

O'Keefe, Bryan and Richard Vedder. 2008. *Griggs v. Duke Power*: Implications for college credentialing. John William Pope Center for Higher Education Policy. www.centerforcollegeaffordability.org/uploads/Griggs_vs_Duke_Power(1).pdf.

Stinebrickner, Ralph and Todd R. Stinebrickner. 2008. The causal effect of studying on academic performance. *The B.E. Journal of Economic Analysis & Policy,* Vol. 8.1. www.bepress.com/bejeap/vol8/iss1/art14.

U.S. Department of Education. 2009. *Evaluation of Evidence-Based Practices in Online Learning: A Meta-Analysis and Review of Online Learning Studies.* Office of Planning, Evaluation, and Policy Development, Washington, DC.

Vedder, Richard. 2004. *Going Broke by Degree: Why College Costs Too Much.* Washington, DC: AEI Press.

Vedder, Richard, and Matthew Denhart. 2009. The real March madness. *The Wall Street Journal.* online.wsj.com/article/SB123751289953291279.html.

Vedder, Richard *et al.* 2010. *From Wall Street to Wal-Mart: Why College Graduates Are Not Getting Good Jobs.* Center for College Affordability and Productivity. www.centerforcollegeaffordability.org/uploads/From_Wall_Street_to_Wal-Mart.pdf.

Washington Post. 2005. Literacy of college graduates is on decline. December 25.

Zemsky, Robert. 2009. *Making Reform Work: The Case for Transforming American Higher Education.* Chapel Hill, NC: Rutgers University Press.

Additional Resources

- *PolicyBot*, The Heartland Institute's free online clearinghouse for the work of other free-market think tanks, contains thousands of documents on higher education issues. It is on Heartland's Web site at www.heartland.org.

- *www.schoolreform-news.org*, a Web site devoted to the latest news and commentary about education policy issues, including higher education reform. Read headlines, watch videos, or join the conversation using Twitter or Facebook.

- *School Reform News*, a monthly publication from The Heartland Institute, focuses on elementary and secondary education but at times addresses higher education. Subscribe online at www.heartland.org.

Directory

The following national organizations support higher education reform and are good sources of additional research and commentary on this issue.

American Legislative Exchange Council, www.alec.org
American Enterprise Institute, www.aei.org
American Council of Trustees and Alumni, www.goacta.org
Cato Institute, www.cato.org
Education Sector, www.educationsector.org
Foundation for Individual Rights in Education, www.thefire.org
Intercollegiate Studies Institute, www.isi.org
John William Pope Center for Higher Education Policy,
     www.popecenter.org
Manhattan Institute Center for the American University,
     www.manhattan-institute.org/html/veritas_fund.htm
National Association of Scholars, www.nas.org

About the Authors

Joseph L. Bast is president of The Heartland Institute and coauthor or editor of 14 books, including *Rebuilding America's Schools* (1990), *Why We Spend Too Much on Health Care* (1992), *Eco-Sanity: A Common-Sense Guide to Environmentalism* (1994), *Education & Capitalism* (2003), and *Climate Change Reconsidered* (2009). His writing has appeared in *Phi Delta Kappan, Economics of Education Review, Wall Street Journal, Investor's Business Daily, The Cato Journal, USA Today*, and many of the country's largest-circulation newspapers. He is publisher of six monthly newspapers: *Budget & Tax News; Environment & Climate News*; *Finance, Insurance, and Real Estate News; Health Care News, InfoTech & Telecom News*; and *School Reform News*.

Matthew Denhart is administrative director of the Center for College Affordability and Productivity, where he has authored several studies examining trends in American higher education. His research has been discussed widely by publications including *The Wall Street Journal, USA Today, The Chronicle of Higher Education, Inside Higher Education*, and *Forbes*. Denhart holds a BA degree from Ohio University in economics and political science.

George Gilder is chairman of Gilder Group, Inc. and a senior fellow at Seattle's Discovery Institute, where he directs Discovery's program on high technology and democracy. Gilder is a contributing editor at *Forbes*, a frequent writer for major business publications, and the author of many books on society, politics, and economics. He wrote the classic *Wealth and Poverty* (1981), a book widely credited with setting the free-market agenda for the Reagan era. Other books include *Microcosm* (1989), *Life After Television* (1990), *Telecosm* (2000), *The Silicon Eye* (2005) and *The Israel Test* (2008).

Leonard Gilroy is a certified urban planner and director of government reform at Reason Foundation. He has worked closely with legislators and elected officials in Texas, Arizona, Louisiana, Utah, Virginia, California, and several other states in efforts to design and implement market-based policy approaches, improve government performance, enhance accountability in government programs, and reduce government spending. Since early 2009, Gilroy has led Reason's partnership with the administration of Louisiana Gov. Bobby Jindal to research and develop a range of privatization opportunities within the Louisiana Division of Administration and develop a statewide privatization program. Gilroy also served as an advisor to Virginia Gov. Bob McDonnell's transition team on budget and government reform issues.

Matthew Glans is director of the Midwest office of the Center on Finance, Insurance, and Real Estate (FIRE) at The Heartland Institute. His responsibilities include interacting with elected officials and staff on insurance and finance issues; tracking new legislation; and drafting responses to emerging issues via talking points, news releases, and op-ed pieces. He previously worked for the Illinois Department of Healthcare and Family Services in its legislative affairs office in Springfield and as a Congressional Intern in the office of U.S. Representative Henry Hyde. Glans earned a Master's degree in political studies from the University of Illinois at Springfield and a B.A. in political science from Bradley University.

Hance Haney is director and senior fellow of the Technology & Democracy Project at the Discovery Institute, in Washington, DC. He spent ten years as an aide to former Senator Bob Packwood (OR) and advised him in his capacity as chairman of the Senate Communications Subcommittee during the deliberations leading to the Telecommunications Act of 1996. He subsequently held various positions with the United States Telecom Association and Qwest Communications. He earned a B.A. in history from Willamette University and a J.D. from Lewis and Clark Law School in Portland, Oregon.

Eli Lehrer is a senior fellow and national director of the Center on Finance, Insurance, and Real Estate at The Heartland Institute. He oversees offices in Chicago, Washington, DC, Tallahassee, and Austin, addressing issues relating to insurance, risk, and credit markets. Lehrer also played a major role in founding the smartersafer.org coalition, a coalition of taxpayer, environmental, insurance, and free-market groups dedicated to risk-based insurance rates, mitigation, and environmental protection. Prior to joining Heartland, Lehrer worked as speechwriter to United States Senate Majority Leader Bill Frist (R-TN), manager in the Unisys Corporation's Homeland Security Practice, senior editor of *The American Enterprise* magazine, and fellow for The Heritage Foundation. He holds a B.A. (cum laude) from Cornell University and an M.A. (with honors) from The Johns Hopkins University.

Adrian Moore is vice president of research at Reason Foundation, where he oversees policy research and conducts his own research on topics such as privatization and regulatory reform. He has testified before Congress on several occasions and regularly advises federal, state, and local officials on ways to streamline government and reduce costs. In 2008 and 2009, Moore served on Congress' National Surface Transportation Infrastructure Financing Commission. He is co-author of *Mobility First: A New Vision for Transportation in a Globally Competitive 21st Century* (2008) and *Curb Rights: A Foundation for Free Enterprise in Urban Transit* (1997). In 2002, Moore was awarded a World Outsourcing Achievement Award by PricewaterhouseCoopers and Michael F. Corbett & Associates Ltd. for his work showing governments how to use public-private partnerships and the private sector to save taxpayer money and improve the efficiency of their agencies.

Daniel J. Pilla is a tax litigation consultant and executive director of the Tax Freedom Institute, a national association of tax professionals. He is admitted to practice before the United States Tax Court. He is the author of 11 books, hundreds of articles, and dozens of research reports on IRS problems resolution and taxpayers rights issues. One of his books, *The IRS Problem Solver,* was ranked by *The Wall Street Journal* as the number one tax book in America. His book *How to Fire the IRS* started the national debate on abolishing the IRS that took place throughout the 1990s. He was on the editorial board of the Institute for Policy Innovation's "Road Map to Tax Reform Project" in 2001 and a consultant to the National Commission on Restructuring the IRS. He has two Web sites, at www.taxhelponline.com and www.taxfreedominstitute.com. He speaks nationwide to tax professional associations, trade associations, and citizens' groups on taxpayers' rights and tax policy issues.

Steve Stanek is managing editor of *Budget & Tax News*. He has been a freelance writer and editor since 1997, producing marketing materials and business articles for corporate clients, as well as feature articles and news stories for Chicago-area newspapers, magazines, and business publications. He has worked as a newspaper reporter and editor at weekly and daily newspapers in Illinois. He is the coauthor of "The State Public Pension Crisis: A 50-State Report Card," published by The Heartland Institute in 2010.

Richard Vedder is distinguished professor of economics at Ohio University in Athens, Ohio. He has written extensively on taxes, regulation, labor, and higher education, authoring such books as *The American Economy in Historical Perspective* (1976) and, with Lowell Gallaway, *Out of Work: Unemployment and Government in Twentieth-Century America* (1997). Vedder has written more than 100 scholarly papers published in academic journals and books. He served as an economist with the Joint Economic Committee of Congress and as the John M. Olin Visiting Professor of Labor Economics and Public Policy at the Center for the Study of American Business at Washington University in St. Louis, and he has taught or lectured at many other universities.

Herbert J. Walberg is distinguished visiting fellow at Stanford University's Hoover Institution and chief scientific advisor to the Center on Innovation and Improvement. He has written and edited more than 65 books and written some 350 articles on such topics as school choice, educational testing and evaluation, and exceptional human accomplishments. He served as a professor at Harvard University and the University of Illinois at Chicago after earning a Ph.D. in educational psychology at The University of Chicago. Walberg has given invited lectures in Australia, Belgium, China, England, France, Germany, Israel, Italy, Japan, the Netherlands, South Africa, Sweden, Taiwan, the United States, and Venezuela. He has frequently testified before congressional committees, state legislatures, and federal courts. He is the only American to have served on the National Assessment Governing Board, which oversees the National Assessment of Educational Progress, and the presidentially appointed National Board for Educational Sciences. He has served on seven boards, including that of the California-based Foundation for Teaching Economics. He currently chairs the boards of the Beck Foundation and The Heartland Institute.

About The Heartland Institute

The Heartland Institute is a national nonprofit organization with offices in Chicago and Washington DC. Founded in 1984, it began as a state-based free-market think tank but soon evolved into a regional and, since 1993, a national organization.

Heartland has policy advisors and supporters in all 50 states. Approximately 120 academics and professional economists participate in its peer review process, and nearly 200 elected officials serve on its Legislative Forum. Heartland currently has a full-time staff of 35 and a 2011 budget of $6.8 million.

The Heartland Institute contacts more elected officials, more often, than any other free-market think tank in the United States. According to a telephone survey of randomly selected state and local officials conducted in 2009, 85 percent of state legislators and 63 percent of local officials say they read and rely on Heartland publications.

Some 120,000 of the nation's most influential people – including every state and national elected official – receive at least one Heartland publication every month. Heartland also operates *PolicyBot,* an online clearinghouse for the work of some 350 think tanks and advocacy groups.

Heartland's full-time staff of government relations professionals interacts daily with hundreds of elected officials across the country, and its public relations and media specialists help shape public opinion by writing and placing dozens of letters to the editor and opinion editorials each week.

Support for The Heartland Institute's programs comes from some 1,800 individuals, foundations, and corporations. Contributions are tax-deductible under Section 501(c)3 of the Internal Revenue Code.

For more information, visit our Web sites at www.heartland.org and www.schoolreform-news.org; call 312/377-4000; or write to The Heartland Institute, 19 South LaSalle Street, Suite 903, Chicago, Illinois 60603.